A KINGDOM FOR A STAGE

O for a Muse of fire, that would ascend
The brightest heaven of invention,
A kingdom for a stage, princes to act,
And monarchs to behold the swelling scene!
                                —Henry V, *prologue*

A KINGDOM FOR A STAGE

The Achievement of Shakespeare's History Plays

ROBERT ORNSTEIN

Harvard University Press
Cambridge, Massachusetts
1972

163134

TO   DORIS

ACKNOWLEDGMENTS

I am grateful to the John Simon Guggenheim Foundation for the award of a Fellowship in 1961 which enabled me to do the research for this book. An associate membership in the Center for Advanced Studies at the University of Illinois allowed me to spend the fall of 1965 on its chapters. I owe much to my colleagues and students at the University of Illinois and Case Western Reserve University with whom I discussed the History Plays. I am indebted also to many earlier critics and scholars of these plays, not the least to E. M. W. Tillyard, with whom I so often disagree in my text. My typist, Mrs. Carol Prael, deserves special thanks for her scrupulous preparation of the manuscript. The dedication of this book to my wife is a way of acknowledging how much she has taught me about the nature of artistic interpretation.

Quotations from E. M. W. Tillyard, *Shakespeare's History Plays* (copyright, 1946, by The Macmillan Company), are by permission of The Macmillan Company, New York; Stephen Tillyard and Chatto and Windus, Ltd. Quotations from John Palmer, *Political Characters of Shakespeare*, are by permission of St. Martin's Press, Inc., The Macmillan Company of Canada, and Macmillan London and Basingstoke.

R. O.

CONTENTS

A KINGDOM FOR A STAGE

1. THE ARTIST AS HISTORIAN

The many books and articles that have been written in the past several decades about the History Plays have rescued them from the relative neglect of earlier years when the tragedies and comedies seemed to monopolize the attention of Shakespeareans. But though appreciation of the History Plays is greater now than it ever was before, so too perhaps is awareness of their flaws and imperfections. In fairly recent years critics have declared substantial portions of the *Henry VI* plays too inferior to have come from Shakespeare's pen. They have also pointed out the makeshift construction of *King John*, the lapses of style in *Richard II*, and the lack of coherence in *Henry VIII*; they have even questioned the seriousness of Shakespeare's artistic purpose in *Henry IV Part II* and *Henry V*. I am ready to leap to the defense of *Henry IV Part II* and *Henry V*, because, like most of the History Plays, they seem to me extraordinary artistic achievements. But rather than argue the greatness of every History Play, I would ask why Shakespeare seems at times less certain a craftsman in this genre than in his comedies and tragedies. Even if we grant that the plays of the first tetralogy probably include his earliest dramatic efforts, we must still wonder why we do not find in them the artistic tact and intuitive sense of form evident in his earliest comedies.

We can beg the question by deciding that Shakespeare had a surer instinct for comedy than history or that he found comedy more congenial than history. Or we can recognize that it was much easier for him to find his artistic direction in comedy than in history because he had landmarks to guide him and a charted territory before him. Lacking the artistic precedents and models which the plays of Plautus, Gascoigne, Peele, and Greene provided in comedy, he had not only to create a suitable dramatic form for the History Play but he had also to recreate that form again and again as his vision of politics and history deepened. He was also, I think, more ambitious and adventurous, more willing to experiment and innovate in his History Plays than in his comedies. Once he found his romantic theme in *Two Gentlemen of Verona*, he was content to vary, refine, and sophisticate it in succeeding comedies. Thus, a reader familiar with *Love's Labors Lost, Two Gentlemen of Verona,* and *A Midsummer Night's Dream* knows pretty much what to expect in the plotting, dialogue, and characterizations of *Much Ado About Nothing*. But there is nothing in the *Henry VI* plays and *Richard III* which allows a reader to anticipate the handling of dramatic form, mood, and characterization in *Henry IV Part I*, just as there is little in *Henry IV Part II* that echoes the poetic style, plotting, and characterizations of *Richard II*. So different, in fact, are the History Plays from one another that it is difficult to generalize about their subject matter, much less about their dramatic and poetic qualities.

If I lay too much stress on what is original and individual in the History Plays, it is because recent scholarship has so often declared them conventional in form and substance and traditionally staid in their political and moral attitudes. We are asked to believe that the Shakespeare who blazed the path in tragedy for Chapman, Tourneur, Webster, Beaumont and Fletcher, Middleton, and Ford was content to follow the lead of the plodding didacticists who supposedly created the genre of the History Play, and like them dedicate his art to moralistic and propagandistic purposes. The pity of this scholarly insistence on the conventionality of the History Plays is that it threatens to turn living works of theater into dramatic fossils or repositories of quaint and dusty ideas.[1] Instead of bridging the gulf of the centuries, the historical approach to the History Plays seems to widen it by identifying Shakespeare's mind and art with a past that viewed through the lens of scholarship appears more remote than ever before.

The problem of scholarly perspective is not unique to the interpretation of the History Plays. When placed in historical context—that is, annotated by reference to Elizabethan ideas—Shakespeare's tragedies and comedies can also be made to seem thoroughly conventional in form and orthodox in substance. But those who would prove by appropriate glosses that *Antony and Cleopatra* is a warning against sensuality prove only their insensitivity to its poetry, and

1. Insisting that the History Plays reveal Shakespeare's "official self," E. M. W. Tillyard remarks also that "the political doctrines of the History Plays fascinate partly because they are remote and queer," *Shakespeare's History Plays* (New York: Macmillan, 1946), p. 146.

those who would have us read Shakespeare's tragedies "through Elizabethan eyes" do not convince us that his tragic vision can be identified with the commonplace moralism of his age or that Elizabethan sermons can teach the proper response to plays as universal as *King Lear*. Are we to accept as valid for the History Plays a method of scholarly explication which strikes us as reductive when applied to the tragedies? The answer can be "yes" only if we believe that by choice or necessity Shakespeare assumed an "official" stance in the History Plays and was more conformist and conventional in attitude in *Richard II* than in *Hamlet* and *King Lear*.

No doubt the History Plays were more topical in their concerns than Shakespeare's other drama. They were also uniquely "public" plays in that they dealt with the political anxieties and patriotic enthusiasms, the shared memories and aspirations which make a people conscious of their oneness and destiny as a nation. Necessarily, therefore, Shakespeare was constrained in these plays by Chronicle "fact" and by accepted opinion. He could no more think of making Richard III a Yorkist Hamlet than he could deny Henry V his praise as a conquering hero. But if one does not expect Shakespeare to be emancipated in his political attitudes or recklessly heterodox in his interpretations of history—an Elizabethan revisionist or debunker of eminent Plantagenets—neither does one expect him to step forward in the History Plays as the laureate of Tudor royalism. One could imagine him in a time of national peril dedicating one or two plays to what he thought were necessary patriotic purposes. Can we believe, however, that he dedicated nine plays—the weightier part of all the drama he wrote before *Hamlet*—to the claims of orthodoxy? And can we imagine that a dramatic form as prescribed and conventional as the History Play is made to seem allowed scope for the artistic development which made him capable of plays like *Hamlet* and *King Lear*?

The scholarly insistence on the orthodoxy of the History Plays would be more tolerable if it were tinged with some regret that the Soul of the Age lent his great art to doctrinaire purposes. But instead of regret, there seems to be pleasure in the scholarly discovery of the orthodoxy of this character's thought and the "correctness" of that character's acts.[2] If there is a left and right wing

2. The triumphant discovery of orthodoxy is evident in Tillyard's *Shakespeare's History Plays*, and to a lesser degree, in Irving Ribner's *The English History Play in the Age of Shakespeare* (Princeton: Princeton Univ. Press, 1957) and M. M. Reese, *The Cease of Majesty: A Study of Shakespeare's History Plays* (London: Ed. Arnold, 1961). Lily B. Campbell also insists upon Shakespeare's orthodoxy in *Shakespeare's Histories: Mirrors of Elizabethan Policy* (San Marino, Calif. Huntington Library, 1947). At its worst, this approach has some of the characteristics of a security investigation and clearance. In his chapter on "The English Chronicle Plays," for example, Tillyard informs us that Marlowe

in the criticism of Shakespeare, one libertarian (or Falstaffian) in sympathies, the other conservative and mindful of the need for authority and discipline, then the party of the right (and of Prince Hal) seems entrenched in the scholarship on the History Plays. Rather than complain of the bias of particular scholars, however, I would point out the inherent bias of the historical method toward what is conventional and orthodox in Elizabethan culture, because any search for the "norms" of Elizabethan thought must lead to a consensus of truisms and pieties. In sketching the main contours of Elizabethan thought, scholarship often smooths out the jagged edges and wrinkles of individual opinion. It does not maintain that all Elizabethans were typical, but it often creates the impression that there were only two categories of Renaissance thought and art—the orthodox and the deviant—and it seems to insist that we place Shakespeare on one side of the angels or another.

What we need is not a less historical approach to the History Plays but a more rigorous methodology for that approach. The insistence, for example, on the pre-Shakespearean tradition of the History Plays seems curious when no one can point to the earlier plays which might have provided Shakespeare with a model or inspiration for the *Henry VI* plays. So few are the possible exemplars of the pre-Shakespearean History Play that Thomas Preston's *Cambises* (c. 1560), which has nothing to do with English history and little to do with dramatic art, is sometimes brought forth as an ancestral form.[3] A more obvious progenitor of the History Plays, we are told, was *Gorboduc* (1561), Sackville and Norton's academic Senecan tragedy; and beyond *Gorboduc* the empty spaces of the tradition yawn, because the only earlier example of the pre-Shakespearean History Play that scholars can cite is John Bale's *King Johan* (c. 1534), an anti-Catholic polemic in Morality form presented at the court of Henry VIII.[4] It is hard to think of a literary tradition quite as meager and

---

in *Edward II* "shows no sense of national responsibility" though he uses "two current political orthodoxies"; he notes further that "On the matters of civil war and obedience to the king, the author of *Woodstock* is ample, explicit, and scrupulously orthodox"—a curious view of a play which applauds armed rebellion against a corrupt monarch. See *History Plays,* pp. 108-9, 118. Ribner, in contrast, notes the unorthodoxy of *Woodstock* (*English History Play,* 2nd revised edition [London, Methuen, 1965], p. 141.) All citations from Ribner are to this edition.

3. See Ribner, who describes *Cambises* as a "clear facet" of the development of "a real native historical drama" in England (*English History Play,* p. 57). On the other hand, Reese sees the "absurd" *Cambises* as "a dreadful warning, perhaps, of what the English history play might have become if the Senecan *Gorboduc* had not given it form and discipline" (*Cease of Majesty,* pp. 76-77). It is difficult, however, to think of an Elizabethan History Play that takes the "form and discipline" of *Gorboduc.*

4. Tillyard is inclined to discount the importance of *King Johan* in the tradition of the History Play because its concern with history is so sketchy and peripheral (*History Plays,*

eccentric as this one, a tradition which produced in the fifty or so years between Bale and Shakespeare only two plays that barely resemble one another. Nor can one think of a similar literary tradition in which there is not one tangible connection or demonstrable relationship between the several works that constitute it.[5] To explain why Elizabethan History Plays do not resemble the works that were supposedly their progenitors, E. M. W. Tillyard remarks that "just as Holinshed seizes on the factual side of Hall and ignores his philosophy, so most of the English Chronicle plays ignore the steady moral bent of *Gorboduc* and exploit the mere accident of successive events."[6] We know that Holinshed used Hall's Chronicle in compiling his own, but we have little reason to think that the writers of Elizabethan History Plays took *Gorboduc* as a guide, and it is impossible to believe that they were willing to follow the artistic example of a play like *Cambises*, which they treated as an object of ridicule.[7] They did not stray from the turgid didacticism of *King Johan;* in all likelihood, they did not even know that Bale's play existed.

The tracing of the genealogy of the History Plays seems almost like an exercise in Renaissance metaphysics. Just as Hooker postulates the sovereignty of the law of nature and then explains why nature diverges from it, so scholarship postulates the pre-Shakespearean tradition of the History Play and then explains why Elizabethan History Plays do not conform to it. Despite repeated assertions that the History Play descended from Tudor Moralities and Moral Interludes, there is a remarkable absence of Morality techniques and echoes in the earliest of the Elizabethan History Plays, where one would expect the ancestral resemblances to be most evident. This is not because Morality themes and conventions had become so sophisticated by the 1580's that they are difficult to discern in the drama, for we can find very obvious pedestrian Morality plays being written at that time. The reason we do not find Morality

pp. 92-3), but both Ribner and Reese see *King Johan* as the beginning of the dramatic genre to which Shakespeare's History Plays belong (Ribner, pp. 33-36; Reese, pp. 69-70).

5. Although Ribner several times speaks of *Cambises* as continuing the tradition or "line" of *King Johan* (*English History Play*, pp. 50, 57), there is not the slightest shred of evidence that Preston referred to Bale's play in writing his own, that he modeled his play on Bale's, or that he even knew of Bale's play, which had been written twenty-five years before and never published. Similarly, there is no evidence that Sackville and Norton knew, imitated, or were influenced by Bale in writing *Gorboduc*. To speak then of *Gorboduc* and *Cambises* as continuing the "line" or tradition of *King Johan* is to make the term "tradition" nearly meaningless.

6. *History Plays*, p. 99.

7. The fact that both Marlowe and Shakespeare explicitly ridicule the ranting style of *Cambises* is proof that they knew the play. Very likely one of the most famous lines of *Henry VI Part III* (which Greene immortalized in parody), "O tiger's heart wrapp'd in a woman's hide!" is a remembrance of Preston's line, "Oh tigers whelp, hadst thou the hart

influence in *The Troublesome Reign of King John* (1591), *The Famous Victories of Henry V* (1587?), and *Henry VI Part I* is that their romantic, heroic, and comic impulses are quite divorced from the didactic intention of the Moralities, and their concern with the flesh and blood reality of politics and history is contrary to the conceptualistic and allegorical impulse of the Moralities. It is only in later History Plays that unmistakable echoes of Morality themes and techniques can be found, and then it is obvious that the echoes are precisely that—tags, epithets, reminiscences of themes and character types, conventions transmuted and adapted to new artistic purposes.

Seeking continuity and pattern in the history of literature, we understandably look for the precedents and influences which shaped Shakespeare's artistic practice. But the insistence on the traditionality of his History Plays so far outreaches empirical evidence that one suspects it is, in part, a special pleading for the didactic and orthodox Shakespeare. If we put aside this special pleading, we must agree with F. P. Wilson "that there is no certain evidence that any popular dramatist before Shakespeare wrote a play based on English history."[8] And even if we grant the possibility that plays like *Jack Straw* or the original version of *The Famous Victories* actually preceded *Henry VI Part I*,[9] we have to say that Shakespeare followed his own artistic bent in the first tetralogy and that he was the supreme artistic influence on the History Plays written in the 1590's by his contemporaries. If he did not originate the form of the History Play when he wrote the *Henry VI* plays, he created its vogue and shaped its tradition. So preeminent was his contribution that, if we omit his History Plays, the tradition very nearly ceases to be artistically significant. No one has admired Marlowe's *Edward II* for its depiction of political realities, and no one

---

to see this childs hart-blood?" because the dramatic contexts for these lines are remarkably similar. York mourns over his murdered son even as the Mother in *Cambises* mourns over her son killed by the King (see *Cambises*, 1.594, in *Chief Pre-Shakespearean Dramas*, ed. J. Q. Adams [Boston: Houghton Mifflin, 1924], p. 653). But it is impossible to believe that Shakespeare used a play as ridiculous as *Cambises* as a model for the *Henry VI* plays.

8. F. P. Wilson, *Marlowe and the Early Shakespeare* (Oxford: Clarendon Press, 1953), p. 106.

9. Since the dates of composition of almost all Elizabethan History Plays are unknown, their order of precedence can only be conjectured. Most authorities date the *Henry VI* plays 1590-91, which places them among the very earliest of their kind. Printed in 1593, *Jack Straw* may have been composed some years before, but there is no hard evidence to support this supposition. *The Famous Victories,* which David Bevington has recently called "probably the first extant English history play" (*Tudor Drama and Politics* [Cambridge, Mass.: Harvard Univ. Press, 1968], p. 196), is generally thought to have been performed in 1587, but again, this is a speculation based on contemporary allusions to a "Henry V" play staged in the 1580's. The only other popular drama on English history which might have preceded the *Henry VI* plays was *The Troublesome Reign of King John,* which was printed in 1591 and may have been written several years before.

could take seriously the portrayal of history in Greene's *James IV*.[10] Apart from the contributions of Shakespeare, Marlowe, and Greene, the tradition of the Elizabethan History Play consists of a handful of anonymous plays which are primarily interesting because of their possible relationship to Shakespearean drama.[11]

When we seek "the effect of the Chronicle Plays on Shakespeare," we are likely, as Tillyard remarks, to discover "something much more like the effect of Shakespeare on the Chronicle Play."[12] But suppose it were the other way around, suppose that rather than one of the chief creators of the Elizabethan dramatic tradition, Shakespeare had been, like Bach, the inheritor and supreme exemplar of a long-established artistic tradition. Could we by studying that tradition recover the historical Shakespeare even as twentieth-century musicologists and musicians have recovered the historical Bach? Certainly the pursuit of the historical Shakespeare through literary research is as valid and necessary as the pursuit of the historical Bach through musicological research, because only scholarship can provide the accurate texts that musical and literary interpretation requires, and only scholarship can free us from misconceptions and misinterpretations that, hallowed by time, seem natural and "right." We cannot hope to perform Bach "Bach's way" if his works are known only in vulgarized transcriptions or editions encrusted with misinformation. Similarly we cannot hope to hear Bach "Bach's way" if his works are performed in nineteenth-century romantic fashion. To recover Bach we have had to reconstruct eighteenth-century instruments, to study the musical conventions of his time, and to ponder all that hints of his musical intentions, tempi, phrasing, and modes of ornamentation and improvisation. In the process we have learned that the mere accumulation of scholarly information does not guarantee "authentic" interpretation, because the demand for historical authenticity may turn musical performance into pedantic demonstration, and strict attention to all the learned rules of Baroque performance may result in a "correctness" that disallows the verve and freedom of Bach's individual genius. The discovery of Bach's art necessarily begins where scholarly research ends; the authenticity of an interpretation cannot be argued with footnotes, it must be apparent in the immediate beauty and power of the musical experience itself. In other words, we do not train ourselves to listen to Bach through

10. Like George Peele's *Edward I* (c. 1591), Robert Greene's *The Scottish History of James IV* (c. 1591) is a romantic pageant with only faint pretenses at historical or political concerns.

11. For example, *The Troublesome Reign of King John*, *The True Tragedy of Richard III*, *Woodstock* (c. 1592), and *Edward III* (c. 1592).

12. *History Plays*, p. 120.

eighteenth-century ears, nor do we cherish in his art outworn musical ideas. Instead we seek to recapture the contemporaneousness of Bach's genius that transcends all changes in musical style; by immersing ourselves in his works, we hope to escape the parochialism of modern tastes and to enlarge our awareness of what music is—and can be.

Can we learn to read Shakespeare "Shakespeare's way," as we learn to perform and listen to Bach "Bach's way?" Can we join historical research and aesthetic awareness in the interpretation of plays as in the interpretation of music? Our task as literary critics is more difficult because we cannot appeal to the "truth" of performance; we do not have a company of actors to stage our interpretations, and often we are arguing not about the performance of a scene but about the proper response to it, though, of course, the one question is intimately related to the other, and our critical interpretation often suggests the way in which a scene should be acted. But the heart of the matter is something else again: an implicit refusal by historical scholarship to grant that the ultimate standard for the interpretation of art is aesthetic. Insisting on the primacy of Shakespeare's didactic intention, scholarship would have us believe that the interpretation of the History Plays does not depend on sensitivity to nuances of language and characterization or awareness of Shakespeare's poetic and dramatic methods; it depends instead on the appropriate annotation of the doctrine of the plays. Where the interpreter of Bach hopes through historical research to transcend history, the literary scholar insists that historicity is *the* goal of interpretation. Convinced that the "Elizabethan response" which he postulates is the authentic one, he assures us that if we were Elizabethan enough in our attitudes, we would have no difficulty in interpreting Shakespeare correctly. If, for instance, we recognized that York's stance in *Richard II* is impeccably orthodox, we would not think his eagerness to have his only son executed unconscionable or, as it seems in the play, somewhat comic.[13]

It is doubtful, however, that a modern audience can be so tutored by scholarship as to become for a time royalist enough to admire the orthodoxy of York's behavior in the last act of *Richard II*. And it is doubtful that even the most dedicated students of literature can teach themselves to look at the History Plays through Elizabethan eyes. By steeping ourselves in Elizabethan culture, we can puzzle out some of the oddities of Elizabethan taste; we can, for example, fathom some of the reasons for the enormous popularity of plays like *Mucedorus*. But this knowledge of Elizabethan tastes does not make the absurdities of *Mucedorus* any more attractive, and if we cannot reorient our

13. See Tillyard, *History Plays*, pp. 261-62.

literary tastes, is it likely that we can alter our moral and emotional responses? A case in point is the scene in *Henry IV Part I* (II.iv), where Hal, aided by Poins, plays a joke on Francis, the drawer. Perhaps it is wrong to be slightly pained by the callousness of Hal's treatment of Francis, but if we are pained, at least we are responding immediately and honestly to the lines which Shakespeare wrote and to a human situation which we can understand because we have experienced or witnessed its analogue in our own lives. We recognize Hal's boredom in the tavern, and his condescension to those who are his inferiors. We recognize, too, the pleasure which he takes in playing cat-and-mouse games with other people—with Poins, Falstaff, and the Lord Chief Justice in *Henry IV Part II*, and with the English traitors and the French Princess Katherine in *Henry V*. Arguing that "we must not judge Shakespeare by standards of twentieth-century humanitarianism," Tillyard would have us believe that Elizabethan audiences (in which apprentices far outnumbered princes) would not have been troubled at all by Hal's conduct because they thought the Francises of the world hardly human.[14] If we accept this dubious generalization about Shakespeare's contemporaries, however, we do not respond "properly" to Shakespeare's representation of life; what we respond to is a learned admonition against modern sentimentality which saves Hal's ideality by degrading Shakespeare's humanity and cheapening his art. If Tillyard is correct, the Francis episode is not a fascinating revelation of Hal's personality; it is an irrelevant and purposeless bit of low humor, which exposes Shakespeare's "Elizabethan" snobbery and coarseness.

Because we do not have the same social attitudes and political assumptions as Shakespeare's audience, it is possible that our responses to his plays are, by Elizabethan standards, somewhat distorted. Too accustomed perhaps to the security of stable political institutions, we may be more tolerant of aberration than were Elizabethans, and we may be inclined to sentimentalize characters like Falstaff whom Shakespeare thought of as threats to order and morality. If this is so, we must hope that the experience of great literature will enlarge our perspective and make us conscious of what is sentimental or romantic in our valuations. To be educated in this way, however, we must have the shock of artistic recognition; we must be convinced by the compelling truth of the artistic portrayal of life. We cannot simply be scolded about our ignorance and assured that if we had an Elizabethan view of serving boys, we too would enjoy

14. According to him (*History Plays,* p. 277), "the subhuman element in the population must have been considerable in Shakespeare's day; that it should have been treated almost like beasts was taken for granted." But apart from the fact that Francis generously gave Hal a pennyworth of sugar and wished that it had been two pennyworth, the only evidence of his character (and subhumanity) is the way he scurries about at Hal's behest.

the sport of baiting Francis. It is worth noting that Poins, Hal's assistant in the game, who is as coarse and common in his outlook as any Elizabethan one would ever want to meet, seems to lack the proper Elizabethan outlook, because he does not get the joke of baiting Francis and asks Hal the point of it.[15]

The appeal to Elizabethan attitudes is frequent enough in the literature on the History Plays for us to wonder why it should be easier to predict the responses of Shakespeare's audience than to interpret his artistic intentions from the thousands of lines which embody them. If we grant that there was in Shakespeare's England a community of shared values and beliefs which scholarship can cautiously describe, we must grant too that a wide range of individual and group attitudes must have existed in his society, which knew more than its share of religious and political turmoil and social and economic change. When we consider how reluctant we would be to generalize about the attitudes of our contemporaries—or to define the beliefs of our next-door neighbors, for that matter—we must be astonished at the confidence with which scholars characterize Elizabethan convictions. Perhaps the Elizabethans seem simpler and more transparent than do our contemporaries, because we know less about the diversity, contradictions, shadings, and facets of their beliefs—or because these nuances are not apparent in the documents and treatises which we consider the repositories of Elizabethan "thought." In any event, Shakespeare's contemporaries sometimes appear in scholarly portraits as a fundamentally naive and credulous folk, who managed to create a highly sophisticated civilization and great monuments of art while retaining simple emotional enthusiasms and stock responses.

More unfortunate still is the curiously Philistine blueprint for Elizabethan culture sometimes implicit in the scholarship that looks always outside the realm of literature to explain and annotate literary ideas. Such an approach creates the impression that Elizabethan poets and dramatists made no significant contribution to the thought of their age, that they found their moral values in sermons and took their psychology from treatises on the humors, their political ideas from the Tudor and Elizabethan Homilies. What an approach to the era of Shakespeare, Marlowe, Spenser, Jonson, and Donne! One cannot imagine Sir Philip Sidney, who eloquently argued that literature may be more philosophical than philosophy and more historical than history, agreeing that the light of artistic intelligence was wholly reflected in his time and not particularly bright. Nor can one imagine the Elizabethan dramatists considering themselves "blessed fellows" (as Hal contemptuously describes

15. "What cunning match have you made with this jest of the drawer?" Poins asks when the game is done. "Come, what's the issue?"

Poins) "to think the way everybody thinks." If not particularly intellectual, the dramatists were shrewd observers of their contemporary scene, and if they were not clever enough to invent political myths, they were clear-sighted enough to discern the contradictions and expediencies of Tudor royalism.

The problem of interpretation does not lie with playwrights as blessed as Thomas Heywood, who did in large measure think the way everybody thought, because even when we cannot share Heywood's bourgeois enthusiasms and antipathies, we know precisely where he takes his conventional stand. The problem lies with playwrights as "eccentric" as Marlowe or as thoughtful as Shakespeare, whose insights were not bounded by the truisms and common-place judgments of their time. It is sometimes suggested that the problem of interpreting Shakespeare results from refractive errors in the vision of modern critics which can be corrected by the lenses of scholarship. *Measure for Measure*, we are told, seems ambiguous only because we do not venerate chastity as Elizabethans did and therefore do not properly admire Isabella's fierce desire to preserve her virginity even at the cost of her brother's life. Perhaps so, but this kind of appeal to Elizabethan attitudes places critical interpretation on very dubious grounds. For if we grant that we may be less sympathetic than Elizabethans were to Isabella's defense of her virginity, we must insist that we are probably more sympathetic to her defiance of her brother than were Elizabethans, who believed that women should be subservient to men. Indeed, if Isabella has lost status as a virgin, she has undoubtedly gained dignity and stature as a woman who passionately defends her integrity against the weakness and tyranny of men. We can not assume that a modern critic lacks the proper cultural orientation to sympathize with Isabella, just as we cannot assume that all Elizabethans automatically shared Isabella's horror and outrage at Claudio's request that she lay down her body for his life. Consider, for example, the subplot of Heywood's *A Woman Killed with Kindness,* in which feminine nobility is exemplified by Susan Mountford's readiness to sacrifice her chastity and then her life to redeem her brother's honor. Nothing in the play indicates that Heywood, a pillar of bourgeois morality, condemns as perverse the brother's demand that his sister pay his debt of honor with her body; and though at first horrified by her brother's request, Susan quickly realizes that her brother's plan is a proof of his extraordinary nobility.[16] I would not suggest that Heywood's fantasizing of aristocratic behavior teaches us how to deal with the complex reality of

16. In Heywood's play, the noble Sir Charles Mountford wants his sister to submit to the lust of his enemy Sir Francis Acton, because Acton paid five hundred pounds to release Sir Charles from debtor's prison. Knowing that this request comes from an

Shakespeare's art; my point is that the task of the critic is to fathom Shakespeare's unique insight and intuition, not to square his plays with a hypothetical norm of Elizabethan attitudes.

It is instructive that although many sensitive critics have been somewhat repelled by Isabella's virtue, very few have ever questioned Cordelia's refusal to humor her father with some comforting words. Possibly our admiration for Cordelia is also too modern a response, because assumptions about parental authority and filial obedience have changed as radically since the Renaissance as have assumptions about chastity. Perhaps because we live in a permissive society we may be too tolerant of Cordelia's recalcitrance and pride for Shakespeare's tastes, and we should judge her behavior by the standards of filial obedience set forth in Renaissance courtesy books. But we need not pore over Elizabethan volumes to interpret the opening scene of *King Lear*, because Shakespeare carefully cues our emotional and moral responses by contrasting Cordelia's honesty to her sisters' oily hypocrisy and by bringing forth Kent and France as witnesses to her nobility and truth. The moral situation in this scene is so transparent that only the dullest reader could be astonished by the absolute generosity and selflessness of Cordelia's behavior later in the play. If we are less certain of the rightness of Isabella's behavior, it is not because we are tolerant of premarital intercourse and therefore expect her to submit to Angelo's disgusting and degrading lust, but because her moral responses are rigid and self-righteous, and because she seems until the last scene of the play incapable of the compassion on which charity rests. As a matter of fact, the knowledge of self which she gains at the close of the play seems to include the awareness that she is not intended for a religious, much less a saintly, life.[17]

While we can only speculate about Elizabethan responses to Cordelia and Isabella, we can determine what sixteenth-century historians, politicians, and artists thought about the historical figures who appear in Shakespeare's plays. We can also assume that Shakespeare was aware of the dangers of portraying these figures and of treating political issues in heterodox ways. Government officials alert to subversive ideas censored and banned dramatic texts and

---

"honor'd mind," which cannot stand to be indebted to one he hates, Susan says (V.i): "I see your resolution, and assent; / So Charles will have me, and I am content." Acton also admires Charles' "honourable wrested courtesy." If the good Elizabethan sister will prostitute herself to save her brother from a sense of obligation, what shall we say of Isabella's response to Claudio's plea for his life?

17. One cannot be certain that Isabella will accept the Duke's marriage proposal in the last scene of *Measure for Measure,* but unless one feels that the proposal is appropriate (that Isabella is less a nun at the end of the play than at the beginning), the Duke will seem either foolish or coarse.

performances, and on various occasions they haled forth the playwrights and actors to be tried for their slanderous or profane libels. But though the fear of censorship, official reprisals, and imprisonment probably dampened rebellious spirits, and though the playwrights and actors were dependent on royal patronage and support, they were not as easily intimidated as the government would have liked. And just as the dramatists were relatively free and sometimes satiric spirits, so too Elizabethan theatergoers had minds of their own, and were no doubt not all of one mind about any performance or any play. What plays and what characters of Shakespeare they loved, we know, even as we know which plays of Jonson they booed. How they interpreted the History Plays, we do not know—or, more correctly, what we know about Elizabethan responses to *Richard II* seems to contradict the chief assumptions of recent scholarship. Embodied in *Richard II*, we are told, is the orthodox view that the deposition of Richard was a heinous sin that brought down on England God's wrath and the curse of civil war.[18] Yet on the eve of Essex's rebellion, his adherents paid a bonus to Shakespeare's company to play *Richard II*, presumably in hope that it would stir the audience to sympathy for the uprising. Quite possibly Essex's followers were so blinded by their fanaticism that they lost sight of the orthodoxy of *Richard II*, but if so they were not the only ones, because we know of Elizabeth's bitter remark about the popularity of the play—a bitterness founded in the knowledge that her enemies identified her and her favorites with Richard and his circle of flatterers.[19]

One can not speak with certainty of Shakespeare's view of Richard II; one can hope only to interpret *Richard II* thoughtfully and sensitively. But one can state with some certainty that the supposedly orthodox view of Richard II, which can be found in Holinshed's Chronicles, is not the view of most Tudor and Elizabethan writers who deal with his character and reign. The anonymous author of *Woodstock* (c. 1592), a play which Shakespeare apparently used for *Richard II*, depicts the youthful Richard as thoroughly despicable and corrupt, and he portrays the barons who rebel against Richard as patriotic defenders of the commonweal.[20] The authors of *The Mirror for Magistrates* (1559) proclaim the sinfulness of rebellion, but they do not exclaim against Richard's deposition. Described in the *Mirror* as a vicious, lecherous, predatory "Kyng

18. See Campbell, *Shakespeare's Histories,* pp. 211-12; Tillyard, *History Plays,* p. 261.
19. Complaining that the tragedy of *Richard II* "was played 40 times in open streets and houses," Elizabeth is said to have remarked in 1601, "I am Richard II, know ye not that?" (Campbell, *Shakespeare's Histories,* p. 191).
20. In his edition of *Woodstock* (London: Chatto & Windus, 1946), A. P. Rossiter notes its quite unorthodox sympathy with armed rebellion against tyranny (p. 32).

that ruled all by lust, / That forced not of vertue, ryght, or lawe," Richard is treated not as a martyred king but as a tyrant whose fate may serve as a warning to lawless monarchs:

> Thus lawles life, to lawles deth ey drawes.
> Wherefore byd Kynges be rulde and rule by right,
> Who wurketh his wil, and shunneth wisedomes sawes,
> In flateries clawes, and shames foule pawes shal light.[21]

Tudor and Elizabethan Chroniclers are less vehement in their condemnation of Richard, but without exception they detail his personal vices and his political rapacity and disregard of law.[22] Knowing that Richard was often cited by sixteenth-century writers as an example of royal lawlessness and incompetence, we can understand why the *Homily against Disobedience and wilful Rebellion* (1574) takes John, not Richard, as its example of English royalty betrayed by disloyal subjects—why Catholic polemicists cited the deposition of Richard in justifying disobedience to tyrants[23] —and why Essex's party wished to have *Richard II* performed on the eve of their uprising.

To understand how an uncharacteristic view of Richard II came to be regarded by scholars as the "orthodox" Elizabethan view we have to retrace the steps by which the Tudor myth of history became prominent in the scholarly interpretation of the History Plays. As early as 1913, the distinguished historian C. L. Kingsford had pointed out the extent to which Hall's narrative of the reign of Henry VI was "mere Tudor fiction based on Yorkist misinterpretation" of the characters of Margaret, Suffolk, and Humphrey.[24] Kingsford noted that Hall's Chronicle (1548) "was intended as a glorification of the House of Tudor" and that Hall grasped the pattern of fifteenth-century English history which "appears also in the continuous cycle of Shakespeare's histories. The downfall of Richard II, the glories of Henry V, the long struggle of Lancaster and York ending in the happy union of the rival houses, were all stages in the preparation for a greater Age."[25] When some decades later

21. *The Mirror for Magistrates,* ed. L. B. Campbell (Cambridge: Cambridge Univ. Press, 1938), p. 120.
22. There is no Tudor or Elizabethan Chronicler who fails to document Richard's personal vices and political failings, his lawlessness and rapacity. The only completely sympathetic sixteenth-century view of Richard, I think, is the idealized portrait in *Jack Straw,* which is not a defense of the character of Richard II but rather an abstracted study in royal fortitude and clemency. The play focuses wholly on the uprising and makes no comment on other aspects of Richard's life or reign.
23. See the discussion of the writings of the Jesuit Robert Parsons in Campbell, *Shakespeare's Histories,* pp. 173-81.
24. C. L. Kingsford, *English Historical Literature in the Fifteenth Century* (Oxford: Clarendon Press, 1913), p. 265.

literary scholars confirmed Shakespeare's use of Hall's Chronicle for the plays of the first tetralogy, they went further than Kingsford in identifying Shakespeare's view of history with Hall's.[26] Where Kingsford saw Hall as an ardent supporter of the Tudors, Lily B. Campbell in her book on the History Plays makes him out to be a propagandist whose "chronicle was undoubtedly written to serve the political purposes of Henry VIII, being directed to teaching political lessons in general and one imperative lesson in particular, the destruction that follows rebellion and civil dissension in a realm."[27] Implicitly identifying the political lessons of Hall's Chronicle with those of the Tudor Homilies, Professor Campbell makes Hall seem a spokesman for Tudor orthodoxy, and she asserts that "each of the Shakespeare histories serves a special purpose in elucidating a political problem of Elizabeth's day and in bringing to bear upon this problem the accepted political philosophy of the Tudors."[28] More sweeping still is Tillyard's claim that the picture of English history in the tetralogies is based on the Tudor myth which Hall promulgated in his Chronicle and which supposedly moralizes the calamity of the War of the Roses in the following way:

Over against Richard [II]'s inability is set Henry IV's crime, first in usurping the throne and secondly in allowing Richard to be killed against his oath. God punished Henry by making his reign unquiet but postponed full vengeance till a later generation, for Henry (like Ahab) humbled himself. But Henry was none the less a usurper and this was a fact universally accepted by the Elizabethans. Hall notes the immediate jealousy of the house of York when Richard was deposed. Henry V by his politic wisdom and his piety postpones the day of reckoning. He learns from the example of past history and chooses good counsellors; he banishes his evil companions; he does his best to expiate his father's sin by having Richard reburied in Westminster. But his wisdom does not stretch to detecting the danger from the House of York. With Henry VI the curse is realised and in the dreaded form of a child being king—"woe to the nation whose king is a child."[29]

Because Tillyard's exposition of the Tudor myth seems to explain the form and comprehend the substance of Shakespeare's tetralogies, it has had an enormous influence on the criticism of the History Plays.[30] To be sure,

25. Kingsford, p. 274.
26. See, for example, W. G. Zeeveld, "The Influence of Hall on Shakespeare's English Historical Plays," *ELH,* III (1936), 317-53.
27. *Shakespeare's Histories,* p. 68.
28. *Shakespeare's Histories,* p. 125.
29. *History Plays,* p. 60.
30. That one or both of Shakespeare's tetralogies is founded on the Tudor myth of

skeptics have pointed out that the pattern of the Tudor myth is eccentrically set forth in the tetralogies, which begin with the funeral of Henry V and end with the famous victory of Agincourt. Others have noted that the political lesson which is supposedly at the heart of Hall's Chronicle and Shakespeare's History Plays is remarkably obscure in the tetralogies. The three brief references to the deposition of Richard II in the first tetralogy scarcely convince us that it was the cause of Henry VI's calamities. And though Shakespeare has the opportunity to drive his lesson home in the Epilogue to *Henry V*, which comments on the tragedy of the War of the Roses, he makes no mention of the original sin committed against Richard II for which later generations supposedly paid with their blood.

There is very good reason to doubt that Shakespeare wrote his tetralogies to set forth what Tillyard calls the Tudor myth of history. There is reason also to question whether the view of history which Tillyard sets forth as the Tudor myth was in fact the Tudor myth and can be attributed as such to Hall. Certainly Hall was familiar with this moralistic interpretation of the past and refers to it in his Chronicle, but he never acknowledges it as his own. Reflecting on the misfortunes of Henry VI, he notes that some say Henry was "a man of no great wit"—an "innocent" more godly than worldly. Some say that he was a coward incapable of ruling.

Other there be that ascribe his infortunitie, onely to the stroke and punishment of God, afferming that the kyngdome which Henry the iiii hys grandfather wrongfully gat, and uniustly possessed agaynst kyng Richard the ii and his heyres could not by very divyne iustice, longe contynew in that iniurious stocke: And that therefore God by his divine providence, punished the offence of the grandfather, in the sonnes sonne.[31]

Nothing indicates that Hall agrees with this last explanation of Henry's calamity, and everything he says earlier about Richard II and Henry Bolingbroke suggests that he did not think the deposition of Richard a dreadful sin for which England suffered. Judging Richard wanton rather than malicious, he laments that Richard was deceived and betrayed by those he trusted and preferred.[32] But he makes quite explicit that Richard's lawless acts were destroying England and he tells that nobility, prelates, and magistrates

---

history has become practically a *donnée* of the scholarship on the History Plays. See, for example, *Narrative and Dramatic Sources of Shakespeare*, ed. Geoffrey Bullough (New York: Columbia Univ. Press, 1960), III, 355.

31. Edward Hall, *The Union of the Two Noble and Illustrious Families of York and Lancaster* (London, 1809), pp. 285-86. Hall's Chronicle was first printed in 1548.

32. Hall, p. 21

"perceavyng daily more and more the realme to fall into ruyne and desolacion (in maner irrecuperable as long as kyng Richard either lived or reigned)" pleaded with the exiled Bolingbroke to return and take the crown of England.[33] Hall adds furthermore that Bolingbroke, who returned to England only after the Archbishop of Canterbury appealed to him to rescue his homeland, was declared king "with one voyce both of the nobles and commons."[34] He describes Bolingbroke as a noble aristocrat whom the people loved and as an excellent king—as a patriot who saved his nation from calamity, not as a guilty usurper.[35] Of course, his patterning of history makes Henry IV the "first aucthor" of the division between Lancaster and York, but by this Hall means only that in accepting the crown Henry necessarily disallowed the Yorkist claim to it as Richard's chosen heirs; and thus willy-nilly he sowed the first seed of the contention for the throne in the time of Henry VI.[36]

Like most Henrician writers, Hall dwells on the horrors of civil war, and on the unnaturalness of dissension, strife, and factionalism in England. He does not, however, propagandize for the Tudor doctrine of obedience; he never postulates the sacredness of royal authority, nor does he exclaim against the sin of rebellion. His central theme is announced in his opening paragraph:

What mischief hath insurged in realmes by intestine devision, what depopulacion hath ensued in countries by civill discension, what detestable murder hath been committed in citees by separate faccions, and what calamitee hath ensued in famous regions by domestical discord and unnaturall controversy . . .[37]

33. Hall, p. 6.
34. Hall, p. 13.
35. Although many scholars insist that he viewed Henry IV as a usurper, Hall does not, so far as I can determine, accuse Henry of usurping the throne. Surely if the guilty consequences of Henry's usurpation of the throne is Hall's chief historical lesson, he should make that guilt unequivocal. Hall's admiring portrait of Henry Bolingbroke contrasts sharply with that of John Hardyng, who suggests in his *Chronicle* (1534) that Bolingbroke won the crown by coercion and kept it by cheating the Percies. Hardyng says that on his deathbed Henry IV thought "nought of repentance of usurpement of the realme, ne of the restorement of ryght heyres to the crowne" (*The Chronicle of John Hardyng* [London, 1812], pp. 351, 369). Hall never speaks of Mortimer as rightful heir or of Henry's "usurpement of the realme."
36. In at least three places, including his title and his dedication, Hall speaks of Henry as the "first aucthor" of the division between Lancaster and York or as "the beginnyng and rote of the great discord and devision." He never accuses Henry, however, of unlawfully taking the crown that belonged to Richard or to his heir Mortimer. What he points out is that Henry, in taking the crown for himself and his heirs, put aside the claim of Mortimer and his Yorkist heirs, a claim that would be pressed in the time of Henry VI (pp. 13, 231).
37. Although Hall returns again and again to the theme of faction and division, he does not speak of the deadly sin of rebellion. His plea for unity is quite different from the Homilies' execration of rebellion.

For Hall, England's tragedy was the result of the emulous pride and rivalry of the houses of Lancaster and York, whom he compares to the Guelphs and Ghibellines. He does not preach the doctrine of nonresistance nor does he anathematize those who take arms against anointed majesty. Pleading for patriotic devotion to the commonweal, he celebrates the unity and the peace which the Tudors restored to a ravaged England.

Like other Chroniclers, Hall finds God's hand and often inscrutable purposes in history. Again and again he points out that retribution follows evil acts and that guilty men are often punished in some fashion for their crimes. But we need only look at the titles which he gave to the reigns of English kings—titles that supposedly influenced Shakespeare's treatment of history—to realize that Hall does not trace a grim pattern of retribution from the deposition of Richard to Bosworth Field, nor does he suggest England was a nation cursed by God because Richard had been deposed. The "unquiet tyme of kyng Henry the Fowrth" is followed by the "victorious actes of kyng Henry the V"; the "troublesome season of kyng Henry the VI" is followed by the "prosperous reigne of kyng Edward the iiij"; the "pitifull life of kyng Edward the V" leads to the "tragicall doynges of kyng Richard the iij," and that to the "politike governaunce of kyng Henry the vij" and finally the "triumphant reigne of kyng Henry the viij." Because he never speaks of God's curse on sinning England, Hall does not have to explain why the curse was lifted during the victorious acts of Henry V and the "prosperous reign" of Edward IV. A devout Protestant, he believes in a just and loving Christian God, not a primitive and capricious deity who exacts horrible vengeances on innocent generations but can be mollified temporarily by the virtue of this or that monarch.

What Tillyard and other Shakespeareans call the Tudor myth of history might more correctly be called the Yorkist myth of history, because it corresponds in essential details to the argument set forth by the Duke of York to the English Parliament after the battle of Northampton, when he claimed the throne as its rightful heir.[38] It is Holinshed in 1577, not Hall in 1548, who accepts this Yorkist view of the past, who condemns Bolingbroke as a usurper,

38. See Hall, pp. 245-47. It is in this speech, not in Hall's commentary on the fall of Richard II, that Bolingbroke is called a usurper and murderer who never afterward enjoyed peace of mind and body. It is also in this speech rather than in Hall's commentary that the War of the Roses is described as a punishment sent by God to scourge an unruly and ungracious people. In the introduction to his new Arden edition of *Henry VI Part III*, A. S. Cairncross, obviously influenced by Tillyard and Ribner, refers his readers to York's oration as an expression of Shakespeare's moral view of English history. See *The Third Part of King Henry VI* (London: Methuen, 1964), p. l, n. 4. In York's oration, Henry V's virtue is acknowledged to have stayed God's wrath, but even Henry is said to have been

and who dwells on the fits of remorse and guilty fears that supposedly plagued Bolingbroke's later years as king. According to Holinshed the "unquiet time" of Henry IV was a fitting punishment on him and his subjects who "were so readie to ioine and clappe hands with him, for the deposing of their rightfull and naturall prince king Richard, whose cheefe fault rested onlie in that, that he was too bountifull to his freends and too mercifull to his foes."[39] One cannot imagine such a reading of history serving the political purposes of Henry VII or Henry VIII because it places too great an emphasis on the principle of legitimacy. That is to say, in condemning Bolingbroke as a usurper, Holinshed implicitly accepts the validity of the Yorkist claim to the throne. He even suggests that the Duke of York was the true claimant to the throne occupied by Henry VI and deserved to be king until he proved too impatient and bloody in his desire to wrest the crown from Henry.[40] Having overthrown the last of the Yorkist kings at Bosworth, the Tudor monarchs could hardly have sanctioned or made official a reading of history which made the Yorkist dynasty the true inheritors and which stained their own Lancastrian ancestry with the sin of usurpation even as it disallowed their claim to the throne by lineal descent. Where Holinshed feels free in 1577 to weigh rival claims or to assume a legitimist stance, the early Tudor apologists, aware that the Tudor claim was not "indubitate," had to avoid the issue of legitimacy by proclaiming again and again the sanctity of de facto royal authority. Rather than condemn the guilt of Henry IV, they dwelled on the villainy of Richard III; and rather than describe Henry VI as the scapegoat for his grandfather's sin, they canonized him as a saintly martyr to Richard's murderous ambition, who foresaw the redemption of England under Richmond. Determined not to set Lancaster's claim against York's, as Holinshed does, they celebrated (as Hall does) the union of Lancaster and York in Richmond's marriage to Elizabeth, a sacramental joining together of the two great houses which was symbolized in the Tudor Rose.

Hall's great theme—the Tudor theme—was reconciliation, not retribution. He regards the English, not as sinners who had to be redeemed, but as a chosen people who had to wander in the desert of civil strife before they were led to

---

punished for his father's sins in that he died young. Surely this is not Shakespeare's view, nor is it the judgment of Hall on the mirror of all Christian kings.

39. Raphael Holinshed, *Chronicles of England, Scotland, and Ireland* (London, 1808), III, 58. This edition is a reprint of the 1587 edition of Holinshed, which Shakespeare used for the plays of the second tetralogy. The *Chronicles* were first printed in 1577.

40. Holinshed, pp. 447-"48." Page 448 is mispaginated as 478, and there are no pages 448-477 in the volume.

their nationhood by the Tudors. When one turns the pages of Holinshed, who begins his account of English history with its legendary beginnings, one has a vivid sense of the conflicts and disorders that plagued so much of England's past. One knows from Holinshed that the reign of Richard II was tumultuous from its start, and that long before Mowbray and Bolingbroke quarreled, Richard was engaged in a bitter struggle for power with his closest kin and most powerful subjects. Wiping away this wretched past by excluding it from his Chronicle, Hall makes it seem as if the dissension that climaxed in the War of the Roses first broke out at the end of Richard's reign. Thus, while political conflict seems an eternal norm of English history, Hall's Chronicle suggests that factionalism and strife are aberrations, diseases of the body politic that can be traced back to a beginning in time and will have an ending in time. He finds in the vicissitudes of history proof of God's providential care because it is the chaos of civil war that actually leads to England's fulfillment as a nation under the Tudors.

Hall's conviction of the working of Providence in history never interferes with his strong common sense. Even as he can find God's judgment in the misfortunes of evil men, he can also condemn the superstition of those bent on moralizing every turn of fate. He is especially contemptuous of those who attribute the illness of Henry IV to divine vengeance: "What shall a man say of such writers," he remarks, "whiche toke upon them to know the secretes of Goddes iudgement?"[41] In Hall's, as in other sixteenth-century Chronicles, moralistic judgments stand side by side with shrewdly realistic observations of political life. Next to pious exclamations and simplistic moral portraits are clear-eyed statements of the Machiavellian facts of political struggle and intrigue. Leonard Dean has pointed out that, even though Tudor Chroniclers appeal to the will of God, they see history primarily as a world of "second causes," of human acts and consequences.[42] Even more mundane is the viewpoint of an Elizabethan like Samuel Daniel, who retains the pious tags and apostrophes of Tudor Chroniclers but approaches politics in a completely pragmatic fashion in his epic poem *The Civil Wars*. The first impression, to be sure, is that Daniel intends to superimpose Holinshed's moralism on Hall's patterning of English history. His Preface to the 1609 edition declares an intention "to shewe the deformities of Civile Dissension, and the miserable events of Rebellions, Conspiracies, and bloudy Revengements, which followed

41. Hall, p. 35.
42. Leonard F. Dean, "Tudor Theories of History Writing," *University of Michigan Contributions in Modern Philology*, no. 1 (1941), pp. 17ff.

(as in a circle) upon that breach of the due course of Succession, by the Usurpation of Hen. 4."[43] But within the poem itself, Daniel proves to be more impartial in his judgments than either Hall or Holinshed. He blames the greedy lawless ambitions of Richard's uncles Gaunt and Gloucester as much as Richard's own frailty, indulgence of flatterers, and indiscretion for the turmoil that climaxed in armed rebellion.[44] Similarly, he is reluctant to accuse Bolingbroke of calculated opportunism, although he questions his purity of motive in returning from exile.[45] Viewing history as a fascinating drama of human motives, acts, and conflicts, he sees very little in it to ascribe to divine intervention.

The many plays and poems written by Elizabethans on English history reveal the variousness of their approaches to the past. The Tudor and Elizabethan Chronicles, as we might expect, are more uniform in temper and outlook, because the Chroniclers draw on common sources, borrow from and plagiarize one another, or simply incorporate their predecessors' accounts in their own. Still, on scores of specific points the Chronicles vary significantly, because each author has his own judgment of historical personalities and each selects and edits his materials in his own way. "Quoting" at length Canterbury's appeal to Bolingbroke to save England, Hall creates the impression that Bolingbroke returned from exile for the highest purposes; omitting that speech, Holinshed makes Bolingbroke's return from exile appear more opportunistic. Similarly, each of the Chroniclers reports Henry IV's quarrel with the Percies in a slightly different fashion—some emphasizing the Percies' malcontent, others noting that Bolingbroke had, as the Percies proclaimed, lied when he swore to them on his landing that he had returned to England only to seek his ducal inheritance. Astute readers could not but notice that Chronicle accounts contradicted one another,[46] and those who read the Chronicles with any care could not but notice the inconsistencies and contradictions of Holinshed, who declares Richard II almost blameless on one page but elsewhere repeats the

43. Samuel Daniel, *The Civil Wars,* ed. Laurence Michel (New Haven: Yale Univ. Press, 1958), p. 67. Citing Tillyard's *Shakespeare's History Plays,* Michel comments that Daniel probably took his view of history from the Tudor myth which Hall promulgated (p. 4). But though Daniel cites Hall among many other Chronicles as sources which he used for his poem and though he patterns history as Hall did, he obviously based his work squarely on Holinshed, who is the only Chronicler aside from Hardyng who explicitly condemns Bolingbroke as a usurper.

44. *The Civil Wars,* pp. 78-84.

45. *Ibid,* pp. 93-95.

46. The author of Mowbray's tragedy in *The Mirror for Magistrates,* for example, calls attention to the discrepancy between Hall's and Fabyan's accounts of the quarrel of Mowbray and Bolingbroke (p. 112).

opinion of earlier Chroniclers that he defiled his life with "fowle enormities," for which he was cut down by the wrath of God.[47] Rather than an authorized version of the past, the Chronicles offered Elizabethan artists a fascinating hodgepodge of significant and trivial facts, of shrewd judgments and fantastic opinions, eclectically gathered and often uncritically repeated. Although the dramatists were in the main faithful to their Chronicle sources they had necessarily to select, edit, and transpose materials to fashion coherent plots out of rambling accounts. Faced with the inconsistencies, contradictions, dubieties, and ambiguities of the Chronicles, they also felt free to alter or elaborate on historical "fact" for artistic purposes.

If Shakespeare's interest in history had been shallow and opportunistic, if he had turned to the Chronicles merely to find plot materials and had been willing to accept without question the judgments of his sources, he would have found all he needed to write his History Plays in a single Chronicle as comprehensive as Holinshed's. Yet he used Hall as his primary source for the first tetralogy, and, in addition to Holinshed, read Stowe, Foxe, the *Mirror for Magistrates*, a host of lesser Chronicles and historical accounts, plays, and poems. One could reasonably conclude that a man who consulted so many source materials and who wrote nine or ten plays about English history and three about Roman history had a very deep and serious interest in the past. But so persistent is the idea of the unintellectual Shakespeare that scholars would rather conjure up the ghost of vanished ur-texts than accept the probability that he read widely in history and thought critically and independently about it. Dover Wilson, for example, suggests that *Richard II* is based upon materials gathered from half a dozen English and French historical sources, but he would have us believe that this research was done by some unknown dramatist whose lost play Shakespeare revised.[48] (If Shakespeare had had Jonson's foresight, he would also have documented his historical scholarship with footnotes.) When one compares Shakespeare's plays with their source materials, one sees that, far from exploiting the merely sensational or theatrical possibilities of history, Shakespeare again and again deepens characterizations and illuminates political issues—again and again his vision of the past is more penetrating and acute than that of the Chroniclers. Yet it is astonishing how often scholars will fasten on minor confusions of names or muddles of fact in the History Plays as evidence of Shakespeare's indifference to historical truth.[49]

47. Holinshed, II, 868-69.
48. See the new Cambridge edition of *Richard II*, ed. John Dover Wilson (Cambridge: Cambridge Univ. Press, 1939, reprinted 1961), pp. lxiv-lxxvi.
49. See, for example, Wilson's introduction to *Richard II*, pp. lxiv-lxv.

Although Shakespeare based the first tetralogy primarily on Hall and the second tetralogy primarily on Holinshed, he did not see history first in Hall's way and then in Holinshed's. Whatever source materials he used, his interpretation of the past was his own. Perhaps we lay too much stress on the ideological influence of the Chronicles on Shakespeare's art because we live in an age of ideologies and mass political movements. Today campaigning and propagandizing are very nearly continuous; the trumpet calls to action and to opposition from the right and the left, and the air is filled with revolutionary battle cries or appeals to moderation. We accept as healthy and necessary the fierce competition of political parties in our democracies, and we assume that the art of politics includes not only the governing of a state but also the wooing of large masses of the populace whose party allegiances are subject to change. We have, in short, systematized faction, moderated it by constitutional restraints, and legitimized it as the basis of democratic politics. So persistent and pervasive, therefore, are political argument and ideology in our times that no one can escape their influence. However judicious and detached our historians may be, they are almost inevitably of one inclination or another; their objectivity is either liberal or conservative, and their political orientations bias, however faintly, their interpretations of the past.

It would be nearly impossible, however, to distinguish the political stances of the Tudor and Elizabethan Chroniclers, to say that Hardyng is more radical than Fabyan or that Hall was more liberal (or conservative) than Holinshed. While the rise of Protestantism had created religious radicals, moderates, and reactionaries in Tudor England, the politics of party and ideology did not really begin until the last decades of the sixteenth century, when Parliament, under militant Puritan leaders, began to assert its independence from the Crown. Up to the Henrician Reformation, English politics had little if any ideological cast. Medieval theorizing about the state (as Machiavelli scornfully noted) was idealistic and divorced from practical realities. While theorists expounded the higher purposes of rule, kings embarked on military adventures to win territory and booty, and barons and churchmen vied for the wealth and power that belonged to the ruling classes of a feudal society. Alliances were pragmatic and opportunistic; sometimes the king and the baronry feuded, sometimes they joined together against the Church, and now and then all three estates banded together to put down peasant uprisings and to extirpate the rare revolutionary movements that threatened the institutions and privileges of the feudal world. As accounts of the War of the Roses indicate, men rallied to the great dynasties and houses according to their local feudal allegiances. Their attachments were familial and regional, not ideological and national.

Under the Tudors the character of feudal politics began to change as the national state gained power at the expense of the great feudal baronry and the clergy. A new aristocracy came into being whose interests were national, not local—identified with the crown, not with the ancient feudal order. The issue of religious reformation, moreover, cut across the boundaries of regional alliances and antipathies, and involved great masses of the population in a political as well as religious controversy. For the first time ideological stances and commitments threatened to become important in English politics as Protestant and Catholic polemicists clamored for the support of Englishmen. But, just as one cannot describe the sixteenth century in England as an era of placid political consensus,[50] neither can one describe it as a time of widespread ideological divisions. Lily. B. Campbell suggests that the question of a people's right to depose a king "was uppermost in men's minds" when Shakespeare wrote *Richard II*.[51] I think it more accurate to say that the theoretical right to disobey or rebel against a king was argued in the 1590's only by a very small and fanatical group of Catholic exiles, even as during Mary's reign the right of rebellion had been argued only by a very small group of Protestant exiles. To be sure, Elizabeth's government could not let the polemical justifications of rebellion and regicide by Robert Parsons go unanswered;[52] and it had to take very seriously the danger of internal subversion when the assassination of the Queen would probably have caused widespread disorders if not anarchy and civil war. Vulnerable to foreign attack and limited in its resources and its effective control of the nation, the regime had to guard vigilantly against the possibility of another uprising on the scale of the Northern Rebellion of 1569, which had for a time endangered the regime.

But we cannot judge from popular hysterias or bureaucratic anxieties the extent to which Englishmen were divided or seriously perplexed over the question of obedience to kings. Impressed by the vehemence of Catholic exiles, the earnest polemics of Elizabethan apologists, the harsh measures enacted against Catholics and other subversives in the 1590's, and the elaborate intelligence systems developed by Elizabeth's ministers which uncovered a number of plots against the state, one might conclude that Elizabethan England was a nation seething with internal strife. One might also conclude from the hysterias of the McCarthy era, the confessions of ex-Communists, the

50. The range of Elizabethan political thinking is evident in Ernest William Talbert's *The Problem of Order* (Chapel Hill: Univ. No. Carolina Press, 1962).
51. *Shakespeare's Histories*, p. 211.
52. See Campbell, *Shakespeare's Histories*, pp. 173-81.

discovery of espionage cells, the security clearances, the Senate hearings, and the multiplication of loyalty oaths, that the rooting out of subversive conspiracy was necessary to the survival of the United States after World War II. In both eras, however, the fear of subversion was largely unfounded, and the search for traitors a symptom of deeply rooted fears and frustrations. Both countries had won great victories against foreign enemies only to find themselves (or to think themselves) under the continuing threat of encirclement and attack. This sense of peril, coupled with the stresses of social and economic change, sorely tried the confidence and unity of England in the 1590's and America in the 1950's, and though security from foreign attack was not to be gained by the rooting out of supposed traitors at home, the hunting down of subversives had its psychological and political uses in both eras.

Can we believe, however, that Shakespeare was so shallow in his assessment of the temper of his countrymen, and so fearful of the threat of incipient anarchy, that he wrote play after play to persuade his audiences of the need for order and obedience? If we may judge from his characterizations of common men in the History Plays, he knew that his fellow Englishmen were neither giddy nor eager for change. He may even have suspected that as a people the English were far more conservative than were their Tudor monarchs, who came to power by armed rebellion, who changed the established religion, radically altered the Church, dissolved the monastic orders, and centralized political power under the throne—all the while proclaiming that whatever is is right. When, as in sixteenth-century England, the government becomes revolutionary, it is likely that those who rebel are conservatives who resort to arms in attempts to restore traditional ways of life.[53] Actually, the Tudor regimes were threatened, not by ideologists who proclaimed from afar the right of rebellion, but by disgruntled aristocrats at home and by impoverished peasants in outlying counties who clung fiercely to the Old Faith. The Catholic earls who led the Northern Rebellion did not proclaim the right of rebellion. They swore that they took arms against those who "abused the queen," and that their goal was to restore "ancient customs and liberties."[54] Shakespeare, I think, understood that men do not easily shrug off the habit of obedience, nor

53. That the two great uprisings of the sixteenth century (the Pilgrimage of Grace in 1536 and the Northern Rebellion of 1569) were essentially conservative protests against revolutionary political, social, and religious changes is noted by Christopher Morris, *Political Thought in England: Tyndale to Hooker* (London: Oxford Univ. Press, 1953), pp. 58-9, and by J. B. Black, *The Reign of Elizabeth* (Oxford: Clarendon Press, 1936), pp. 103-8.
54. Black, *Reign of Elizabeth*, pp. 107-108.

do they easily renounce time-honored oaths of allegiance and fealty. All men—and rebels not the least—consider treason abhorrent, but there are occasions when ambition irresistibly beckons or when men think themselves so terribly wronged or threatened that they must take arms to defend the right and reform the regime. Marching against the King, they act and speak like the rebels in *Richard II*, who challenge law and appeal to ancient traditions. Ready to stoop to true authority, they are also ready, however, to contest violently the legitimacy of the authority which oppresses them. As is so often apparent in the Chronicles, rebels come not as rebels but as patriots, saviors, and restorers of order, determined to protect their monarch from his evil counselors if they have to dethrone him to do so. And if, as will happen, they depose him, they very quickly discover that he never belonged on the throne to begin with.[55]

Because the Tudor claim to the throne was not unquestionable, and because opportunists and enemies of the regime often used the pretense of restoring the true inheritor to the throne, a trace of the blood royal and a connection to the throne proved fatal to many gentlemen and women in Henrician days. But the plots and the attempted coups on behalf of this pretender or that failed because Englishmen were not inclined to risk their lives and England's peace for the sake of a subtly argued genealogy. Knowing his countrymen, Shakespeare does not suggest that men chose sides in the War of the Roses according to their beliefs in de facto authority or legitimacy. They took sides because of their feudal attachments, because of the appeal of family honor and pride, or as they were prompted by ambition, greed, patriotism, or revenge. In the sixteenth century as in earlier times Englishmen were willing enough to support the existing government so long as conditions were reasonably tolerable. They preferred to suffer the political evils they knew than to risk the unknown terrors of civil war. I doubt, however, that the Tudor doctrine of de facto political authority inspired fierce loyalty to the regime, for men (as Shakespeare realized) will not eagerly sacrifice their lives to preserve the existing regime, when they know that they will be able, in good conscience, to support the rebels if they succeed.[56] Despite Tudor efforts to make rebellion unthinkable, men did think about it, and the wittiest of them understood that in rebellion, as in most human enterprises, nothing succeeds like success. A

55. It was a time-honored custom for usurpers to bastardize those they overthrew. Richard III, for example, spread rumors of the illegitimacy of Edward IV, his own brother.

56. See Act III, scene i, of *Henry VI Part III*, where the gameskeepers explain their loyalty to Edward IV to their former king Henry VI.

successful rebel, John Harington shrewdly observed, is no rebel at all: "Treason doth never prosper; what's the reason? / For if it prosper, none dare call it treason." This cynical epigram is not the gospel according to Machiavelli—it represents good, though maliciously phrased, Tudor theology: God defends the right of whoever wins.

Hardly cynical in his portrayal of human behavior, Shakespeare nevertheless records in the History Plays the ease with which men turn their coats and alter their allegiances and yet remain men of conscience. He allows us to savor the irony of ingenious political rationalizations, but he is not quick to brand equivocations of loyalty hypocrisy. He knows that politics is the art of accommodation and survival, and he knows too that because political theoreticians invoke metaphysical absolutes it is difficult for them to adjust to changing circumstances without seeming to abandon their principles. At various times during the sixteenth century, for example, the radical Protestant and Catholic positions on obedience to kings turned about face. The zealous reformers who in Henrician days promulgated the Lutheran doctrine of obedience to princes, preached the right of resistance during Mary's reign, and with the accession of Elizabeth once again vehemently insisted on the religious duty of nonresistance to kings. But as the century wore on and Elizabeth refused to prosecute the cause of total Reformation, the Puritan faction became again an opposition party, and half a century later Puritan revolutionaries used the arguments of the Marian exiles to justify the execution of Charles.[57] When the official religious policy of the Tudor monarchs bent and twisted and reversed itself, it was impossible for men of religious zeal to walk a strait and narrow path.

Although a belief in the sinfulness of rebellion undoubtedly exerted a powerful influence on the behavior of men in sixteenth-century England, the Tudors survived their parlous times largely because their subjects rejected the attempts of controversialists to make political loyalty conditional upon religious allegiance. Since a century of Tudor and Stuart dogmatizing about the holy duty of obedience did not save Charles I from his God-fearing enemies, we can assume that had there been compelling political reasons or had Elizabeth been as tactless and inept as Charles in dealing with her opposition, she too might have been dethroned and perhaps even executed. For century after

57. See the discussion of the "Puritan Protest" in Morris, *Political Thought,* chs. 2, 6, 8; see also Franklin Le Van Baumer, *The Early Tudor Theory of Kingship* (New Haven: Yale Univ. Press, 1940), pp. 91, 112-113, for the reversals of Catholic and Protestant positions during the sixteenth century.

century theologians and philosophers had proclaimed the sacredness of royal authority; and for century after century English and European history had been dyed in the blood of kings. But despite the facts of political life the idea of divine right persisted because it was useful to all who wielded power, and because devout men could always find God's purposes in events and thereby prove that whatever happens in history is providential and right. The authors of *The Mirror for Magistrates*, for example, can explain why God permits rebellions even though they are contrary to his law:

For in dede officers be gods deputies, and it is gods office which they beare, and it is he whiche ordeyneth thereto suche as himselfe lysteth, good whan he favoreth the people, and evyll whan he wyll punish theim. And therefore whosoever rebelleth agaynst any ruler either good or bad, rebelleth against GOD, and shal be sure of a wretched ende: For God can not but maintein his deputie. Yet this I note by the waye concernyng rebelles and rebellions. Although the devyll rayse theim, yet God alwayes useth them to his glory, as a parte of his Iustice. For whan Kynges and chiefe rulers, suffer theyr under officers to mysuse theyr subiectes, and wil not heare nor remedye theyr peoples wronges whan they complayne, than suffreth GOD the Rebell to rage, and to execute that parte of his Iustice, which the parcyall prince woulde not.[58]

The Puritan leaders in Parliament in the 1580's and 1590's no doubt shared the conviction of the heinousness of rebellion expressed in *The Mirror for Magistrates*. Yet that conviction did not prevent them from opposing Elizabeth's policies or deter them from attempting to legislate about the succession and the religious establishment—subjects forbidden to them by Elizabeth's edicts. We cannot explain the behavior of such men simply by reference to sixteenth-century postulates about the duty of subjects to obey. We must keep in mind that while the royalist doctrines promulgated in the reign of Henry VIII and reinforced in the Elizabethan Homilies remained fixed in their official mold, the relation between the crown and the nation changed in significant ways during the century. In Henrician times the crown was the symbol of national unity and independence, and of Protestant defiance of a hated Papacy. So long as the threat of foreign intervention and civil war seemed immediate, so long was the power of the throne the key to England's survival. When the threat of invasion diminished after the defeat of the Armada, a loyal opposition to the crown and a more critical view of royal authority became permissible.[59] Where King and Parliament had been united

58. *Mirror*, p. 178.
59. See the discussion of the "Cult of Authority" in sixteenth-century England in Baumer, *Tudor Theory*, p. 90.

in Henrician days in a common will to Reformation, the Queen and the Parliament were recurrently at odds in the late Elizabethan days, and again and again Elizabeth was forced to admonish or veto the bills of Parliaments intent upon matters that were the prerogative of the Crown.[60]

Earlier scholars were too quick to find oblique allusions to contemporary political issues and intrigues in Shakespeare's plays. Of late scholars have been too ready to suggest that Shakespeare, oblivious to contemporary political realities, gained his knowledge of politics from Erasmus, Elyot, and the Homilies. As we would expect, religious concepts of authority and obedience are set forth in some of his plays, but not in a way that would convince an audience to suffer gladly the evil that kings do.[61] And for all the stress that recent scholarship has placed on Shakespeare's orthodoxy, the fact remains that no other Elizabethan writer so acutely and extensively portrays the weakness, folly, incompetence, and wickedness of English kings. Unwilling to propagandize by making all who oppose a king villains and all who support the existing government heroes, Shakespeare knew that political issues are much more complex than the Homilies would allow—that honorable men must sometimes compromise their principles because their choices are limited and ambiguous.

I doubt that Shakespeare needed Machiavelli's tutelage to see the uglier realities of political life, but he was conscious, I think, of the challenge of the Florentine's thought to traditional assumptions.[62] Like Machiavelli, he sees the contention for power as one of the eternal facts of history, and he realizes that pious professions simply mask the dominant role of self-interest in politics. But he knows also that ideals of honor and loyalty can inspire men to rise above their selfish interests and that principles of right and justice have since time immemorial exerted their influence on English life. Living in a country that had achieved the political unity and independence which Machiavelli hoped would some day come to Italy, Shakespeare was not inclined to accept the degraded politics of a fifteenth-century Italy as a universal norm. Knowing how Englishmen cherish the past and how stubbornly they cling to established ways and values, he could not think the majority of men as pliant and credulous, or as easily duped and cowed as Machiavelli suggests. He realizes that decency

60. See Black, *Reign of Elizabeth*, pp. 179-94; J. E. Neale, *Elizabeth I and Her Parliaments 1584-1601* (London: Jonathan Cape, 1957), pp. 298-312, 363-75.
61. It is the regicide Claudius who speaks in *Hamlet* of the divinity that hedges a king. Equally unconvincing is Richard II's fantasizing of his omnipotence when he returns from Ireland to face the threat of rebellion.
62. Estimates of Machiavelli's influence on the History Plays vary from Tillyard's belief in his "irrelevance to the age of Elizabeth" (*History Plays*, p. 22) to John F. Danby's belief that *King John* and the second tetralogy are profoundly influenced by Machiavelli's

may not be virtue enough in a ruler as incompetent as Henry VI, but he realizes also that the Machiavellian virtuosity of a Richard III provides no lasting basis for rule because it offers nothing to the people, who are the ultimate source of power in any state.

Addressing himself always to fact and historical example, Machiavelli thought there could be no appeal from the dictates of Necessity; Shakespeare realized, however, that Necessity is as the mind conceives and rationalizes it. Where Machiavelli insisted that seeing was believing, Shakespeare understood that in politics believing is often seeing. He knew that political rituals are not just shows designed to pacify or dupe the populace; they are the tangible expressions of political mystery, the ceremonies which invest authority with religious awe. Whatever role the Prince may play—magus or scapegoat—the King's Body is the living presence of the nation and his royal We a communion of multitudes. He is the Host upon which a people feed, in whose veins flows the blood of twenty thousand or a hundred thousand men, and whose illnesses infect his meanest subject. His sacred right is a mystery of blood that raises the throne above the gross purchase of political ambition but that makes the common weal subject to accidents of birth and death. Dynasties fall when the heirs to warrior kings are sybarites or saints, and anarchy overwhelms a nation whose "true inheritor" is an incapable child.

A master of theatrical spectacle, Shakespeare could appreciate the need for spectacle in politics, for the ceremonies which make all the world a stage for the mystery of power. He could also appreciate the mythopeic genius of the Tudors, who traced their descent to legendary kings and who consciously imitated the splendor of Plantagenet rule in their courtly pomp and stately progresses. Where Henry VII had ascended the throne as a savior-bridegroom whose marriage to the Yorkist princess Elizabeth reunited the royal houses of England, Elizabeth presented herself to the nation as the bride of England—as the Virgin Queen who loved her people so well that she would accept no other husband. Aware that all successful leaders create their personal mythologies, Shakespeare does not hesitate to grant the Lancastrian kings the political instincts of the Tudors. Where the Chronicles tell of a Prince Hal whose youth was misspent but who put on a new man when crowned, Shakespeare depicts a prince who deliberately fashions the legend of his prodigality and miraculous reformation, even as his father had artfully made himself seem a man of destiny who obeyed heaven's will in becoming King.

political ideas (*Shakespeare's Doctrine of Nature* [London: Faber & Faber, 1961], pp. 69-113).

If we ask, "Did Shakespeare believe in the myth of Tudor deliverance from the tyranny of Richard III?" the answer must be, "Yes, even as Americans believe in the myth of their deliverance from the tyranny of George III." For the sense of the past is almost always touched by mythic memories, and without epic legends of heroism and sacrifice a nation's history lacks meaning and form. But I do not think that Shakespeare was content to serve as the spokesman for an official version of history in the tetralogies. Rather he makes the memory of Agincourt and the memory of Bosworth the polarities of a personal mythic interpretation of England's history. The triumph at Agincourt epitomizes the heroic impulse of a people beginning to embark again on the adventure of empire. The victory at Bosworth recalls the hope of reconciliation and brotherhood among Englishmen that was still unfulfilled at the close of the sixteenth century and that would grow more remote in the seventeenth century as political and religious antagonisms intensified.

The tetralogies are too separate and too different from one another to be regarded as the complementary halves of a single oddly constructed panorama of English history. Each has a distinctive architectural unity that evolves, like the unity of a medieval cathedral, through the wedding of new form and conception to old; and each embraces a multitude of unities because it is made up of plays that have their own artistic integrity and individuality of theme, style, and structure. So extraordinary is the evolution of form and conception in the plays of the tetralogies that I cannot believe Shakespeare ever chafed at the "conventionality" of the History Play or had to flee its limitations to gain the larger horizons of his tragedies.[63] His progress in the History Plays was a journey of artistic exploration and self-discovery that led almost unerringly beyond politics and history to the universal themes and concerns of his maturest art.

To see in the tetralogies the same openness of mind and breadth of humanity that we find in the comedies and tragedies is to know that in writing the History Plays Shakespeare surrendered nothing to the dictates of orthodoxy. Only in *King John* and again in *Henry VIII* can we find what seems to be a stooping to or uncritical veneration of majesty. But the apparent royalism of *King John* is more likely the result of Shakespeare's boredom with his artistic task than of any eagerness to exalt the monarchy. The royalism of *Henry VIII*

63. This view is expressed in Granville-Barker's influential British Academy Lecture "From Henry V to Hamlet," first printed in 1925, revised in 1933, and reprinted in *Studies in Shakespeare*, ed. Peter Alexander (London: Oxford Univ. Press, 1964), pp. 71-102.

is more difficult to explain, or, at least, to attribute to Shakespeare, because it is at once solemn and facetious; it makes the king an object of idolatry and a subject of smutty innuendoes. Completely alien to Shakespeare's temper, such archness is but one of the many evidences of Fletcher's responsibility for the design of *Henry VIII*, to which Shakespeare lent a handful of scenes and (more important to the King's Men) his great name as a writer of History Plays.

2. THE HENRY VI PLAYS

One way to avoid the controversy over the authorship of the *Henry VI* plays is to admit the possibility that many of their scenes might have been written by Greene, Nashe, and Peele working as Shakespeare's collaborators. But the most cogent argument for multiple authorship, set forth by Dover Wilson in the new Cambridge editions of *Henry VI,* does not suggest a simple collaboration in which Shakespeare played a dominant role. Instead it suggests that Shakespeare was the reviser of "basic texts" of the *Henry VI* plays that had been plotted by Greene, and composed by Greene and Nashe, with some assistance from Peele.[1] Such a theory does more than disintegrate the texts of these plays; it casts doubt on their very ascription, because the kind of revision which Wilson attributes to Shakespeare could not have transformed the essential natures of the "basic texts." Indeed, if Wilson's hypothesis were correct, we would have to regard the *Henry VI* plays as the unacknowledged masterpieces of Greene and Nashe rather than the remarkable first fruits of Shakespeare's genius.

Wilson's arguments are too complex to be easily summarized. Particularly intricate and ingenious is the marshaling of evidence and supposition to support his contention that *Part I* was written after *Parts II* and *III* were performed.[2] But at the risk of oversimplification, these salient points of his textual analyses of the plays can be listed. Wilson sees no trace of Shakespeare's hand in more than a third of *Part I* and attributes only three of

1. The main burden of Wilson's argument is contained in his introduction to *The Second Part of King Henry VI.* It is continued in the introduction to *The Third Part,* and further evidence is supplied in the introduction to *The First Part.* The three texts were published by Cambridge Univ. Press in 1952.
2. Introduction, *The First Part of Henry VI,* pp. ix-xxi.

its scenes wholly to him.[3] He implicitly grants the dramatic structure of *Part II* to Greene and Nashe by discovering vestiges of the "basic text" in every scene.[4] He finds little or nothing of Shakespeare's composition in substantial portions of *Part III*, and suggests that his major contribution is confined to the last act, which he recast and rewrote.[5] In theory, Wilson's disintegration of the plays rests on a variety of evidences: echoes of Greene and Nashe in lines of the play, inconsistencies in the texts, contemporary allusions, and so forth. In practice, however, his analysis of text is a sorting out of sheep and goats, a distinguishing between poetry good enough to be Shakespeare's and that too labored and pedestrian to be assigned to him. Such an approach can be as nearsighted as it is meticulous, because it does not pay sufficient attention to the plays as artistic wholes. Although Wilson repeatedly questions whether Shakespeare could have written this scene or these lines, he does not ask whether Greene, Nashe, or Peele were capable of creating the kind of plots which Shakespeare supposedly found in the "basic texts." We do not know what Shakespeare's earliest and crudest poetry was like, but knowing the very height of the dramatic abilities of Greene, Nashe, and Peele, we can scarcely imagine their conceiving the epic political and moral dramas that, according to Wilson's hypothesis, must have existed in the basic texts of the *Henry VI* plays.[6]

If we assume that Shakespeare was born a poet,[7] we can use the quality of the poetry in the *Henry VI* plays as a touchstone to authorship. But this assumption begs the crucial question of Shakespeare's artistic development, for we have no reason to think him a second Marlowe who conquered the stage through his poetic verve. The envious Greene would have us believe quite the contrary: that the young Shakespeare was "an upstart Crow" who plagiarized other writers' styles and was "beautified with [their] feathers."[8] Blessed with

3. The notes to *The First Part* ascribe only II.iv., IV.ii, and IV.v wholly to Shakespeare; in all other scenes Wilson finds evidences of the original lines of the "basic text."

4. Notes to *The Second Part of Henry VI*. Although willing to attribute all the prose of the Cade scenes (IV.ii-IV.x) to Shakespeare, Wilson thinks that even here he is revising a basic text by Nashe.

5. Notes to *The Third Part of Henry VI*.

6. Whatever their poetic deficiencies, the *Henry VI* plays are masterpieces of dramatic form and profound studies in politics and history compared to Greene's *James IV* and Peele's *Edward I*, plays which hardly qualify for the title of History Plays and are as scattered in dramatic form as they are lacking in seriousness of theme and historical insight.

7. According to Wilson, Shakespeare had "three things . . . by nature and could no more dispense with than he could dispense with breath or heart-beat: I mean the poet's tongue, the poet's ear, and the poet's eye" (Introduction, *The Third Part of Henry VI*, p. xiv).

8. Wilson offers a more ingenious and dubious explanation for Greene's accusation (Introduction, *The Second Part*, pp. xiv-xix). It is difficult to see why Shakespeare was accused of beautifying his work with Greene's feathers if his crime was to rewrite basic

a remarkable ear and gift for mimicry, Shakespeare, I think, began his career as dramatic poet with a blank verse that was largely derivative and consciously literary—dignified with classical allusions and Senecal flourishes. It is quite likely that his dramatic instincts were at first superior to his poetic abilities, though he very quickly developed a mastery of the blank verse line and his own distinctive way with language and metaphor. Even in *Henry VI Part I*, however, his verse is not a hodgepodge of various styles, for what he borrows he fashions to his own artistic purposes, and though his lines often stumble, they are nearly always sufficient to their dramatic and rhetorical purposes. Shrewd about his limitations as a poet, he relies on exciting physical action to engross his audience's attention, and he casts many scenes as formal ceremonial occasions for which a stiff declamatory style is quite appropriate.

It is better to accept the poetry of the *Henry VI* plays as Shakespeare's earliest (and rapidly maturing) efforts than to save his reputation as a poet by suggesting that he was an opportunistic botcher of other men's plays, who was content to touch up some lines here and some scenes there, while he allowed much that was inferior to pass by. If we assume that the *Henry VI* plays were written by Shakespeare in their normal order, as does A. S. Cairncross in his illuminating introductions to the new Arden editions,[9] then we find a natural progression in Shakespeare's art—a growing sureness and refinement of technique and dramatic idea. If we assume, as Wilson does, that *Part I* followed *Parts II* and *III*, then we can find no satisfactory explanation for the fact that *Part I* is so much more primitive artistically than its "predecessors." In the process of explaining away relatively minor inconsistencies in these plays, Wilson creates major perplexities. His appeal to opportunistic motives[10] and his thesis of makeshift revisions cannot account, moreover, for the ambitious unities, the spacious historical design, the impressive consistencies of character portrayal, and the careful articulations of plot in the tetralogy: these all point to the working of a single remarkable artistic intelligence.

---

texts originally composed by Greene and others. If Shakespeare imitated lines, phrases, and stylistic mannerisms of his predecessors, then he did, as Greene claimed, beautify himself with other men's pens (or plumes). If, however, Shakespeare rewrote texts by other men, then he beautified their work with his plumes, and Greene's metaphor is askew. See the astute refutation of Wilson's hypothesis by A. S. Cairncross in the new Arden edition of *The Second Part of King Henry VI* (London: Methuen, 1962), pp. xlii-xlv.

9. *The First Part* was published in 1962; *The Third Part* in 1964.

10. Wilson suggests, for example, that *Part I* was probably written to exploit the popularity of *Part II* and *Part III*; through some underhanded dealing, *Part I* was supposedly given to Shakespeare to be hurriedly revised while its seige scenes were still immediately topical (Introduction, *Part I*, pp. xiv-xx, xlviii-l).

Part I

The earliest efforts of other Elizabethan playwrights were no doubt too poor to deserve publication. Shakespeare's artistic powers were such that his rudest apprentice work succeeded and survived in the *Henry VI* plays. There is enough that is skillful, lively, and thoughtful in *Part I* for us to say that here is Shakespeare's apprentice craftsmanship, were it not for the presence of the Temple Garden scene (II.iv), which is so superior to all else in the play that it makes all else seem less than "Shakespearean." In this scene the language grows terse and economical, the blank verse becomes fluent and edged with irony, and the stylized rhetoric effectively communicates the controlled rage of sophisticated antagonists. We cannot, however, attribute the power of the Temple Garden scene simply to its poetic style, when so much depends upon the building of dramatic tension, the inspired ironic use of the language of flowers, and the convincing representation of political conflict.[11] What prompts the quarrel we never learn and need not know, because at stake is not a point of law but feudal enmity and ambition—Somerset's pride and York's humiliation as the son of an attainted traitor. Recalling the treasons of an earlier generation, the quarrel prefigures even more dangerous conspiracies to come, for there is no sign of principle in the barons who jest cynically about law and who will accept no judgment except that rendered by the sword. Other scenes show how violent feuds mar the facades of courtly decorums. The Temple Garden scene takes us behind those facades as witnesses to the covert alliances and antagonisms which will surface only with the outbreak of civil war.

A triumph of the dramatic imagination over the inartistic formlessness of Tudor historiography, the Temple Garden scene adumbrates the danger of York and of divisive factionalism before that danger historically existed. In Hall, the early years of the reign of Henry VI have no particular political character. The tide of battle in France shifts back and forth; sometimes the noble English armies are checked by a lack of supplies and reinforcements, sometimes they are defeated by the treachery of the French. The English court is repeatedly disturbed by Gloucester and Winchester's quarrels, but their feud seems to have no special significance. No great figures dominate the political landscape: Henry is a child, and York, whose role in events is minor, is only a

11. Something in the power of the Temple Garden scene reminds me of comparable moments of verbal conflict and irony in Kyd's *The Spanish Tragedy.* In the Temple Garden scene as in scenes in *The Spanish Tragedy,* the dramatic conception, not the poetic style, is memorable.

latent threat. It is Shakespeare who brings York to the fore by inventing the quarrel in the Temple Garden scene, and the following one in which York meets with the dying Mortimer. It is Shakespeare who also magnifies the impact of York's quarrel with Somerset by making York, quite unhistorically, a party to the betrayal of Talbot in France. Boldly ignoring chronology and Chronicle "fact," he interweaves the destinies of Talbot, Joan of Arc, and York by making Talbot, Joan's adversary and victim, and York, Joan's nemesis and counterpart. Where she invokes the powers of darkness, he plots a Machiavellian conspiracy that will send ten thousand souls to hell. In this complex moral design, which pits chivalry against policy, England against France, and, most tragically, Englishmen against Englishmen, Talbot plays a major role, but rather than the protagonist of the play, he is the last exemplar of England's vanishing chivalric greatness.[12] First Salisbury falls, then Bedford, and when Talbot and his son die, the plant and seed of English heroism are lost.

A flesh and blood hero, Talbot descends from the epic figures of medieval romance, not from the didactic figures who people *Gorboduc* and the Tudor political Moralities. His death is a page out of Malory, or, perhaps out of the *Chanson de Roland,* whose hero is similarly betrayed. Like Gawain in another respect, Talbot proves himself in the trials of lust by conquering the treacherous French Countess, who would have kept him in her *daunger.* Immediately afterward, there is a more sardonic remembrance of romance in the Temple Garden scene, which uses the setting and allegory of the *Roman de la Rose* to dramatize deadly enmity.[13] Talbot has the two-dimensional quality of a literary memory and type. Other characters in *Part I* have more of the psychological substance and individuality of observed life. With a strong instinct for human realities, Shakespeare makes no attempt to conceptualize and allegorize virtues and vices in the manner of earlier Moralities. Even with his very limited artistic powers, he seeks to differentiate the emotional drives of the English opportunists—for example, Winchester's gnawing sense of inferiority from Suffolk's urbane cynicism and sensuality. Where Tudor didacticists drive home their Morality lessons by stark contrasts between good and evil, Shakespeare shades his melodramatic portraits. On the one hand, he

12. See Cairncross' refutation of the notion that *Part I* is a "Talbot play" (Introduction, *The First Part,* pp. xl-xli).
13. There is no reason to believe that Shakespeare is concerned in the *Henry VI* plays with such abstractions as "Respublica." The only echoes of medieval allegory in *Part I* are of the allegory of love. While nothing in *Part I* smacks of the Senecan turgidities of *Gorboduc,* various incidents, characters, and situations recall the motifs of chivalric romance.

allows the diabolical Joan her measure of greatness; on the other, he shows the irascible pride that flawed Gloucester's nobility. And just as the choleric Gloucester profanes the funeral rites of Henry V by pursuing his quarrel with Winchester, the chivalric Bedford has his moment of vainglory in the opening scene. When the news comes of Talbot's capture, Bedford exclaims, "His ransom there is none but I shall pay."

Fortune plays its role in *Part I* in such accidents as the untimely death of Henry V, or in the killing of the great Salisbury by a mere boy. But the tragical rhetoric of the play provides a literary atmosphere rather than a philosophical perspective. What happens happens because the characters are what they are and do what they do. If England is "doomed" to calamity, it is because the Englishmen *we see* are careless of their principles and untrue to their traditions. There is not the slightest hint that present ills are a retribution for earlier guilts, nor is there any intimation that England is cursed because three generations ago its people deposed their king. Only once in the play is the deposition of Richard II mentioned, and then it is by the dying Mortimer, who whispers to York a very partisan view of Bolingbroke's ascent to the throne and of the Percy rebellion that followed.[14] Quite obviously York does not aspire for power because he is convinced that he is a true inheritor. Malcontented before he learns about his link to the throne, he finds the justification for his conspiratorial ambition in Mortimer's account of the Yorkist claim to the succession, a claim that must be whispered fearfully because no others question Henry's title. It is Henry's failure to rule that makes his authority weak, not the flaw in his title that prevents him from ruling effectively. How else could Shakespeare have presented it, when history tells that Henry reigned for thirty years before his right to the throne was challenged by York?

The breakdown of political order in *Part I* proves the ancient truism: woe to a kingdom ruled by a child. The later years of the reign are even more disastrous because, though Henry grows older, marries, and fathers a son old enough to participate in the battle at Tewkesbury, he remains for too long a child, weak-willed and indecisive. Innocent and kindhearted, he is a paragon of virtue compared to most of his barons and to the Dauphin of France, but he is unable or unwilling to act the king. Desiring the public good, and seeing clearly enough what that good is, he never exerts his authority to achieve it. When Gloucester and Winchester and their servants quarrel in his presence, he asks them to join their hearts in amity. He pleads when he should demand, and his

14. According to Mortimer (II.v), the Percies rebelled to "plant [him] the rightful heir" on the throne. That is not the view of their motives in *Henry IV Part I*.

appeal is to men's sympathies, not to their allegiances. He would rather command his subjects' pity than their obedience:

> Can you, my lord of Winchester, behold
> My sighs and tears and will not once relent?
>
> (III.i.107-8)[15]

Against swords and masculine fury, Henry employs a woman's arsenal of sighs and tears, and he is too ready to accept at face value transparently hypocritical pledges of love and friendship. To underline Henry's lack of judgment, Shakespeare alters the Chronicle account of York's feud with Somerset. According to Hall, their feud began after York had been appointed Regent in France. In *Part I*, however, Henry appoints York and Somerset commanders in France after they have quarreled violently in his presence. Then, condemning their feud, he pointlessly (or witlessly) antagonizes York by deciding to wear a red rose. Of course, Shakespeare no more blames Henry for England's calamity than he makes York his villain. Despite Henry's naiveté, order might have survived had the great nobles of the realm been less factious and unscrupulous; conversely, York might have satisfied himself with a lesser greatness had Henry been more fit to rule.

In portraying Henry's personal decencies and public failings, Shakespeare does not accept Machiavelli's differentiation of individual and political morality. He does not suggest that Henry's decency is politically irrelevant or a hindrance to political competence, nor does he suggest that Henry would have been more successful had he been more ruthless. Henry is not "too good" to rule; he is unable to translate his goodness into political action. His sixteenth-century counterpart was the ineffectual pietist Henry III of France, whose vacillations enraged Elizabeth. "Jesus," she wrote to him, "Was there ever a prince so smitten by the snares of traitors without the courage or counsel to reply to it?"[16]

Where Hall and Holinshed are content to report the contradictory views of Henry's character without concluding whether he was a fool or a saint, Shakespeare makes of him a consistent and credible figure, one who was incapable of ruling but was capable of spiritual growth so that his innocence in time attained to saintliness. York, the instigator of civil war, is also given his share of nobility. More dangerous than the other opportunists of *Part I*, who aim at lesser spoils, York is nevertheless a patriot who identifies his cause with

15. All quotations from Shakespeare's plays are taken from *The Complete Works of Shakespeare*, ed. G. L. Kittredge (Boston: Ginn, 1936).
16. Black, *The Reign of Elizabeth*, pp. 316-17.

England's, whereas Suffolk, Winchester, and Somerset casually sacrifice the national good to their ambitions. Unlike the malevolent Winchester, who is a teeth-gnashing caricature of a popish Machiavel, York is a true politician, cautious, patient, able to conceal his purposes and keep his own counsel. Where Winchester defies the world, York knows the need for alliances and virtuous appearances. Foresighted enough to accept present humiliations if they further his plans, he would be content to be denied his dukedom if he could make "his ill th'advantage of his good." Where others break out in open mutinies, York is willing to bide his time until his faction is strong and Henry's cause weak. In the meantime, he vows humble allegiance to the King: he pledges that he will thrive as Henry's foes fall.

In the first three acts of *Part I*, York and the other politicians scheme at Court while heroes like Salisbury, Bedford, and Talbot fight in France. In the last two acts the worlds of policy and chivalry come together as York, Somerset, and Suffolk assume command of the armies in France. Superficially the curve of action is upward because English arms triumph despite Talbot's fall: Joan is destroyed, and the French accept English rule. Nevertheless, the concluding ceremonies of peace and concord are sham, because the Dauphin merely pretends obedience to Henry, and the English barons are more discontented than before. Winchester vows to sack the country with a mutiny; Gloucester is infuriated by Henry's betrothal to Margaret; and York is enraged by the ignoble terms of the peace treaty with France. Henry's marriage threatens, moreover, to demean the royalty of England, for his bride is dowerless, her grandiloquent titles empty, and her sponsor the scheming, lustful Suffolk.

Having captured the noble essence of romance in Talbot's gests, Shakespeare burlesques it in Suffolk's encounter with Margaret, a scene of outlandish Petrarchan postures and passions and ludicrous asides. Why Shakespeare conceived the moment so broadly is difficult to say. Possibly the mingling of the comic and erotic echoes the bawdy insinuations of the Dauphin's first encounter with Joan, for Margaret enters the play as Suffolk's captive just after York captures Joan, who was a more dangerous French enchantress.[17] But the parallel between Margaret and Joan is very faintly suggested, and there is no intimation here of Margaret's tigerish destiny, nor any hint that she merely

17. There is a specific link between Joan and Margaret in the text of the play. To save herself from execution, Joan declares herself pregnant by Reignier, Margaret's father. But one would hardly expect an audience to make much of this accusation when Joan previously accuses the Dauphin and Alençon of being her paramours.

plays at innocence. The dissembler is Suffolk, who pretends to plead Henry's love even as he plots to have Margaret as his mistress and to gain control of England by manipulating the King.

When Joan dies, the Dauphin becomes more his own master. When Suffolk speaks of Margaret's beauty, Henry succumbs to a vicarious passion. Before, his sins were of omission: he did not act the king. Now, seduced by Suffolk's words, he willfully dishonors his throne by breaking a pledge of marriage. Before, he protested that he was too young to love but was ready to enter any marriage that tends "to God's glory and my country's weal." Now, careless of God and country, he would have Suffolk compound any terms necessary to obtain Margaret and he allows Suffolk to collect as his reward an exorbitant "tenth" from the people. Deaf to Gloucester's good counsel, he is swept helplessly, he claims, by the tide of amorous desire:

> Her virtues, graced with external gifts,
> Do breed love's settled passions in my heart;
> And like as rigour of tempestuous gusts
> Provokes the mightiest hulk against the tide,
> So am I driven by breath of her renown
> Either to suffer shipwreck or arrive
> Where I may have fruition of her love.   (V.v.3-9)

Before this moment, the currents of dissension swirled around the King; now dissentious emotion wells within his breast:

> I feel such sharp dissension in my breast,
> Such fierce alarums both of hope and fear,
> As I am sick with working of my thoughts.   (V.v.84-6)

This illness is graver than the conventional malaise of the Petrarchan lover, because Henry in love is less manly than ever. When Gloucester and Exeter protest the marriage, Henry protests his helplessness to do other than he wishes. Previously he had made emotional appeals to his barons' moral instincts; now his emotionality is a refuge from political and moral responsibility. Deaf to Gloucester's protests, he wishes to be led "from company" where he "may resolve and ruminate [his] grief." Wrapped in grief, Henry will again flee from the Parliament in *Part II*, leaving the innocent Gloucester to be arrested by his enemies. Once an ineffectual moral chorus to the quarrels of his courtiers, Henry collaborates in the last scene in their betrayal of the common weal. The crowing Suffolk has the final prophetic words of the play. He is off to France to play Paris to Margaret's Helen and Henry's Menelaus:

> Margaret shall now be Queen, and rule the King;
> But I will rule both her, the King, and realm. (V.v.107-8)

Part II

The popularity of *Henry VI Part I*, which was probably composed about 1590,[18] must have been considerable—or at least considerable enough to encourage Shakespeare to continue his dramatic history of the War of the Roses. The success of *Parts II* and *III*, written not many months later, was extraordinary enough to excite Greene's envy. Now other playwrights hastened to beautify their History Plays with feathers plucked from Shakespeare's poetic wings, and more determined plagiarists exploited his success by publishing pirated and shortened memorial reconstructions of *Parts II* and *III*.[19] In a very brief space, the apprentice Shakespeare had become a teacher of his contemporaries, though he was not yet fully in command of his own artistic purposes.

The first two acts of *Henry VI Part II*, for example, seem diffusely and episodically plotted; they unfold a mosaic of events rather than a unified dramatic action. Some scenes document Henry's naiveté; others suggest that York is secretly publishing his claim to the throne. Casual incidents expose Suffolk's ruthlessness and Margaret's restless urge for power, which is matched by the high-vaulting ambition of Eleanor, Gloucester's wife, who is like Joan in her masculine spirit and faith in witchcraft. The first blow of the civil war is struck by Margaret when Eleanor deliberately insults her majesty. The first martial conflict is the combat at arms between the Armorer and his Man. In the third act the plot against Gloucester winds together the separate threads of the dramatic action, and once Gloucester is murdered and Suffolk banished, the plot belongs to York, who foments the Cade rebellion before he openly challenges Henry's right at the battle of St. Albans.

Dover Wilson makes much of minor discrepancies and inconsistencies in *Parts I* and *II*.[20] I think it more just to point out the carefulness with which

---

18. See Cairncross' discussion of the date of *Part I* in his edition of the play, pp. xxxvii-xxxviii.

19. *The First Part of the Contention betwixt the two famous Houses of York and Lancaster* (1594) and *The True Tragedy of Richard Duke of York* (1595), thought by Malone to be the pre-Shakespearean versions of *Henry VI Part II* and *Part III*, are now recognized as Bad Quartos of Shakespeare's plays. Echoes of *Part II* and *Part III* and of these Bad Quartos can be found in most of the succeeding Elizabethan History plays.

20. See, for example, Wilson's introduction, *The First Part*, pp. xii-xiii.

Shakespeare preserves the integrity of his dramatic conception from play to play. *Part I* ends as Suffolk is sent off to France to make a treaty of peace and obtain Margaret as Henry's bride. *Part II* opens with the presentation of Margaret as Henry's Queen and with the reading of the shameful terms of peace, which stirs again the rage of Gloucester, York, and other noblemen. Suffolk, who declared himself a truant to the law in the Temple Garden scene, now gives scope to his lawlessness as Henry's minion, and the mockery of legal judgment in the Temple Garden scene threatens to become a norm as Gloucester is falsely indicted and slain, Suffolk is outlawed by mob violence and lynched, and the rebel Cade, prompted by York, leads an insurrection that substitutes kangaroo trials for legal proceedings.

The climax of *Part II*, as of *Part I*, is the betrayal of England's champion by politic noblemen, only Gloucester, whom the Chronicles term "the good Duke Humphrey," plays Talbot's role. In *Part I* Gloucester's patriotism was sullied by his irascible temper and his eagerness to feud with Winchester. In *Part II* Gloucester is not more amiable toward Winchester but takes his duty as Protector to the youthful King more seriously. Though his temper flares again in the first scene, when he learns of the terms Suffolk has compounded with France, he schools his anger and allows only a silent gesture of outrage: he drops the parchment and finds an excuse not to continue reading it. Only when Henry, Margaret, and Suffolk exit, does Gloucester reveal his anger to the other English barons, and when Winchester breaks in to resume their quarrel, Gloucester leaves to avoid their "ancient bickering."

Gloucester is, from the start, a somewhat older and wiser man in *Part II*. Margaret first enters very much like the youthful innocent whom Suffolk encountered in *Part I*, but when she next appears she speaks bitterly to Suffolk of Henry's unmanliness. Restless, disillusioned, and exasperated by her husband's timidity and piety, she wants the power that Henry is reluctant to exercise. Mated to Suffolk in ambition and sensuality, she joins with him and the other conspirators against Gloucester, who protects the realm from their predatory appetites; and even here she demonstrates the fierceness of spirit that will make her equal to the Yorkists in ruthlessness and brutality in *Part III*. Margaret's evolution during the tetralogy from romantic stereotype to pitiless Fury is a remarkable achievement for an apprentice playwright, because the pathological warping of her character is acutely and convincingly portrayed. Not born the she-devil the Chronicles describe, Margaret becomes one as frustration and vindictive rage coarsen her passionate nature.

One doubts that the months between the composition of *Part I* and *Part II* lengthened Shakespeare's psychological perceptions. What did develop was his sense of the possibilities of characterization and his range of dramatic and poetic techniques. With more understanding of his medium and a more flexible blank verse, he no longer has to limit himself in *Part II* to bold strokes of characterization; he need not always extrovert passion or inflate it with hyperboles. He still aims at the bravura in Margaret's operatic speeches and in York's Marlovian soliloquies, but he is also capable of nuance of tone, and he knows how to use figurative language to delineate shadings of emotion. Some of the finest touches in *Part II* appear in what seem at first to be artificial set speeches. Suffolk's farewell to Margaret at the close of Act III, for example, echoes the Petrarchanism of their meeting in *Part I*, with a psychological difference. He does not confess his adulterous passion, but his Petrarchan language and conceits bespeak erotic memories and longings. And though he and Margaret adopt the neoplatonic postures and the pseudo-spiritual vocabulary of Petrarchan devotion, their hunger of the flesh shows through. Kissing Suffolk's hand, Margaret declares that they are "loather a hundred times to part than die." Suffolk's lines leave no doubt about his willingness to "die" with her:

> If I depart from thee, I cannot live;
> And in thy sight to die, what were it else
> But like a pleasant slumber in thy lap?
> Here could I breathe my soul into the air,
> As mild and gentle as the cradle-babe
> Dying with mother's dug between its lips;
> Where, from thy sight, I should be raging mad
> And cry out for thee to close up mine eyes,
> To have thee with thy lips to stop my mouth.
> So shouldst thou either turn my flying soul,
> Or I should breathe it so into thy body,
> And then it liv'd in sweet Elysium.
> To die by thee were but to die in jest;
> From thee to die were torture more than death. (III.ii.388-401)

Suffolk's eroticism is witty like Donne's. Margaret's eroticism takes a more macabre form when later she fondles the severed head of Suffolk on her "throbbing breast." Unable to embrace his body, she will embrace revenge and in *Part III* enjoy the satisfaction of putting York's head on the gates of the city of York.

The obvious consonances of Margaret's and Suffolk's speeches declare their meetings of true minds and adulterous bodies. More subtle is the clash of tonalities in Margaret's dialogue with Henry when both respond to the report of Gloucester's death. The anguished Henry speaks of his desire

> to chafe [Gloucester's] paly lips
> With twenty thousand kisses and to drain
> Upon his face an ocean of salt tears,
> To tell my love unto his dumb deaf trunk.   (III.ii.141-4)

The same hyperbole appears in Margaret's "lamentation," but there it is sinister rather than pathetic, for her conceit lingers on the physical horror of Gloucester's suffering and violent death:

> And for myself, foe as he was to me,
> Might liquid tears or heart-offending groans
> Or blood-consuming sighs recall his life,
> I would be blind with weeping, sick with groans,
> Look pale as primrose with blood-drinking sighs,
> And all to have the noble Duke alive.   (III.ii.59-64)

To perform *Part II* Shakespeare's company had to learn a subtler language of emotional inflection and gesture. The actors, in turn, schooled his audience in more sensitive responses so that they could distinguish nuances—differentiate between a genuine and an imagined frustration. Unable to protest the shameful treaty with France, York compares his situation to that of a merchant robbed by pirates:

> Pirates may make cheap pennyworths of their pillage,
> And purchase friends, and give to courtesans,
> Still revelling like lords till all be gone,
> While as the silly owner of the goods
> Weeps over them and wrings his hapless hands
> And shakes his head and trembling stands aloof
> While all is shar'd and all is borne away,
> Ready to starve and dare not touch his own.
> So York must sit and fret and bite his tongue
> While his own lands are bargain'd for and sold.   (I.i.222-31)

Henry expresses a similar helplessness just before he leaves Gloucester, falsely accused, to his fate:

> And as the butcher takes away the calf
> And binds the wretch and beats it when it strays,
> Bearing it to the bloody slaughterhouse,
> Even so remorseless have they borne [Gloucester] hence;
> And as the dam runs lowing up and down,
> Looking the way her harmless young one went,

And can do naught but wail her darling's loss,
Even so myself bewails good Gloucester's case
With sad unhelpful tears, and with dimm'd eyes
Look after him and cannot do him good,
So mighty are his vowed enemies.   (III.i.210-20)

York's manner of speech is characteristically practical and unsentimental. His frustration is real in that he can no more revoke the treaty Suffolk has made than a captured merchant can save his goods from the pirates. Henry's vignette of the cow and the calf expresses a more tender heart, but his pathetic analogy is false and his tone self-pitying. Unlike York, Henry is helpless only because he is too weak and too timid to act against Gloucester's "mighty" enemies. He knows that Gloucester is innocent, that his accusers "seek subversion of his harmless life." But though he has the power to save the "good Humphrey" (the calf who will be butchered), he cannot outface his wife and her fellow conspirators. As so often before, sorrow is Henry's refuge. Imagining himself the helpless dam, he weeps as much for his loss of Gloucester as for Gloucester himself.

The conspiracy against Gloucester begins with the opening scene of the play, which choreographs the intrigues of the court in very stately measures. First Margaret, Suffolk, and Henry command attention. When they exit, Gloucester steps to the center of the stage to denounce the treaty and the marriage. When Gloucester leaves the stage, Winchester takes the lead in plotting against him; and when Winchester exits, Somerset and Buckingham form their private faction to seize power when Gloucester falls. The tide seems to turn momentarily when they exit, because the Nevils declare themselves for Gloucester; but when they leave York has the last conspiratorial word. As the stage clears, the audience's attention is focused on progressively smaller groups of characters until at last it fastens on York, the last to leave, the last to speak here, as again in the opening scene of Act III.

There are only glimpses during the play of the covert meetings and bargaining with which York wins the Nevils to his cause and turns Salisbury, an honorable patriot, into a fellow conspirator. In the opening scene the Nevils are outside the factions of the court and ready to support Gloucester against his enemies. In their second appearance they still seem neutral although they argue for the appointment of York rather than Somerset as Regent in France. But even there Warwick's arrogance and ambition are apparent. Hurling his contempt at Winchester he boasts that he may live to be the best of all. In their third appearance the Nevils commit themselves to York's cause as they acknowledge his claim to the throne and kneel before him. By this time they can listen without a murmur to York's plan to stain his sword in Lancaster's heart-blood. When York predicts that the other conspirators will find their death in snaring "the shepherd of the flock, / That virtuous prince, the good Duke Humphrey," the Nevils do not recoil with horror. Salisbury merely remarks, "We know your mind at full." Here the bargain of power is ratified. Warwick pledges to make York king; York pledges that Warwick will be "the greatest man in England but the King."

Because the Nevils acquiesce in the plot against Gloucester and Henry merely wrings his hands, the assault on Gloucester can be brutally direct. The accusations hurled against him are patently false, the slanders gross and incredible. Yet the conspirators bow to no one in their moral earnestness; seeking only the common good, they are determined to strip way Gloucester's disgusting pretense of virtue, for "who cannot steal a shape that means deceit?" Their common-sense, prudential view of politics is reflected in their homely saws: "Smooth runs the water where the brook is deep"; "The fox barks not when he would steal the lamb." And since they cannot find a "color" for Gloucester's death in what he is—Brutus' very predicament—they come to a Brutus-like conclusion: that the guiltless Gloucester must die *before* he can fulfill his murderous nature:

> Let him die in that he is a fox,
> By nature prov'd an enemy to the flock,
> Before his chaps be stain'd with crimson blood,
> As Humphrey, prov'd by reasons, to my liege.   (III.i.257-260)

Men of judgment and "reasons," they know, like Goneril, it is better to fear too far than trust too far.

Another Elizabethan dramatist would have staged the actual murder of Gloucester as the tragic climax of his action.[21] Shakespeare's plotting is more daring and imaginative. Having foreshadowed the terrible deed in recurrent allusions to snaring, liming, trapping, and slaughtering that verbalize the horror of a court turned into a hunting ground and a shambles, he allows the murder to occur offstage, so that he can make the discovery of the murder his climactic moment. Then one long, superbly fashioned dramatic sequence poses Henry's grief against Margaret's hypocrisy and Suffolk's brazenness against

21. As does the anonymous author of *Woodstock,* who makes the murder of the Duke of Gloucester by Richard II the climax of his play. Unlike the choleric, ambitious magnate whom the Chronicles describe, the idealized Gloucester of *Woodstock* very clearly seems modeled after the good Duke Humphrey of *Henry VI Part II.*

Warwick's accusations, which begin with a vivid description of the death agony etched on Gloucester's face. The scene opens with the stealthy conversation of Gloucester's murderers hastening to tell Suffolk of their deed. It rises to a crescendo of excitement as Suffolk and Warwick duel and the clamor of the offstage mob threatens the palace. The tension subsides when Henry banishes Suffolk, and the scene closes on a quiet note as Suffolk and Margaret, who have found the success of their plot against Gloucester an ironic peripeteia, bid one another farewell.

Hall attributes Suffolk's banishment to the outrage of the commoners at the murder of the good Duke Humphrey. Shakespeare intimates that the mob is the Nevils' instrument, even as the Nevils are York's ladder to the throne. Although they do nothing to prevent the crime, the Nevils spring into moral action against Suffolk once Gloucester has been murdered. Turning public prosecutor, Warwick builds a case against Suffolk with the same homely adages that Suffolk had used in condemning Gloucester:

> Who finds the heifer dead, and bleeding fresh,
> And sees fast-by a butcher with an axe,
> But will suspect 'twas he that made the slaughter?
> Who finds the partridge in the puttock's nest
> But may imagine how the bird was dead,
> Although the kite soar with unbloodied beak?   (III.ii.188-93)

Warwick's pose of selfless patriotism disintegrates, however, when he trades personal insults with Suffolk and so forgets his devotion to Henry that he draws his sword against Suffolk, an insult to the King's majesty. Shrewdly questioning the Nevils' role as his prosecutors, Suffolk notes that Salisbury is glad to play the orator and that the ultimatum he brings Henry is obviously too polished to have been composed by a mob. Henry prefers to accept the Nevils at face value. He exits talking of great matters to the "good Warwick," who will next appear on stage with York's army to challenge Henry's right to rule.[22]

The banishing of Suffolk is at best a partial and ironic justice. Margaret, Winchester, and York, the other conspirators, are not accused or judged. The Nevils' role of King's Counsels is a sham, and Suffolk's trial is a farcical proceeding, because no witness except Warwick appears against him, and no

---

22. Tillyard also accepts Warwick's moral outrage at face value (*History Plays*, pp. 182-83). But how can we look on him as a choric moral spokesman when Suffolk calls attention to the dubiousness of the Nevils' part in the proceeding, and when Warwick's words and acts in this very scene cast doubt on his pose of selfless patriotism?

real evidence of his guilt is brought forth. Cowering before the threat of mob violence, Henry sentences Suffolk, even as later, cringing before the threat of York's armies, he imprisons Somerset. A triumph of policy rather than of justice, Suffolk's banishment brings England one step closer to chaos because it removes the only nobleman strong enough to oppose York. Indeed, there is only a short step from the uproar of the commoners in the palace to the violence and anarchy of the Cade rebellion, when justice will be meted out by lynch mobs to those guilty of knowing how to read.

The scenes of *Part I* tell all we know and need to know about the intrigues of the court. The scenes of *Part II* present only the visible surface of the iceberg of York's intrigues, an economy that allows Shakespeare more scope in his representation of Gloucester's fall. But since York is to emerge as the supreme antagonist of the play, he cannot be too elusive or shadowy a presence; and since the plot demands that York be offstage during half of Act III and all of Act IV, he must tower over the other characters when on stage so that he is not out of mind when out of sight. In short, York needs the special relation with the audience and the extra dimension of personality which his florid soliloquies provide. Sent to lead the army in Ireland, he gloats over this opportunity to realize his politic schemes:

> Now, York, or never, steel thy fearful thoughts
> And change misdoubt to resolution.
> Be that thou hop'st to be; or what thou art
> Resign to death: . . .
> My brain more busy than the labouring spider,
> Weaves tedious snares to trap mine enemies.
> Well, nobles, well! 'tis politicly done
> To send me packing with an host of men.
> I fear me you but warm the starved snake,
> Who, cherish'd in your breasts, will sting your hearts.
> 'Twas men I lack'd, and you will give them me.
> I take it kindly. Yet be well assur'd
> You put sharp weapons in a madman's hands.
> Whiles I in Ireland nourish a mighty band,
> I will stir up in England some black storm
> Shall blow ten thousand souls to heaven or hell;
> And this fell tempest shall not cease to rage
> Until the golden circuit on my head,
> Like to the glorious sun's transparent beams,
> Do calm the fury of this mad-bred flaw.   (III.i.331-54)

If this hyperbolic rage for destruction does not square with York's sober machinations, it does give him the mythic largeness of the Marlovian superman, and it reinforces the contrast between his temper and Henry's. Where Henry is weak, York is strong. Where Henry is compassionate, York is ruthless. Where Henry is naively credulous, York is a cunning dissembler and manipulator of others. Where York is a man able to keep his own counsel, Henry is a child whose tears flow in the first scene at the sight of Margaret, and who weeps even as he abandons Gloucester to his murderous enemies.

If Henry really were too innocent and child-simple for this world, his case would be merely pitiable. But though he is easily duped, he can tell the very obvious: he knows that the good Gloucester is falsely accused. Nevertheless, he thanks the conspirators for their care and allows Gloucester to be arrested. His conscience tells him that Gloucester's life is threatened by his enemies, but it does not insist that he must protect him from judicial murder. His heart "drown'd with grief," he tells the conspirators, "My lords, what to your wisdoms seemeth best / Do or undo, as if ourself were here" (III.i.195-6).[23]

When the King will not defend the right, the people grow muddied, ready to take justice into their own hands or to redress grievances with force. When the King cannot lead, the commoners will follow a Warwick or a Cade or a York. In the Chronicles the English people appear to be a fickle lot who change allegiances easily. Shakespeare sees the commoners more as the victims of disorder than as its many-headed beast and senses that their instinct is for survival, not for giddy change. Although he spares no detail of the atrocities committed by the Cade rebels, he does not make them appear any worse than their aristocratic betters, who more deliberately subvert the law and murder their enemies. Compared to the malevolent impulses and acts of Margaret and York, the mindless violence of the rebels is almost innocent. Shrewd, good-humored, and clear-sighted about their leader, the rebels want excitement, booty, and some revenge on those with money, privilege, and education. Since they are not revolutionaries and they do not want Cade as their king, they quickly return to obedience when Clifford reminds them of the spoils they can win in France:

> To France, to France, and get what you have lost!
> Spare England, for it is your native coast.   (IV.viii.51-2)

Here is the first intimation in the History Plays of the virtue of foreign wars which legitimize pillage and ennoble the cutting of throats.

23. Lest we ignore this astonishing retreat from responsibility, the Queen exclaims immediately afterward, "What, will your Highness leave the parliament?"

Cade's ramshackle army is the antimasque to York's rebellion even as Cade's claim to royal descent is a parody of York's pretension to the throne. Cade's neighbors joke about his fictitious ancestry and follow him nevertheless. The Nevils, York's allies, take a more serious view of his claim to be the true inheritor. By the indirections of his genealogical arguments in II.ii, they find directions out and declare his claim a "plain proceeding." It is quite clear, however, that the Nevils do not support York because they are legitimists; rather they are "legitimists" because they support York. When Henry asks how they can dishonor their oaths after a lifetime of obedience, they plead a care for their immortal souls:

It is a great sin to swear unto a sin,
But greater sin to keep a sinful oath.   (V.i.182-3)

As scrupulous as Sir John Falstaff, they will not be damned for any Lancastrian prince in Christendom. There is nothing theoretical in their attachment to York, who promises them power and greatness, just as there is nothing theoretical about York's claim to the throne when he faces Henry in the last act. His argument is that Henry is "not fit to govern and rule multitudes," while his own hand was made "to hold a sceptre up."

The battle of St. Albans marks the end of intrigue and conspiracy, and the outbreak of civil war. Now all enmities and ambitions are declared and all conflicts openly waged. The eruption of the impostume of disorder fails, however, to relieve the diseased state, even as the call to arms fails to resurrect England's chivalric greatness. Where Talbot achieved a heroic apotheosis in defeat, Clifford, the Lancastrian champion, rages for destruction after St. Albans and swears to revenge his father's death on York's babes. The age of chivalry is dead, and the time will soon be at hand when political conflict descends to vendetta, when the murder of children will become common-place, and severed heads will be casually tossed down as trophies of victory. Yet, even while moral restraints threaten to disappear, some kind of moral order asserts itself in the destinies of evil men. Suffolk is exiled and lynched, Winchester dies maddened by the fear of a last judgment, and Cade ends his life a starving fugitive. Shakespeare takes little satisfaction, however, in pointing out that blood will have blood, because he has no taste for the ghastly retributions that fall on innocent children, and he does not believe in the providentiality of barbarous acts. The Chroniclers speak of the divine judgment that fell on Suffolk, who was beheaded by Exeter's soldiers. Shakespeare turns these agents of retribution into freebooters, who parcel out their prisoners as booty and extort ransom by threats of death. Their captain invokes the cause of York and the memory of Richard II in "sentencing" Suffolk, but the trial is a kangaroo proceeding and the executioner a sullen pirate who would slaughter all the prisoners to "revenge" the eye he lost in attacking Suffolk's vessel. However one may moralize it, the murder of Suffolk is, in the play, a "barbarous and bloody spectacle." More thoughtful about human nature than the Chroniclers, Shakespeare knows that when crime answers crime, morality is debased. The hope of the future does not depend on the tally of horrible "retributions" which Margaret draws up in *Richard III*; it depends upon the capacity of men to forgive their enemies and to forego the promptings of hatred and revenge.[24]

Part III

Shakespeare's instinct for dramatic form, so evident in the shaping of the plot of *Henry VI Part I*,[25] was apparently unable to check the onward rush of the historical narrative in *Part II*. His plot races across the pages of the Chronicles without a backward glance, and when it reaches its destination, the battle of St. Albans, its point of departure seems a distant speck. Most of the characters prominent in the first half of the play do not survive the third act, and a new cast of characters appears in the last act as the Cliffords become the chief supporters of the King, and York's sons, Edward, Richard, and Clarence, join the Nevils as the mainstays of his cause. Thus, while the battle of St. Albans is the culmination of the factious and conspiratorial politics of the first four acts, it is less a conclusion to an era than a prologue to the civil war which will rage in the scenes of *Part III*.

The plot of *Part III* seems even more episodic and long-winded than that of *Part II*, although the plays are approximately the same length, because *Part III* does not have the central core of action provided in *Part II* by the unfolding of York's conspiracy. As one battle leads to the next and one atrocity prompts another, the historical narrative meanders; the tide of fortune shifts this way

24. In a fine discussion of the *Henry VI* plays, J. P. Brockbank suggests that Shakespeare ironically questions the Chronicle idea of providence by investing the acts of retribution in *Part II* in an atmosphere of evil. See "The Frame of Disorder—'Henry VI,'" in *Early Shakespeare*, ed. J. R. Brown and B. Harris (London: Ed. Arnold, 1961), pp. 82, 86.

25. See Hereward T. Price's splendid discussion of the dramatic construction of *Part I* in "Construction in Shakespeare," *University of Michigan Contributions in Modern Philology*, no. 17 (1951), 1-42.

and that, as first York and then Lancaster triumphs on the battlefield. Although York falls at Wakefield, his heir Edward wins control of the kingdom at Towton. The captured Henry is dethroned, later restored to seeming rule by Warwick (who changes sides), captured again, and finally murdered. Edward is crowned after Towton, then captured by Warwick, rescued by Richard, and with his brothers able to win a decisive victory at Tewkesbury. Not content simply to chart this zigzag course, Shakespeare gives the power struggle in *Part III* another crosscurrent of action by allowing Richard to embark on his treacherous quest of the throne before the Yorkist victory is assured. Even as the conflict between York and Lancaster draws to a close, Richard plans a campaign against his own flesh and blood which will beggar the earlier horrors of civil war.

The perfunctory quality of some of the plotting in *Part III* makes one suspect that Shakespeare is more interested in developing Richard as Machiavellian conspirator than in chronicling the final events of the civil war. He also seems less concerned with creating a satisfying dramatic form in *Part III* than with laying the groundwork for Richard's brilliant scheming in *Richard III*. This is not to suggest that Shakespeare treated *Part III* as nothing more than an obligatory task which he had to perform before he could plunge into More's fascinating narrative of Richard's rise and fall. But certainly the peaks of poetic and dramatic inspiration in *Part III*—the great ritual scenes at Wakefield and Towton and Richard's bravura soliloquies—stand out among much else that seems relatively uninspired. Lacking Richard's brilliance, the other politicians in the play mimic each other in their posturing and double-dealing, so much so that the ironies of political maneuver threaten to become repetitious.

Characteristically, Shakespeare is not interested in expounding or explaining political doctrines. Instead of weighing Lancaster's claim against York's, he presents the ironic drama of their attempts to convince themselves that their expedient turns and turnabouts constitute the strait and narrow way. He recognizes that neither side in the War of the Roses had a consistent or logical ideological stance. Altering their principles as circumstances required, they did not hesitate to adopt their enemy's arguments. In the first scene, York and his allies speak as legitimists. Proclaiming the inviolability of the succession, they insist that Richard II could not have lawfully disinherited his line to make Bolingbroke his heir. Nevertheless, they are willing to let the usurping Henry rule during his lifetime if he adopts York as his heir. At Towton the antagonists trade positions. The Lancastrians, who claim the throne through Henry IV, Richard II's "adopted" heir, now argue that Henry VI cannot adopt York as his heir, while the Yorkists, who once claimed that a king cannot disinherit his natural heirs, now claim the succession to the throne as Henry's adopted heirs. Henry is not more scrupulous than his followers; he confesses that his title is "weak," and then agrees to disinherit his son if he may be allowed to continue as king. York assents to the bargain and honors it until he is convinced by Richard that his oath of allegiance to Henry is "frivolous and vain." For Richard, who pretends to shudder at the thought that his father "should be for sworn," such sophistry is an ironic joke. For others splitting hairs is a very sober business. Lewis of France, for example, has no doubt of the justice of Margaret's cause until Warwick arrives at his court with the proposal that Lewis' daughter marry Edward. Then the prospect of a royal alliance raises sudden scruples in his mind about Henry's title. A good monarchist, he feels compelled to support the existing Yorkist government—and to find in Edward's success proof of God's approval and defense of the right. Although we can say about Lewis what Joan said about Burgundy in *Part I*: "Done like a Frenchman—turn and turn again!" Lewis' premises are English and his casuistry "orthodox."

When barons and kings prove faithless, who can blame simple people for swimming with the tide? The commoners, one feels, are deserted by Henry before they desert him and pledge allegiance to the stronger and more capable Edward. Rather than condemn their slipperiness, Shakespeare pities their pawnlike helplessness. They do not choose badly; they have, in truth, no political choice at all. Reluctant soldiers, they are enlisted on one side or the other by the accidents of feudal allegiances which make a father Lancastrian, a son Yorkist. While great earls hunt their personal enemies at Towton, common soldiers strike blindly at whoever stands against them. They have nothing to fight for except their lives and what small booty they can take from those they kill.

The action of *Part III*, which begins as Richard flings down Somerset's head, is rich in atrocities that make the murder of Gloucester in *Part II* seem, by contrast, a relatively innocent act. Even York, who once seemed the archimmoralist, now appears relatively mild compared to the tigerish Margaret and the pitiless Clifford, who is in turn stalked by Richard, the fiercest predator of all. Where York could patiently bide his time, his enemies are quick in rage and blasphemous in their revenges. The Chronicles describe only one ritual atrocity during this period: the deliberate parodying of the Crucifixion by Margaret and Clifford, who place the captured York on a molehill, grace him with a paper crown, and taunt him with a handkerchief stained with the blood of his child Rutland before they murder him. Following this cue Shakespeare casts other atrocities in the form of perverted and sacrilegious ceremonies. The defenseless Rutland is murdered by Clifford as he prays for mercy. Edward, Richard, and Warwick then kneel to pledge vengeance on the Lancastrians for the murder of York. Later they take turns taunting the dying Clifford, and still later take turns stabbing Edward, Henry's son. In the last act, Richard, fresh from the "execution" of Henry, plants a Judas kiss on the cheek of Edward's son, who will suffer Rutland's fate in days to come.

By casting the atrocities of *Part III* in ritual form, Shakespeare focuses attention on the moral perversity rather than the physical horror of the crimes. We shudder more at the sadistic deliberateness of Margaret's taunting of York than at the sudden fury of Clifford's murder of Rutland. Where Clifford satisfies an individual bloodlust, Margaret fashions a blasphemous communal rite appropriate for the dispensation of vendetta. After the savagery at Wakefield, both sides celebrate the rites of violence and find their communion on the battlefield when they hunt down and torment their enemies, each repeating the other's curses and sword strokes. In earlier days men tilled the soil and increased nature's bounty. Now they clear the land of enemies by cutting down their foes like scrub growth. It is not enough for the antagonists to topple mighty oaks like Clifford and York. Victory and security will be achieved only by extirpating the rival line. So York and Lancaster aim their swords at innocent children—at the very roots of their enemies lives—just as a son strikes at the root of his life in slaying his father at Towton, and a father destroys his seed by killing his son. Few escape the taint of communal guilt or the retributions that punish it. Men die cursing their enemies, and in time the curses fall due, but once again retribution comes in the form of brutal deeds, so that crime is answered with crime, murder with murder. There can be no hope of lasting peace or reconciliation when the victors are drenched in blood, and when the defeated, like Northumberland and Oxford, swear that they will never kneel before those who slew their fathers.

The atrocities of *Part III* do not prove that rebels are impious villains, for Lancaster tutors York in savagery, and both sides are degraded by the bitterness of the protracted struggle. Yet compassion does not vanish, for while the Lancastrians gloat over the captured York, he weeps for his murdered son and is joined in tears by Northumberland, one of his tormentors. And as Richard commits himself to unspeakable villainies, Elizabeth, the first gentle, tender-hearted woman to appear in the tetralogy, triumphs over Edward's lust.

Most of the characters sacrifice some part of their humanity to gain their ends, but Henry, abandoning his power as a king, completes his spiritual journey as a saint.

Although an ineffectual figurehead, Henry does not easily renounce his royal position; he enjoys his role as king and wants others to respect his flimsy pretense of majesty. Cowed by his enemies and intimidated by his wife, he is ignored or despised by his supporters; he complains before Towton that no one will let him speak, and he scurries away from the battle a comic figure:

> Nay, take me with thee, good sweet Exeter,
> Not that I fear to stay, but love to go
> Whither the Queen intends.   (II.v.137-9)

Incapable of bloody deeds, he can urge others to perform them. No sooner does he swear to adopt York as his heir than he wishes that Margaret would take revenge on York, and reminds Northumberland and Clifford of their vows of vengeance against York. Yet when York's severed head appears on the gates of the city of York, Henry recoils: "Withhold revenge, dear God! 'Tis not my fault, / Nor wittingly have I infringed my vow" (II.ii.7-8). Unable to admit his share of responsibility for the bloodshed, he laments that he will be wrongly blamed for the slaughter at Towton: "How will the country for these woeful chances / Misthink the King, and not be satisfied!" (II.v.107-8).

Ignorant of himself, Henry can cling shamefully to the crown and sigh for the retired joys of a shepherd's life while he observes the killing at Towton. Unlike the good yeoman Iden in *Part II*, who spoke convincingly of homely pleasures during the Cade uprising, Henry knows nothing of the contentment of quiet walks. His pastorality, as his diction reveals, is literary and artificial. The king who could not shepherd his own flock creates in imagination an idyllic world where there is no biting wind, no hunger, no predators. His mind lulled by the almost hypnotic repetitions of his speech, he escapes into a reverie in which the sound and fury of battle are distantly perceived as in the blurred landscape of a dream:

> This battle fares like to the morning's war,
> When dying clouds contend with growing light,
> What time the shepherd, blowing of his nails,
> Can neither call it perfect day nor night.
> Now sways it this way, like a mighty sea
> Forc'd by the tide to combat with the wind;
> Now sways it that way, like the selfsame sea
> Forc'd to retire by fury of the wind . . . .

Would I were dead, if God's good will were so!
For what is in this world but grief and woe?
O God! methinks it were a happy life
To be no better than a homely swain;
To sit upon a hill, as I do now,
To carve out dials quaintly, point by point,
Thereby to see the minutes how they run . . . .
So many hours must I tend my flock,
So many hours must I take my rest,
So many hours must I contemplate,
So many hours must I sport myself;
So many days . . .   (II.v.1-35)

We hear the very rhythm of Henry's lines again when Richard II, at Flint Castle, spins out his self-pitying fantasy of renunciation in elegant antitheses and alliterations. Henry would aid the grieving father "tear for tear." Richard would "make some pretty match with shedding tears" with Aumerle.

Henry must lose his crown to find himself because he is incapable of discerning his true state as a king. Even after the terrible defeat at Towton, he can sigh for the trappings of majesty: "No bending knee will call [me] Caesar now, / No humble suitors press to speak for right" (III.i.18-19). And when he is finally able to relinquish his royal power, he does not suddenly "see all," for he naively appoints the turncoat Clarence and "the good Warwick" protectors of the realm. Yet his vision lengthens from first to final act. He predicts the failure of Clifford's ethic of violence, and he knows that Margaret's words will not prevail with Lewis, because she comes to beg while Edward has favors to give. He is even capable of irony when he bids the gamekeepers who capture him not to break their oath of allegiance to King Edward.[26] Thus the impercipient King, who once marveled at the Simpcox hoax, becomes the seer who can prophesy Richmond's role as England's savior.

As Henry approaches saintliness he becomes less a dramatic character than a moral symbol. Richard's development is more paradoxical, because even as he seems to turn into a villainous stereotype, he gains a new psychological complexity. Despite references to his misshapen body and unnatural birth, Richard does not limp on stage a monster. Even More, who anathematized him, had grudgingly to admit that during the civil war he was "none evill captain." Shakespeare more generously allows the youthful Richard a full measure of

26. Humbly yielding himself to his captors, Henry decides not to try to persuade them to break their oaths to the new King Edward, because he would not have them guilty of such a sin (III.i.90ff.).

wit, enthusiasm, and ability. No scoundrel at first, he is set off from the others by a candid and thoroughgoing cynicism. Where others pay lip service to pious ideals, he mocks them with witty unction; when Clifford rages at the close of *Part II*, Richard counsels him to prepare for his end: "Fie! Charity, for shame! Speak not in spite, / For you shall sup with Jesu Christ to-night" (V.i.213-4). In *Part III* Richard is more openly contemptuous of the Christian ethic. He declares that he puts his faith in steel and accomplishes his good works with a sword which tells his devotion on his enemies' heads. His motto is "Priests pray for enemies, but princes kill."

The death of York is Richard's spiritual turning point because it leaves him without a single emotional attachment. He is contemptuous of Warwick, who fled the battle where York was captured, and he openly questions whether Edward is York's true heir. The only goal left for Richard is revenge, but he finds no satisfaction in destroying Clifford and no joy in the victory which makes Edward king. His cynicism, his warped body, and his vindictive fury on the battlefield prepare us for his choice of villainy in Act III. Even so, his metamorphosis into cunning conspirator seems a sudden radical alteration of character, because up to this point Richard has been too restless, too impatient with words, and too impetuously eager to assault his foes to follow in York's politic footsteps. Moreover, when Richard abruptly turns Machiavel, he develops a *sang-froid* that makes York seem by contrast a slave of passion. Where York's soliloquies in *Part II* were Marlovian exercises in hyperbole, Richard's soliloquies in *Part III* are relatively controlled revelations of a terrifying inner self. Where York gloated over his diabolical powers, Richard meditates soberly on the obstacles in his path—the many lives between him and the throne. He needs to flatter himself with impossibilities, however, to put his personal world in joint: "My eye's too quick, my heart o'erweens too much, / Unless my hand and strength could equal them" (III.ii.144-5). Declaring that "love foreswore me in my mother's womb," he will not make his heaven in a lady's lap, and he sees his brothers' sexuality—the "issue of their bodies"—as the barrier to the crown. Love is his antagonist:

> And, for I should not deal in her soft laws,
> She did corrupt frail nature with some bribe
> To shrink mine arm up like a wither'd shrub;
> To make an envious mountain on my back,
> Where sits deformity to mock my body;
> To shape my legs of an unequal size;
> To disproportion me in every part,
> Like to a chaos, or an unlick'd bear-whelp,

That carries no impression like the dam.   (III.ii.154-62)

Since this earth, according to Richard,

             affords no joy to me
But to command, to check, to o'erbear such
As are of better person than myself,
I'll make my heaven to dream upon the crown
And whiles I live, t'account this world but hell
Until my misshap'd trunk that bears this head
Be round impaled with a glorious crown.   (III.ii.165-71)

This pre-Freudian intuition of the compensatory drive for power may be remarkable in its way, but the welling of hatred in these lines astounds because nothing in the earlier portrayal of Richard hints of this tormented sense of abnormality and inferiority. Twice his enemies sneer at his deformity without provoking his wrath. When Clifford in *Part II* refers to him as a "heap of wrath, foul indigested lump, / As crooked in thy manners as thy shape," Richard does not reply. When Margaret in *Part III* describes him as a "foul misshapen stigmatic," he calmly rebukes her vulgarity of mind and tongue. One can imagine a gifted actor suggesting by nervous gesture and grimace or malevolent sneer that beneath Richard's apparent pleasure with himself in the first half of *Part III* is an anguished knowledge of his inadequacy. But this contradicts every indication of the text and sacrifices our pleasure in the earlier Richard, whose high spirits and confident assurance in his abilities ring absolutely true. Fortunately, Richard does not continue to snarl at the world; once he vents his contempt for Edward, he calmly considers the possibilities open to him and decides that his situation is like that of a traveler who must hew his way out of a thorny woods. His axe will be necessarily bloody because the tormenting thickets that stand in his way are his brothers and their children. After elaborating this chilling conceit, Richard grows a bit more rhetorical and conventional. Preening himself on his virtuosity, he struts like the Jew of Malta, promising by cunning dissimulation and wholesale homicides to "set the murtherous Machiavel to school." With this brag, a melodramatizing star is born who takes a kingdom as his stage and later counterfeits the deep tragedian with Buckingham.

The play within the play in *Part III* actually begins when Richard and Clarence play audience and comic interlocutors to Edward's wooing of Elizabeth. More proof of Richard's dramatic talents comes in the last two scenes of the play, where he stages the murder of Henry in the Tower and then takes his Vice-like role in Edward's tableau of familial love. His cat and mouse game with Henry recalls the cruel pleasure with which Clifford and Margaret taunted York, and York's sons in turn amused themselves with Prince Edward before they killed him. Richard's games, though, have a special flavor that sets them apart from more ordinary sadistic entertainments. The other characters allow their passions rein or are goaded to strike by insults. Only Richard commits and takes pleasure in a wholly coldblooded crime. The other characters join in communal acts of vengeance; Richard plays a lone hand in this crime and takes a gourmet's delight in his bloody supper in the Tower. Yet the scene does not wholly belong to him. Courageous at the last, Henry speaks so tellingly of Richard's moral and physical deformity that his tormentor cuts short the dialogue with his sword.

The Richard who can murder an innocent so matter-of-factly is very nearly the villain who will send Clarence and Hastings packing in *Richard III*. The only compassion he knows is the "purple tears" his sword "weeps for the poor King's death!" Yet he cheerfully confesses that Henry's description of him was true, and he is, in a terrible way, more likable than before because he no longer regards his criminality as his revenge upon life. In the next play he will thank God for his humility; here he gives thanks for his deformity, which provides a perfect excuse for his career as villain:

> For I have often heard my mother say
> I came into the world with my legs forward.
> Had I not reason, think ye, to make haste
> And seek their ruin that usurp'd our right?
> The midwife wonder'd, and the women cried
> "O, Jesus bless us! He is born with teeth!"
> And so I was; which plainly signified
> That I should snarl and bite and play the dog.
> Then, since the heavens have shap'd my body so,
> Let hell make crook'd my mind to answer it.   (V.vi.70-9)

Decorum, not chaos, is Richard's aim, a twisted behavior answerable to his misshapen body. Since he resembles no other man, he renounces all human ties: "I have no brother, I am like no brother." And since he has a long and difficult journey to make to the throne, he rejoices that he travels light—without pity, love, or fear. A world unto himself, he exults blasphemously in the isolation which will ultimately unnerve him: "I am myself alone." Even now Richard plans the murder of his relatives, but he does not intend to cut their throats himself. Just as York used the other conspirators to gain his ends, Richard will use Edward's suspicions to be rid of Clarence, and after Clarence, he will manage "the rest."

This preview by Richard of coming attractions foreshortens history in that it makes the reign of Edward, but newly begun, little more than a prologue to Richard's career as Cain. What Hall termed the "prosperous reign" of Edward IV consists in *Part III* of the brief ironic concluding scene; the next time Edward appears (in *Richard III*), he is a dying man. The Chronicles describe Edward as a gallant chivalric leader and successful ruler. Shakespeare's portrait is less flattering. Reckless in war, careless and unscrupulous in politics, Edward is shallow enough to think that the slaughter of the Lancastrians at Tewkesbury has "swept suspicion from our seat," and hubristic enough to list his fallen enemies as if they were so many trophies. This done, he would put out of mind the hatreds he has stirred and the treacheries and atrocities just recently committed. Commanding his brothers to love his Queen, he arranges a tableau of familial devotion, in which the twice-turned Clarence and the sinister Richard pledge their loyalty by kissing Edward's infant son. More fatuous still in *Richard III*, he will arrange other moral ceremonies in which mortal enemies protest their devotion to one another. His last act in *Part III* is to banish Margaret, but like the past which she comes to symbolize, she returns to plague the Court, and though Edward would have "mirthful comic shows" to initiate his "lasting joys," Richard is determined on more tragical scenes.

There will be more suffering before Englishmen rediscover their need for brotherhood, and there will be more bloodshed before peace returns to the divided land. Yet the contention of Lancaster and York does end at Tewkesbury. The next battle will be fought by Englishmen united in their will to overthrow the tyrannical Richard.

3. RICHARD III

A stunning success in Shakespeare's time, *Richard III* has been a favorite of succeeding generations of actors and audiences. Like *Hamlet*, it has never failed to hold the stage because it is superbly theatrical—inspired by the stage and by an actor's awareness of the power which a virtuoso performer has over his audiences. It is also daringly conceived to mingle contrarieties: gothic shapes and Renaissance energies; tragic pathos and ironic comedy; high-spirited farce and Senecan gloom. Not content simply to allow Crookback to display his melodramatic genius before he falls into his destined role of scapegoat, Shakespeare endows Richard's tragic career with monumental artistic form. He imagines the darkness before the dawn of Tudor deliverance as the setting for a vast revenge tragedy which unfolds with prophesies of doom and choric lamentations, a full freight of medieval moralizing, a chilling figure of Nemesis, and a pageant of accusing ghosts. For the first time in *Richard III* Shakespeare's plotting in the History Plays has vertical as well as horizontal form, because each step of Richard's rise and fall offers a fresh discovery of political and moral reality. Seemingly sure-footed in his ascent to the throne, Richard suffers an astonishing vertigo at the pinnacle of his career and regains his equilibrium again only when he touches ground—when he fights on foot against overwhelming odds at Bosworth.

In Richard III Shakespeare had a historical subject worthy of his rapidly maturing powers. He found in More's *History*[1] a brilliant characterization and a biography that had already been given an artistic shape and interpretation.

1. *The History of Richard III*, first printed with Hardyng's *Chronicle* in 1543, was incorporated in Hall's Chronicle and again in Holinshed.

Having made use of More's conception of Richard in developing his portrait of Gloucester in *Henry VI Part III*, he could now fashion his plot directly out of More's terse, coherent, absorbing historical narrative and directly appropriate More's ironic humor and penetrating insights. Fascinating as is More's account of the sinister, misshapen Richard, Shakespeare's portrait is more dazzling and memorable still. For, though More is willing to grant Richard his cleverness, sardonic humor, and theatrical instinct, he describes him as an explorer might describe a rare and horrifying species of poisonous snake. Never allowing his reader to savor Richard's histrionic performances, More makes each of Richard's successes an occasion for moral outrage, disgust, and scorn. It is Shakespeare who endows Richard with his exuberance and extraordinary vitality. It is Shakespeare who makes him an engaging, heroic, and honest villain, one who opens his heart to the audience in soliloquies and asides and who plays the moral teacher for quite a long time before he becomes the moral lesson of the play.

In speaking of Shakespeare's transformation of the "accepted view" of Richard, we should keep in mind that More's was not the only portrait current. Almost certainly Shakespeare read *The True Tragedy of Richard III* (printed in a debased version in 1594), in which Richard is portrayed more like a conscience-ridden Macbeth than the vicious monster whom More describes.[2] Shakespeare does not go half as far in humanizing More's villain; what he does is make Richard's perversity credible and, more than that, enjoyable, for the heartless murderer More depicts becomes in Shakespeare's play a humorist and a comedian so cheeky, frank, and enthusiastic in his wickedness that most of his betters seem unpardonably dishonest and dreary. A gloating dissimulator in *Henry VI Part III*, he is in *Richard III* a thoroughly accomplished *farceur*, an urbane masquerader who literally plots the course of the dramatic action, which he dominates from beginning to end. He is the supreme individualist; the other characters, with the exception of the harridan Margaret, are variations on a theme. They cannot fathom him, but he can play them at sight; and none of them can stand against him until they have been schooled by his treachery. Even after Richmond enters the play, Richard is the only antagonist worthy of Richard and destined to be his own nemesis.

Although more the superman than before, Richard leaves behind the

2. *The True Tragedy* probably gave Shakespeare the inspiration for the pageant of ghosts which visits Richard during his nightmare on the eve of Bosworth. Other verbal echoes are identified by Geoffrey Bullough in the footnotes to his excerpts from *The True Tragedy* in Volume III of *Narrative and Dramatic Sources of Shakespeare*, pp. 317-45.

Marlovian hyperboles of his soliloquies in *Henry VI Part III*. When he walks out on stage to open the play, his speech is measured, his figures neatly contained within the caesuras of his blank verse lines. He can wield words like a rapier, but he has no passion for the grandiose. His bent of mind, like that of the other characters, is rhetorical rather than poetic, and when, late in the play, he grows dull, his rhetoric grows as artificial and as tedious as theirs. Since Richard at his best is incomparable, one wonders why more of the play is not cut to the measure of his brilliance. Often his speeches are the only flashes of life and energy in the tedious bickering of the Court, and that bickering seems highly dramatic compared to the turgid formality of the choric and ritual scenes. Even if we grant that Elizabethans had more taste than we do for sententiousness and rhetorical flourish, we must still wonder why calamity in *Richard III* must be so full of words, why every moral account in the play must be explicitly summed and every irony pointed out and underlined. It is almost as if Shakespeare, unwilling to trust his audiences' perception of the subtle ironies of his plot, provides a more obvious key to the moral drama in Margaret's prophecies and the ostentatious hypocrisies of the courtiers, who damn themselves in swearing falsely. Although the sense of the past evoked in the rhetoric of the choric and ritual scenes is necessary to the play, it is a burden on modern audiences, who must sort out current intrigues and factious alignments even as they try to make sense of the references made to earlier events—the atrocities committed at Wakefield, Towton, and Tewkesbury. We need not assume, however, that Shakespeare's audiences were so familiar with *Henry VI Part III* or with the Chronicles that they could interpret each of the allusions to the past. Nor need we attempt to provide extensive historical notes for modern audiences, because the play provides what information they need. It does not matter precisely what crimes Clarence, Hastings, Rivers, or Grey committed (or allowed) in the past; what matters is that all were involved to some degree in the atrocities of the civil war. Some participated in the murder of children, others watched; few hands are clean in Edward's court, and few pious protestations can be taken at face value.

Of course, the days of vendetta are long since over, and even the memory of atrocity is blurred and fragmentary, because except for Margaret, who nurtures her ghastly memories, the characters of *Richard III* would turn their backs on the past and forget the ways in which they rose to eminence and power. Opportunists for the working day and Christians enough for their world, they do not rage against their enemies and plot their destruction as York did. Moderate in their factionalism, they would be part-time accomplices of the

Protector and settle for minor portions of the spoils. Hastings, loyal to Edward and his sons, would be content with a high position and the power to punish his enemies. Buckingham, less scrupulous and less loyal, would be satisfied with the earldom of Hereford—if he did not have to murder the Princes. Although such men bicker, backbite, and scheme against each other, they leave the commission of murder, judicial or otherwise, to Richard, and they know the pangs of belated conscience, because they would die well even though they live ill. The survivors of catastrophe, they have all learned how to bend with the wind; they have all mastered the art of accommodation which enables a man successfully to turn his coat. They know when to be obtuse and when to equivocate or turn casuist. The noble Buckingham can argue with conviction that innocent children do not deserve the sanctuary which is the right of criminals, and the dying Edward can lament that none of his courtiers prevented him from condemning his brother Clarence. All know the importance of seeming earnest, and all have the gift of fine words. Clarence is an accomplished and unctuous orator, Buckingham a master of the political platform, and Richard a very genius at sanctimony.

John Danby makes the penetrating comment that "in Richard . . . the corruption of his time is made aware of itself. This is the ambiguity of his role: to be the logical outcome of his society, and yet a pariah rejected by that society; a hypocrite, yet more sincere in his self-awareness than those he ruins and deceives."[3] If it were true, however, that Richard takes "the average practice of his world" and erects it "into a conscious principle of action," then England would be like him irredeemable. Although seemingly a very man o' the time, he is not its archetype; on the contrary, his plots are an attempt to call back the yesterday which the other characters shudder to remember. Men like Hastings and Buckingham can enjoy the pleasures of rank and influence, but Richard, bored and restless in "this weak piping time of peace," wants to relive again the thrilling danger of the battlefield. Like Margaret, he is an anachronism, a creature for whom time has stopped; and when he must fully reveal himself by his deeds and words, he resembles no one else in the play—he is very obviously an aberration, uniquely deformed in spirit as in body. Richard falls, among other reasons, because he is not enough like other men and women to know how they think and feel. Although he can manipulate those who are credulous and corruptible, he does not know the difference between his absolute unscrupulousness and the lesser equivocations of his accomplices and

3. *Shakespeare's Doctrine of Nature*, p. 60.

victims. Utterly cynical, he cannot gauge the force of their halfhearted principles or predict their hesitations, and he makes a catastrophic error in thinking that the people can be mollified by pious shows when they know that he has committed unpardonable crimes.

In *Richard III*, as in *Henry VI Part III*, Richard is still the outsider. If he seems now to belong, it is not because his society is made up of men like him but because time has rubbed smooth the sharp edges of his malcontent. Able to get along with men as well as to get rid of them, Richard is completely at ease with himself as well as with others. No longer envious of those of better person, no longer itching to hack his way through his own flesh and blood, he takes a detached, ironic, almost kindly, view of such victims as "simple plain Clarence." One does not feel that Richard has become so skillful at duplicity that he completely masks the hatreds he voices in *Henry VI Part III*; one simply cannot imagine the suave plotter of *Richard III* raging at the world. An entrepreneur and impresario of villainy, he is always removed from the murderous acts he perpetrates. His wit flashes rather than his knife; he kills with words rather than swords, and though we have no doubt that he could stab anyone, he is too fastidious to bloody his hands needlessly. He enjoys entrapping Hastings and allows others the pleasure of beheading him. Instead of eating a bloody supper in the Tower, he is content to beg some good strawberries from Ely's garden and look at Hastings' severed head before he dines.

Acting as prologue as well as puppetmaster, Richard introduces the action he contrives and dominates; and when he lets the audience in on stratagems he dares not reveal to any one else, they enjoy the confidence because his ambition is devoid of personal malice or envy:

> But I, that am not shap'd for sportive tricks
> Nor made to court an amorous looking glass;
> I, that am rudely stamp'd, and want love's majesty
> To strut before a wanton ambling nymph;
> I, that am curtail'd of this fair proportion,
> Cheated of feature by dissembling Nature,
> Deform'd, unfinish'd, sent before my time
> Into this breathing world, scarce half made up,
> And that so lamely and unfashionable
> That dogs bark at me as I halt by them—
> Why, I, in this weak piping time of peace,
> Have no delight to pass away the time,
> Unless to see my shadow in the sun
> And descant on mine own deformity.

And therefore, since I cannot prove a lover
To entertain these fair well-spoken days,
I am determined to prove a villain
And hate the idle pleasures of these days.   (I.i.14-31)

Is this a man tormented by the deformity which he describes with such humor and sweet reasonableness? Or one driven to seek power by a gnawing sense of his own inferiority? If there is any burden of anguish in this frank declaration, it is very deeply submerged, for Richard sounds bored, not embittered. He wants work, an opportunity to bustle, a goal worthy of his extraordinary energies and talents. His calculated changes of mood are unpredictable; his melodramatic gestures are lightninglike, but he is never impulsive. His style is elegant and even studied. He savors, and stamps with his fastidious personality, the alliterations, antitheses, and rhetorical flourishes which are conventional in the speeches of others.[4] An instigator of disorder, he seems, until his failure of nerve, immensely rational and self-controlled, so much so that his aplomb is more frightening than his sudden squalls of passion, which are as calculated as his sudden fits of piety. Unlike the gormandizing Falstaff, who affects a Puritanical preciseness, Richard is genuinely ascetic in his appetites. He does disapprove of lechery, whether Edward's or Hastings'—or rather he despises men who waste their time chasing women.

A born teacher, Richard delights even as he instructs. His mimicking of pious cant is so perfect that, though we are not seduced, we are amused by revelations that should horrify us. The snarling Richard of *Henry VI Part III* was less threatening, because his pathology conformed to and confirmed traditional moral assumptions. A creature warped from birth, he could be explained by Freudian theory as well as Elizabethan ethical psychology as a slave to monstrous passions. But the Richard who makes a cheerful vocation of the evil to which he is drawn by natural instincts and gifts is not so comfortably explained away. To be sure, his posturing is absurdly theatrical; he is a melodramatist who can be enjoyed because he is so patently "fictitious." Yet even as we cheer ourselves with the thought that Richard is unreal, we know he is a more credible and convincing representation of human nature than is Richmond. No stereotype of villainy,[5] Richard has his

4. Olivier caught very well the fastidiousness of Richard's manner in his film version of *Richard III*. As Richard, he spoke in a somewhat high-pitched voice and phrased his lines precisely and elegantly.

5. It is one thing to trace a part of Richard's "ancestry" to the figure of the Vice, with whom Richard identifies: "Thus, like the formal vice, Iniquity, / I moralize two meanings in one word" (III.i.82-3). It is another thing to explain Richard and his successes by

individual bent of speech, a sinister command of homely phrases and a sardonic humor. More "observed" than conceived, he speaks of our own world, and we laugh at his ingenious strategems partly because they lay bare eternal truths of political and moral behavior. Some critics believe his cheerful dedication to a life of evil is a fiction invented to soothe his lacerated ego. Others suggest that he is tormented secretly by his deformity, which he treats as a badge of his uniqueness and a convenient excuse for his inhumanity. But it is hard to imagine that Richard hungers to be normal or that he seeks power as a compensation for his sexual inadequacies, when his conquest of Lady Anne suggests that, had he applied himself to seduction, he might have rivaled Casanova.

Perhaps, like Iago, Richard needs to believe in his reasonableness and cannot admit the sense of inferiority that sparks his malice. But whom does Richard envy? There is no beauty in Hastings' or Buckingham's life that makes his seem ugly, and it is impossible to equate the elegant aristocratic Richard with the vulgar, lying, cheating Ancient. If Richard's self-acceptance is only a mask, it is a mask that does not, like Iago's pose of robust cynicism, slip to disclose a perverted and lacerated ego. What is revealed on the eve of Bosworth is not Richard's long concealed bitterness and spite but his despairing sense of isolation. Unlike Iago, Richard in conversation and in soliloquy is very much the same creature; because he lacks Iago's insistent need for self-justification, he does not lie to himself about his motives or about how he feels or acts. And because he lacks Iago's sadistic cravings, his pleasure in using people is almost wholly impersonal and professional. He does not need to degrade them; he has no knack for gratuitous cruelty. To enter, as Freudian critics will, the subterranean corridors of Richard's psyche is to lose contact with the Richard of the play or to mistake him for the more conventionally conceived malcontent who briefly appears in the last acts of *Henry VI Part III*. Like Elizabethans, we may wish to believe that heartless criminals lead lives of quiet desperation, for if we must have unconscionable villains, we would prefer them warped and tormented, just as if we must have extermination camps, we would have them run by sadists and perverts, not by fussy bureaucrats who take pride in their fanatical efficiency, in an unpleasant job well done. We do not want to believe that men may commit horrible acts just because they are lacking in

---

reference to the conventional figure of the Vice as Bernard Spivack seems to do in *Shakespeare and the Allegory of Evil* (New York: Columbia Univ. Press, 1958), pp. 393-407. At almost every moment Richard's triumphs are convincingly real; we do not have to invoke the convention of the Vice to explain his deception of others, because very few characters in the play are really deceived about his nature.

emotional sympathies or moral sensitivity, because, like Richard, they regard other human beings as objects to be manipulated, acquired, or disposed of.

The cool, ironical Richard of the first acts is not the whole of Shakespeare's portrait. The more he reveals himself during the play, the less attractive he appears. Even before the lines of strain mar his splendid composure, his brilliance loses its fascination; even before he reaches the crown, the "moral holiday" of the opening scenes, created by his witty, conscienceless audacity and preposterous poses, draws to an end. Or rather there is never in *Richard III* a moral holiday comparable to the escape from moral judgments which Lamb finds in Restoration comedy. If we check our morals with our coats when we see a performance of *The Country Wife*, it is because moral judgments are irrelevant to Wycherley's characters. His wives and sweethearts may prove unfaithful, but they cannot be seduced from scruples of chastity because they do not have any; they cannot be corrupted because they are never innocent. Similarly, the victimized husbands and lovers do not arouse our pity because they are too gross to be cheated and too insensitive to be pained. Because Wycherley's point of view is insistently arch and his situations artificial, he threatens nothing by his farcing of adultery. He amuses and titillates; he allows us to enjoy a very bourgeois dirty joke even while we think ourselves very sophisticated and worldly.

Richard III evokes a more complex response because its perspective is moral and because an audience's pleasure in Richard's brilliant plotting is countered by some measure of sympathy for his victims. Even Clarence, the first of Richard's dupes, is a dignified and poignant figure. Little more than a shallow opportunist in *Henry VI Part III,* he has on the night of his murder some touch of poetry and even some unconscious intuition of Richard's treachery.[6] Stirred by remorseful memories and fearful of his life, he prays that his innocent children will not suffer for his misdeeds. One does not feel too sorry, however, for Clarence, who confesses himself false and perjured, because his murderers are so entertaining and so much more brutally honest with themselves about the nuisance of conscience. The balancing of tones in the scene is daring; one moment we sigh for Clarence, the next laugh at the joke of the butt of Malmsey, in which he will have wine enough. At first Clarence would play the orator with his assassins and dissuade them with finespun casuistry, theological

6. Although Clarence is duped by Richard's pretenses of brotherly concern, he dreams on the night of his death that he is "accidentally" drowned by Gloucester. Perhaps this is just an ironic touch, but the play does deal again, in a profounder way, with unconscious thoughts when Richard is tormented by a nightmare on the eve of Bosworth.

arguments, and moral exhortations. But when he appeals to God, they remind him of his crimes and declare themselves instruments of divine justice. The slickness of Clarence's pious sentences and the hypocrisy of the assassins' replies are a sardonically amusing exposure of the moral way of the world. At the very last, however, the joke of scruple and remorse turns out to be no joke at all, for the more reluctant of the murderers is appalled by his deed and will have none of the reward that earlier stilled the whisper of his conscience.

The comedy of Richard's initial successes is enjoyable because there is an ironic justice in the fates of men like Hastings and Buckingham, who think themselves Richard's accomplices, not his puppets, and who betray themselves by their vanity and ambition. The confidence game Richard plays could not succeed if men like Hastings and Buckingham were as moral as they claimed to be or less eager for illicit gains. Delighted to have a seat in the inner circle, and savoring their power to destroy other men, they are fatuously confident that they can outwit Richard or use him to their own ends. Poor Hastings thinks Catesby is *his* spy, and, pleased by the executions of Rivers and Grey, he plans, amidst some pious exclamations, to send a few more packing. Buckingham, a tragic figure in More's *History*, is more comic in *Richard III*, where he preens himself on his political genius when he is only running Richard's errands and parroting his ideas. Ironies multiply as Hastings and Buckingham play their studied roles at the council that is to choose a date for the coronation of Edward's son. Taking a page from Richard's book, Hastings chooses to appear as childish-foolish and naive as the Protector; he remarks to the others about the openness of Richard's feelings. Also playing the innocent, Buckingham declares (more truly than he knows) that he and Richard know each other's faces but not each other's hearts.

Clinging to their shabby ends of morality, Hastings and Buckingham must lose their heads to find themselves—or at least to recognize the vanity of their politic careers. Completely honest with himself, Richard is fully conscious of his hypocrisies and pretenses. Where Hastings shudders at the crimes he contemplates, Richard openly enjoys the company of murderers; and his frank sanctimony is a refreshing breeze in the stifling cant of the Court. He does not release an audience from the burden of morality; he frees it from the burden of the simpering hypocrisy that often passes for moral conviction, from the clichés of brotherhood and charity that substitute for generous thought and Christian deeds.

Iago's plans succeed because Othello and others believe he is honest; Edmund's plots prosper in *King Lear* because he appears a loyal and natural son. Richard's successes are more ironic still because everyone except his gullible brothers knows pretty much what he is and fears him. His counterfeit professions pass current, nevertheless, because in a world of surfaces, of facile words and meaningless oaths, no man can afford to question another man's gestures. We know what Richard believes because he speaks his mind. What the others actually believe is difficult to say. Does Anne really believe when she surrenders to Richard that she does not know his heart? Is the Archbishop of Canterbury convinced that innocent children do not deserve sanctuary? Does Hastings think that Richard lacks guile or the Mayor believe that Hastings is guilty? The will to self-deception is strong when there are advantages to being obtuse, and when accommodation and pliancy are the wisdom of the times.

Cleverer than all the rest, free from sham, and flawless in his Machiavellian virtuosity, Richard surmounts incredible obstacles to the throne. Like Marlowe's Tamburlaine, he seems a transcendent and irresistible force, so resourceful that every challenge or rebuff affords an opportunity for another dazzling performance. Other Elizabethan villains—Marlowe's and Jonson's, for example—overreach in obvious ways; infatuated with their successes, they underestimate their opponents or hoist themselves with their own petards. Richard is too witty, however, and too skeptical to grow infatuate with success. He knows, even as he relishes the seduction of Anne, that he is no thing of beauty, and he takes the accurate measure of almost all of his opponents. He does not gloat like a Barabas or a Guise over his power to destroy: Nothing too much is his political philosophy. Yet he falters at the very moment of his ultimate triumph, and his fall is as precipitous as his ascent was meteoric.

The geometry of Richard's career has a superb logic as well as an artful symmetry. His fall is the mirror image of his rise because the very techniques which carry him to the throne ensure that he will not keep it long. His is the politics of faction and corruption. His plots feed on the intrigues and rivalries of the Court, which provide him with both accomplices and scapegoats. At first he can easily enlist the support of Hastings and Buckingham, who hate the Queen's relatives, and he can win the reluctant assent of Rivers and Grey to his apparently reasonable proposals about the Princes. With each step Richard takes toward the crown, however, his ambition grows more transparent, his accomplices fewer, and his enemies more numerous. He uses his brother Edward to eliminate Clarence; then he uses Hastings to get rid of Rivers and Grey. Buckingham helps him to murder Hastings, and finally he rids himself of Buckingham. Thus, each of Richard's triumphs is purchased with a diminishing

Machiavellian capital, and though his political debts are self-liquidating, so too are his political assets. When he gains the pinnacle of power, he stands alone, isolated from other men by his criminality, and hated by those whose allegiance he nominally commands. Not once could he gain the support of ordinary men like the Scrivener, who immediately sees the fraud of Hastings' indictment. At the Guildhall, the citizens failed to respond to Buckingham's exhortations; and their silence was so ominous that the Mayor, we are told, began to back away from Richard's campaign. Another man might have hesitated at this point, but Richard plunged on because he was too self-confident to value the aid of others. Convinced that shows of piety and popular support were enough, he finds at Bosworth that he has on his side only such shows of loyalty as Stanley offers.

Richard's fall is not political in any conventional sense. He is not toppled from power by the superior forces of Richmond or deposed by his subjects. His defeat at Bosworth puts the seal on a catastrophe that begins the moment he takes his place on the throne. In More's *History* as in Shakespeare's play, the murder of the Princes is the turning point of Richard's career. More relates that after the murder of his nephews, Richard had no rest or quiet of mind, only the torment of conscience and cowardly fears.[7] Shakespeare alters this conception by placing Richard's crisis of confidence before the murder of the Princes, not after it. When Buckingham does not immediately consent to their death in the coronation scene, Richard, who did not blanch at the report of the citizens' silence in the Guildhall, grows angry, gnaws his lip, and speaks for the first time of fear and uncertainty, even though he wears the crown. His response is strikingly out of proportion to its cause. He does not need Buckingham to commit the murders when there are willing cutthroats in the Court, nor does he need his consent or compliance. Yet when Buckingham hesitates, Richard grows furious enough to commit a disastrously unpolitic act. Unwilling to wait for Buckingham's reply (which will soon enough be volunteered), he treats his old ally with brutal insolence. Indeed, he goes out of his way to humiliate Buckingham by denying him the earldom of Hereford, which Richard had specified as his henchman's reward. How extraordinary that, even while he declares that his kingdom stands on brittle glass, Richard insults and casts off the accomplice whose army might have tipped the scales at Bosworth. After this peevishness, Richard grows even more irritable and indecisive. Lethargic, and unable to concentrate, he responds in a confused and

7. See More's description of Richard's fearfulness and sleeplessness after the murder of his nephews, reprinted in Holinshed's *Chronicles,* III, 403.

uncertain fashion to reports of impending invasion and disaffection among his people. What a fall is there from the masterly Richard of the first act to the cringing despondent general of the last act, who seeks reassurance from the men he should lead and who stoops to spying on his own troops.

John Palmer sees Richard as unnerved by his own success. Having achieved the impossible in gaining the throne, Richard, he suggests, finds himself with no new worlds to conquer, and no goal worthy of his extraordinary energies.[8] I would put this a slightly different way, because it seems to me that Richard is unnerved, not because he has nothing left to win, but because having won, he has now everything to lose. An instinctive gambler, he delights in winning Anne "all the world to nothing"; and having won her, he will wager his "dukedom to a beggarly denier" on his good looks. In the same vein, he declares that he "will stand the hazard of the die" at Bosworth because he has bet his life on victory. He is at his best, as in the seduction of the Lady Anne, when the impossibility of a venture challenges his daring. Needing the odds against him, he recovers his old vitality at Bosworth, when with the battle nearly lost, he can again stake everything, including his life, in an impossible venture. What shakes Richard's confidence as he ascends the throne in the coronation scene is an awareness that he is now on the defensive: he must stop all growths that threaten him. Better equipped to seize the crown than wear it, he lacks, as he ironically predicted in a moment of mock self-deprecation, the ability to rule.[9]

Although Richard's failure of nerve betrays itself in his psychological responses, the crux of the coronation scene is unmistakably moral. In More's *History*, Richard falls out with Buckingham over political issues that have no connection to the murder of the Princes. Richard fears and mistrusts his chief ally, More relates, because the ambitious Buckingham was a potential rival, and the earldom of Hereford, which he claimed was "interlaced with the title to the crowne."[10] In *Richard III* Buckingham, too docile to inspire suspicion, aims no higher than the reward which Richard had earlier promised. But he does enrage Richard in the coronation scene when he refuses to consent immediately to the King's request for the murder of his nephews. Earlier Richard had wooed the Lady Anne and had sent Catesby to court Hastings. Now as King he finds it necessary to woo Buckingham to commit a horrid deed, and he discovers to his chagrin that Buckingham knows how to play the bashful

8. John Palmer, *Political Characters of Shakespeare* (London: MacMillan, 1952), pp. 103-104. Although sometimes patronized as an "amateur" effort in Shakespearean criticism, this book is a treasure of acute insight and penetrating interpretation.
9. In III.vii, Richard, descanting to Buckingham on his incapacities to rule, speaks of his poverty of spirit and his mighty and many defects.
10. Holinshed, III, 403.

maiden as well as he. Given the nature of the request, Buckingham's coyness and obtuseness are understandable: at this point any man might pretend dullness. More puzzling is Richard's oblique manner of wooing, because suddenness once was his supreme tactic. Now he moves sideways like a crab towards his goal and stoops to playing guessing games with his puppet. He wants Buckingham not only to consent to the murder of Edward's sons but also to volunteer to perform the deed which Richard is unwilling to call by its name. And, though Buckingham is not shocked by the idea of killing the boys, Richard is enraged by his hesitation, which forces him to state his purpose openly.

This revelation of Richard's nature is extraordinary. He has no scruples in the ordinary sense of the word; only once does he speak of sin and shudder at the thought of wading through blood. But he has the need—the "moral" need—for Buckingham's company in hell. To ascend the heights of power Richard has had to ascend the heights of villainy. Each step upward demanded a crime worse than the last, and at each step another accomplice faltered or held back. First one of the murderers of Clarence fled, then Hastings refused to see Richard crowned. When Buckingham draws away from the murder of the boys, as do Tyrrel and the hired assassins, Richard finds himself without another damned soul. The other crimes Richard willed. The murder of the Princes is one which he must commit whether he wills it or not, because he *needs* the Bastards dead. For the first time he is not in control of his destiny; he is commanded by the necessities which his ambition created. Now he speaks of what he must do:

> I must be married to my brother's daughter,
> Or else my kingdom stands on brittle glass.
> Murther her brothers, and then marry her—
> Uncertain way of gain! But I am in
> So far in blood that sin will pluck on sin.   (IV.ii.60-4)

In *Richard III* as in *Henry VI Part III*, the murder of children is a crowning villainy which only a Richard could coldbloodedly plan and only a Margaret rejoice in. Despite his qualms, Richard keeps to his dreadful course and, though he has no stomach for this crime, invites Tyrrel to come to him after dinner to describe how the boys were murdered. Contemptuous of Tyrrel's show of remorse, Richard greets him sardonically as "kind Tyrrel" and "gentle Tyrrel," but the mockery will not stick because Tyrrel's remorse is genuine. Before, the very frankness of Richard's dedication to evil had a certain charm. Now the pitilessness of his response to Tyrrel is horrifying. Wanting the natural touch, Richard is unable to feel anything for another human being.

The portrayal of Richard's loss of control in the coronation scene is masterful. Thereafter, his uncertainties grow repetitious and his hesitations undramatic. I do not think that Shakespeare becomes bored with his plot at this point. Rather he becomes too interested in working out the symmetries of Richard's pyramidal career. Wanting to fashion a literal peripeteia, to make Richard's decline a precise inversion of his ascent, he devotes too much space to his wooing of the widowed Elizabeth in Act IV, hoping perhaps that his audience will grasp the subtle ways that Richard's failure parodies his triumphant seduction of the Lady Anne. Measured against ordinary reality both wooing scenes are preposterous because no man in his right mind would attempt to seduce women even as they mourned for those whom he has murdered. But the attempt on Anne is something of a lark, a *jeu d'esprit*, in which Richard flatters himself with impossibilities, whereas his encounter with Elizabeth is a political necessity; he must win her daughter to shore his tottering state.

Richard's success with Anne can be made more credible if she is thought of as the "everlasting trollop." [11] But we cannot look at her in this way when every character except Richard treats her with respect and sympathy even after she has married him. Shallow in her grieving over Henry VI, whose corpse she abandons to Richard at the close of the scene, she is not so foolish that she believes Richard's outrageous lies, nor so pliant that she yields to his arguments loathing his nature. His triumph is more of a rape than a seduction, for though he seems to cringe and fawn, he bullies and intimidates and mocks her high moral tone by appeals to Christian charity. Instead of attempting to persuade her of his sincerity, he shakes her belief in her own scruples by answering her hyperboles of outrage with hyperboles that are outrageous. In *Henry VI Part III* he played the chorus to Edward's courtly wooing of Elizabeth. Now he assumes the ludicrously incongruous pose of a sighing Petrarchan lover and casts Anne as his Laura, his saint, his cruel fair who pretends disdain where she means love. And how can she remain cruel when he confesses that he has performed the ultimate service of love—murdered her husband and father-in-law to win her? She cannot believe the fantastic lie that he did all for her

---

11. Palmer remarks of this scene: "The eternal bully speaks to the everlasting trollop—and knows that he will prevail" (*Political Characters*, p. 83). But surely Anne is nobler than this.

beauty, but she must prefer to accept its flattery than to admit the brutality of Richard's contempt for her.

Richard's knack of improvisation is dazzling: Anne's talk of killing him prompts his Petrarchan posturing, and it is only a step from the cliché of her killing eyes to the cliché of his helpless tears. She is vulnerable because she can not match his brutal will except with words; and even as his exaggerated passion is a mere tissue of words, so too her hatred seems at last nothing more than words, for she cannot bring herself to kill him even when he offers her his sword and volunteers to kill himself if she commands him to:

> Nay, do not pause; for I did kill King Henry—
> But 'twas thy beauty that provoked me.
> Nay, now dispatch. 'Twas I that stabb'd young Edward—
> But 'twas thy heavenly face that set me on.
>   *She falls the sword.*
> Take up the sword again, or take up me.   (I.ii.179-183)

The frankness of his confession shatters her last defense. Flattered, humiliated, and terrified, she can escape from knowing herself only by pretending not to understand Richard: "I would I knew your heart."

It is a far less confident and resourceful Richard who claims in Act IV to be a jolly, thriving wooer. Now he faces a worthy antagonist in Elizabeth, who knows Richard's heart and has been schooled in vindictiveness by the railing Margaret. This time the match is even, because it pits realist against realist. Or rather, from the beginning, it is uneven, because Elizabeth has Richard's former strength while he has Anne's vulnerability. He comes armed only with conventional sentiments, platitudes, and hypocritical rationalizations, while Elizabeth speaks with shrewd and bitter cynicism of her willingness to degrade her daughter and to slander herself. Before Richard was the Petrarchan wooer; now Elizabeth, who would teach him how to woo her daughter, suggests that he use the Petrarchan emblem of a pair of bleeding hearts, an appropriate conceit for the murderer of her sons. As the rhetorical patterning of the lines reveals, Richard is on the defensive. It is Elizabeth who interrupts him, who has the brilliant unanswerable ripostes and the last stichomythic words, while he pleads with her not to mock him or confound his meanings. When the arguments and poses that dazzled Anne do not succeed—when casualness and candor are impossible—Richard must stoop to outright falsehood, lying oaths, and disgusting bribes. Accustomed to dealing with human beings as objects, he tries to bargain with Elizabeth like a peddler: so much recompense for so much

loss, so many grandchildren to come for children murdered. Because he is
unable to love, he cannot judge the horror of his commerce of flesh and blood
or the futility of his cynical promises of profit:

> If I did take the kingdom from your sons,
> To make amends I'll give it to your daughter.
> If I have kill'd the issue of your womb,
> To quicken your increase I will beget
> Mine issue of your blood upon your daughter.
> A grandam's name is little less in love
> Than is the doting title of mother.
> They are as children but one step below,
> Even of your metal, of your very blood. . . .
> Again shall you be mother to a king,
> And all the ruins of distressful times
> Repair'd with double riches of content.
> What, we have many goodly days to see.
> The liquid drops of tears that you have shed
> Shall come again, transform'd to orient pearl,
> Advantaging their loan with interest
> Of ten times double gain of happiness. (IV.iv.294-324)

Although Richard speaks of womb, fruit, and harvest, he is the enemy of
increase. His state is threatened by the growth of hopes, and his nature is as
kind "as snow in harvest." Once careful to avoid the hypocrisies that damned
Hastings and Buckingham, now, desperate and bankrupt, he writes out a
canting promissory note that falls due at Bosworth field:

> As I intend to prosper and repent,
> So thrive I in my dangerous affairs
> Of hostile arms! Myself myself confound!
> Heaven and fortune bar me happy hours!
> Day, yield me not thy light, nor, night, thy rest!
> Be opposite all planets of good luck
> To my proceeding if, with dear heart's love,
> Immaculate devotion, holy thoughts,
> I tender not thy beauteous princely daughter![12] (IV.iv.397-405)

Knowing that Elizabeth mocks him, Richard has to believe nevertheless that he
has won her over, though she promises only to send her answer. There is no
pleasure, however, in this "triumph," none of the exuberant self-congratulation

12. The wording of Richard's oath is a precise echo of the false protestations which
earlier damned Hastings and Buckingham. See II.i.11, and 32-40.

that followed the winning of Anne, only a sneering contempt for this "relenting fool, and shallow changing woman." But the joke is on Richard, and so certain was Shakespeare that his audience would understand it that he makes only a casual reference later in the play to Richmond's betrothal of Elizabeth's daughter.[13]

It is appropriate that Richard, who deceived so many others, should at last deceive and confound himself. And it is fittingly ironic that, having cast off all human ties, he is cursed and disowned by the woman who bore him. Once he put on the role of childish-foolishness, but now he finds himself like a child afraid of the dark, and he is unable to trust anyone including himself. Indeed, he is more frightened by the shadows of his own thought at Bosworth than by Richmond's army. Prompted perhaps by *The True Tragedy of Richard III*, Shakespeare stages Richard's "dreadful and terrible dreame" on the eve of Bosworth as a ghostly pageant in which Richard's victims, each in his proper turn, bless Richmond's enterprise and curse Richard. Thus, the past returns to bear witness against Richard, and the nightmare becomes a ritual of excommunication, in which he is anathematized and cast out by the dead as he has been by the living.

The pageant of ghosts seems an appropriately archaic device with which to recapitulate the past; the attempt to make Richard bear witness against himself as he awakens is less successful:

> What do I fear? Myself? There's none else by.
> Richard loves Richard: that is, I am I.
> Is there a murtherer here? No. Yes, I am.
> Then fly. What, from myself? Great reason why—
> Lest I revenge myself upon myself?
> Alack, I love myself. Wherefore? For any good
> That I myself have done unto myself?
> O no! Alas, I rather hate myself
> For hateful deeds committed by myself.
> I am a villain. Yet I lie, I am not. (V.iii.183-192)

These broken, disjointed phrases and abrupt contradictions express too crudely and rhetorically a very sophisticated and "modern" psychological conception. Like one of Dostoevski's heroes,[14] Richard sneers at the slave morality in his

13. Although various critics have been convinced that Elizabeth is suborned by Richard, the outcome of the scene has to be unambiguous. Otherwise Shakespeare would not have dared announce the espousal of the princess Elizabeth to Richmond so coincidentally in the brief scene that follows (IV.v.7-8).

14. I am thinking in particular of Raskolnikov in *Crime and Punishment,* though Ivan Karamazov is also haunted by terrible dreams.

waking thoughts but cannot escape the reckoning of his unconscious nature that takes the form of terrible dreams. That Richard would suffer from nightmares at the crisis of Bosworth seems reasonable enough.[15] It is harder to accept Anne's assertion (IV.i.83-85) that he was often afflicted with "timorous dreams," because this revelation does not square with Richard's personality; we cannot imagine the nerveless villain of the first three acts taking more than ten minutes to fall soundly asleep. Only later will the bankruptcy of Richard's credo of ego become evident. Only in the last scenes will it become clear that the supreme egotist does not know how to love himself.

Richard's spiritual failure is England's salvation, because even as he falls apart, others unite against him. Repaying perjury with perjury, treachery with treachery, murder with murder, he has settled all the criminal accounts of the past except his own; and then with perfect justice he becomes his own nemesis. At Bosworth he stands alone for sacrifice, the only one left with bloody hands, a scapegoat laden with all the sins of his time. At Towton and Wakefield both sides committed vile acts. At Bosworth field, however, the moral oppositions are as clearly drawn again as they were in *Henry VI Part I*, where chivalry opposed witchcraft and was betrayed by policy. When Richmond and Richard share the stage, good stands against evil, love opposes hate, and the communal impulse is set against the predatory instincts of the lone wolf.

Those who want proof that virtue is stronger than vice must find it somewhere else, however, because *Richard III* dramatizes Richard's failure rather than Richmond's success. Hardly a mention is made in the play of the preparations for Richmond's campaign which have so important a place in More's *History*, and Richmond does not even appear until the fifth act. I do not mean that Shakespeare risked angering Elizabeth by slighting Richmond's part in bringing peace and unity to England, only that he keeps his focus on Richard and does not conceive of Richmond as another Talbot or as England's champion in a Morality combat between the forces of darkness and light. So little emphasis, in fact, is placed on Richmond's military prowess that, were it not for the stage direction of the last scene of the play, we would not know that he kills Richard in combat.[16] Under the banner of the Red Cross Knight,

15. Sen Gupta complains, however, that "there is no inner connexion between the man who mocked conscience and the man who is [at Bosworth] mocked by it" (*Shakespeare's Historical Plays* [London: Oxford Univ. Press, 1964], p. 97).

16. When Shakespeare wishes to make the triumph of good over evil important, as in Macduff's victory over Macbeth in single combat, he makes the confrontation genuinely dramatic, a clash of words and personalities as well as of swords. That Richmond should defeat Richard in single combat is not essential to the moral design and dramatic resolution of *Richard III*.

Richmond sallies forth against a dragon who is already doomed—deserted by his followers, sapped of vitality, and sick at heart. Even before Richmond enters the play, moreover, York and Lancaster make peace with one another as Margaret, Elizabeth, and the Duchess of York join together to grieve their losses. No less symbolic of the reunification of England is the pageant of ghosts, Yorkist and Lancastrian, who make common cause against Richard and for Richmond. The future belongs to Richmond, not because he is the greater soldier but because he answers the longing of the nation that there be an end to violence and rage. Richmond's mission is to deliver England not only from Richard's tyranny but also from the hatreds of the past that live on in Margaret's thirst for vengeance.

In a sense Margaret is the presiding genius of the revenge plot in *Richard III*, who makes explicit its pattern of crime and punishment, sin and retribution. But that pattern of vengeance is sickening, because it includes in Margaret's mind the murder of innocents, and because the instrument of this vengeance is Richard, who "punishes" the guilty by making them the steppingstones to his bloody tyranny. Loathesome physically and morally, Margaret is a Senecan Fury, let shrieking out of hell, whose cry for revenge is the direct antithesis of Richmond's appeal for reconciliation. Even when she joins the widowed Elizabeth and Duchess of York in lamentation, she is isolated by her warped emotions. Wanting an eye for an eye, and capable of relishing the suffering of others, she prays to a pitiless deity whose "justice" is an unmitigated horror:

> O upright, just, and true-disposing God,
> How do I thank thee that this carnal cur [Richard]
> Preys on the issue of his mother's body
> And makes her pew-fellow with others' moan!   (IV.iv.55-8)

Where Richard can speak of Elizabeth's children as so much merchandise, Margaret can balance out the murder of children as if she were counting sacks of grain. When the Duchess of York protests that she has wept for Margaret's losses, Margaret continues her sickening arithmetic:

> Bear with me! I am hungry for revenge
> And now I cloy me with beholding it.
> Thy Edward he is dead, that kill'd my Edward;
> The other Edward dead, to quit my Edward;
> Young York he is but boot, because both they
> Match'd not the high perfection of my loss.   (IV.iv.61-6)

From Margaret, Elizabeth can learn to curse and forego sleep. The greater lesson of mercy, so necessary to England's future, requires a nobler teacher, Richmond.

By portraying Richmond as a spiritual leader who brings a new dispensation of mercy to England, Shakespeare avoids the ticklish question of the Tudor claim to the succession and Richmond's role as "rebel." In his oration to his army Richmond does not offer a theoretical justification for rebellion; he portrays the battle against Richard as an act of self-defense by which Englishmen protect their homes and families against a ravening predator. And Richmond need not expound his claim to the throne because his "legitimacy" is moral, not genealogical. The time of rival claimants is past; the new age demands a new royal house, one untouched by dynastic feuds. Thus, while contempt is heaped on Englishmen who support the French invaders in *King John*, England's salvation in *Richard III* can come from France and with French aid, because England needs an "outsider" as king, a monarch who has not bloodied his hands in the civil wars.

In themselves, Richmond's speeches sound conventionally pious. In dramatic context, justaposed against the collapse of Richard's cynical schemes, they have a genuine power. To bring *Richard III* to a close, Shakespeare does not retreat from political realism to moral clichés. The chorus of weeping women and the pageant of ghosts recall the toll of violence, so even as we rejoice in the rescue of the young George Stanley, whom Richard would have executed, we remember Rutland, Margaret's son, Richard's nephews, and all the innocents who were not spared. The mood at the end is one of somber reflection, not of joyous celebration. Instead of proclaiming the Tudor millennium, Richmond prays that England will escape a past when

> The brother blindly shed the brother's blood;
> The father rashly slaughtered his own son.
> The son, compell'd, been butcher to the sire.   (V.v.24-6)

Although there is no doubt that the heavens to which Richmond prays have had their part in England's deliverance, the moral drama of the last scenes is acted out by men on earth. The victory at Bosworth is won, not by armies of angels, but by a people determined to be rid of their oppressor; and if Richard is damned, it is to a spiritual hell on earth from which he can find no exit except the excitement of battle. Despite his nightmare, he is unregenerate on the morrow; having recovered his old zest in combat, he finds at Bosworth the heroic death that was his only possible fulfillment.

In the *Henry VI* plays the well-being of England seemed to depend upon the valor of its legendary champions. But when chivalry died in *Part I*, and the battlefield became a setting for atrocity in *Part III*, heroism ceased to be an ultimate value. Chivalric deeds will not in themselves rescue a country inured to violence; there must be an end to the appetite for war which is Richard's and England's sickness. Thus, while the tetralogy begins with eulogies of the mighty Henry V, whose "brandish'd sword did blind men with his beams," it concludes with Henry VII's invocation of a peaceful agrarian world in which men may enjoy "fair prosperous days" and taste "this land's increase." Once again at Bosworth, as at Wakefield and Towton, men band together to hunt down their foe, only now the hunt is the communal act of peace-loving men who join forces to kill a savage boar. After Bosworth men pray, not for an England once again united and invincible, but for an England in which concord and brotherhood will at last prevail.

4. KING JOHN

It is impossible to determine just where *King John* belongs among the History Plays. A revision of *The Troublesome Reign of King John,* an anonymous play which was printed in two parts in 1591,[1] *King John* was mentioned by Meres in 1598. But there are no records of Elizabethan performances and no topical allusions in the text or contemporary references to the play which enable us to date it with any assurance. The internal evidence of style and craftsmanship is too confusing and contradictory to be very helpful, for though the verve and spontaneity of the Bastard's speeches represent a fairly sophisticated and "mature" poetic style, much else in the poetry, characterizations, and plotting of *King John* seems pedestrian, if not actually "primitive."

One way of explaining the inconsistency and unevenness of the artistic achievement of *King John* is to hypothesize that its text is Shakespeare's revision of a play which he wrote very early in his career.[2] What is dull, stale, or unprofitable we assign to the "basic text," composed perhaps about 1592; what is lively, vivid, and colorful we say was "revised" at a later date, perhaps

1. E. A. J. Honigmann argued unconvincingly in his new Arden edition of *King John* (London: Methuen, 1954) that *The Troublesome Reign* is the Bad Quarto of a play based on *King John* rather than the source of Shakespeare's play. Dover Wilson points out, however, that "the case for *King John* as the original version is a hopeless one"; see his introduction to the new Cambridge *King John* (Cambridge: Cambridge Univ. Press, 1954), p. xxxii.

2. Wilson argues the probability of a "second revision" by Shakespeare in the introduction to his edition of *King John,* pp. xlviii-lvii. He would date the original revision 1590, the second 1594. Tillyard suggests the possibility that *The Troublesome Reign* is a Bad Quarto of an earlier version of *King John* composed by Shakespeare about the time of *Henry VI Part I* (*History Plays,* p. 217).

about 1594—between the composition of *Richard III* and *Richard II.* Unfortunately a hypothesis of revision creates as many contradictions as it explains away, for if the disparities of style in *King John* are the result of a revision, that revision must have been so haphazard and illogical as to be almost eccentric. Can we assume that Shakespeare was willing to rewrite substantial portions of his "original" text and yet made no effort in his revision to correct the serious flaws in the plot of *King John*? Can we believe that at some point in his career he reworked hundreds of lines in *King John* and yet left untouched the muddle of the last scenes of the play, which offer a disjointed, almost shorthand version of John's tragic catastrophe?[3]

Attempts to treat *King John* as if it were an Elizabethan palimpsest necessarily fail because its duller passages cannot be equated with Shakespeare's "early style." Nothing in the *Henry VI* plays, for instance, is quite as monotonous as Pandulph's appeal to the King of France to turn against John:

> O, let thy vow
> First made to heaven, first be to heaven perform'd,
> That is, to be the champion of our Church!
> What since thou swor'st is sworn against thyself
> And may not be performed by thyself;
> For that which thou hast sworn to do amiss
> Is not amiss when it is truly done;
> And being not done where doing tends to ill,
> The truth is then most done, not doing it.
> The better act of purposes mistook
> Is to mistake again. Though indirect,
> Yet indirection thereby grows direct,
> And falsehood falsehood cures, as fire cools fire
> Within the scorched veins of one new burn'd.   (III.i.265-278)

This is not apprentice versifying, stiff and halting in its movement. The handling of the iambic pentameter line is fluent enough, but the passage is lifeless and nearly impossible to follow as dramatic dialogue. We might say that the dreariness is deliberate—Shakespeare's way of characterizing a tedious casuist. Yet about two hundred lines later Pandulph's speech grows racy and vivid, and his political insight chillingly acute and cynical as he explains to the

---

3. Tillyard perceptively analyzes the failures of plotting in the last two acts of *King John* (pp. 215, 232) and suggests the possibility that the play lacks proportion because in rewriting his original version of *King John,* Shakespeare expanded the materials of the first three acts and therefore had to huddle together and compress the materials for the last two acts (p. 218).

Dauphin that John's fears of Arthur will make possible a French conquest of England:

> Now hear me speak with a prophetic spirit;
> For even the breath of what I mean to speak
> Shall blow each dust, each straw, each little rub,
> Out of the path which shall directly lead
> Thy foot to England's throne; . . .
> How green you are and fresh in this old world!
> John lays you plots; the times conspire with you;
> For he that steeps his safety in true blood
> Shall find but bloody safety and untrue. . . .
> O, sir, when [John] shall hear of your approach,
> If that young Arthur be not gone already,
> Even at that news he dies; and then the hearts
> Of all his people shall revolt from him,
> And kiss the lips of unacquainted change,
> And pick strong matter of revolt and wrath
> Out of the bloody fingers' ends of John.   (III.iv.126-168)

We could hypothesize that the first speech (a political oration) is Pandulph's deceptive public mask, and the second one (a private confidence) reveals his true Machiavellian nature, except that Pandulph has no reason to pretend dullness in his oration when his purpose is to persuade France of the truth of his argument. His chop logic must seem convincing enough, moreover, to make France renounce the political advantage of his alliance with John.

One cannot find an aesthetic justification for the sudden changes in Pandulph's style, for what is involved is not simply an inconsistency of characterization but also a failure of characterization. Except for his single conversation with the Dauphin, Pandulph is a blank, a mere counter of the plot fashioned out of papier-mâché. Most of the other characterizations in the scenes at Angiers are equally bland and conventional. France, Austria, the Dauphin, Blanch, and Arthur have little individuality of temperament and little depth of personality. They speak, therefore they exist; but their existences are only rhetorical and their problems of choice conventional rhetorical dilemmas. France is torn between obedience to the Church and the dictates of honor; Blanch does not know whether to be loyal to England or to the Dauphin, her new husband. If the mere expostulation of emotion or the mere striking of emotional attitudes created a vivid impression of character, then Constance would seem a memorable figure. But her macabre conceits are so artificially elaborated that they project no sense of personality; and it is easy to understand why other characters in the play find her arias of frantic grief somewhat strained:

> Death, death, O amiable lovely death!
> Thou odiferous stench! sound rottenness!
> Arise forth from the couch of lasting night,
> Thou hate and terror to prosperity,
> And I will kiss thy detestable bones,
> And put my eyeballs in thy vaulty brows,
> And ring these fingers with thy household worms,
> And stop this gap of breath with fulsome dust,
> And be a carrion monster like thyself.   (III.iv.25-33)

One has only to compare this grandiloquence with the speeches of Margaret in *Henry VI Part II* and *Part III* to realize that Constance and her fellow rhetoricians bear little resemblance to Shakespeare's earliest characterizations. Figures like Blanch and France are simply the puppets of *The Troublesome Reign* carried over into the plot of *King John* in very much their original form. To account for the artistic discrepancies of *King John,* then, we need not hypothesize that Shakespeare revised it some years after he first composed it. We need only recognize the many evidences that his revamping of *The Troublesome Reign* was a halfhearted effort.

Because the artistic contradictions and failings of *King John* are unique, we cannot by comparing it to *The Troublesome Reign* hope to discover Shakespeare "in the workshop."[4] Nor can we believe that the greatness of *Richard II* (or of the *Henry VI* plays, for that matter) resulted from similar revampings of "basic texts,"[5] In no other known instance does Shakespeare use a source play as he uses *The Troublesome Reign.* Although he borrows phrases, details, bits of plot, and characterizations from *Woodstock* and *The Famous Victories* for his History Plays, he follows his own inspiration and freely transforms what he takes. Only in *King John* does he accept the authority of another man's plotting; and only in *King John* does he plod patiently along in the footsteps of his source, scene by scene, so that his

4. Believing that behind many of Shakespeare's plays there is a lost ur-text which he revised, Wilson is prepared to treat Shakespeare's revision of *The Troublesome Reign* as a typical example of his methods of composition (*King John,* pp. xxxiv-xlvii). But *King John* is very untypical of Shakespeare in its artistic inconsistencies and failings.

5. To compare the plotting of any of the *Henry VI* plays to that of *King John* is to erase any suspicions that the *Henry VI* plays were revisions of plays sketched out by dramatists inferior to Shakespeare. The primitiveness of the plotting in *King John* would be mirrored again and again in the plays of the first and second tetralogy if Shakespeare had composed them in the manner of *King John.*

dramatic action is frequently as clumsy and giddy as that of the old play. Although compared to most anonymous Elizabethan playwrights, the author of *The Troublesome Reign* had a masterly sense of dramatic form, he could not create a dramatic action which has the logic and the inevitability of the meanest of Shakespeare's plays. His crude machinery of plot is cranked along by wholly unanticipated turns of events and by sudden unexpected entrances of characters who send the dramatic action careening off in new directions. No sooner are great international conflicts announced in the opening scene than attention is diverted to minor matters with the arrival of the Bastard and his brother seeking judgment from the King. Their quarrel over their inheritance is an ironic parallel to the graver challenge made by France to John's title; and the parallel grows more significant when the Bastard is revealed to be the natural son of Richard the Lionhearted, John's older brother and royal predecessor. But the interruption of the Bastard and his brother does not add a new dimension to the political drama of John's quarrel with France nor does it successfully parody it. It simply crowds the main action of the play off stage and temporarily replaces historical drama with domestic farce. Even in the *Henry VI* plays Shakespeare's plotting has a finer decorum. When he mingles comedy and history, he expands the imaginative compass of his plots; he does not allow trivial episodes to intrude upon and upstage great events.

Incapable of Shakespeare's kind of plotting, the author of *The Troublesome Reign* depends upon the collision of major and minor characters to energize the simple chain reaction of his plot. Because he uses his minor characters as his kinetic forces, he creates the impression that they are the prime movers of history, an impression that exists also in *King John,* where kings turn this way and that as they are manipulated or persuaded by their underlings. The bold challenges and bitter wrangling at Angiers anticipate a bloody struggle between John and his opponents. This struggle no sooner begins, however, than it is halted by the Bastard's suggestion that France and England join forces to subdue Angiers. This new tack is reversed once again by the Citizen of Angiers' proposal of a politic marriage between the Dauphin and Blanch, John's niece, a proposal that turns the rage of battle into the farce of ironic wooing. And the marriage is no sooner announced than Pandulph appears, bringing with him a new and unexpected religious issue. With Pandulph's arrival, everything turns completely around again, as once more, but for different reasons, France becomes England's enemy. The whirligig of plot spins as dizzily in the last act, for just when John's cause seems hopeless, it is rescued by the French General Melun, who reveals to the English rebels the Dauphin's vicious schemes. This good deed is countered, however, by the wicked deed of the nameless monk who poisons John. But all is not lost, because John's son, whose existence was never once mentioned, suddenly appears to become England's salvation.

The plots of *Henry VI Part I* and *Part II* evolve out of the tensions of their opening scenes, in which the feuding of arrogant courtiers endangers the well-being of England and foreshadows disaster in days to come. The first scene of *King John,* however, does little more than begin the story of John's conflict with his foreign enemies. It does not characterize the Court, though it hints that John and his mother are unscrupulous. It does not suggest whether the people are restless or contented, loyal or disloyal; and it reveals almost nothing about the English noblemen who will play a major political and moral role in the events of the last two acts. Even as the opening scene lacks prophetic overtones, it creates no historical perspective, no sense of the past such as exists in the plays of the first tetralogy. Although John's right to the crown is being contested, there is not the slightest intimation that he fears for his throne or doubts his subjects' loyalties, just as there is no hint of any personal vulnerability in his swift, decisive response to the challenge of France. Launched in this fashion, the plot of *King John* is subject to change without prior notice. Even the characters seem to materialize only when their presence is required on stage; they exit into an outer darkness when their dramatic stint is ended.

If we did not have *The Troublesome Reign* for comparison, we could not understand the "falling off" of Shakespeare's artistry in *King John.* But *The Troublesome Reign* does not in itself explain the characteristics of *King John* any more than *Woodstock* explains the characteristics of *Richard II.* To account for *King John* we must explain why a playwright as original and prolific as Shakespeare chose to rewrite *The Troublesome Reign* in the way that he did. The answer perhaps is that Shakespeare had no choice in the matter—that he was asked to revamp *The Troublesome Reign* by his company, which hoped to capitalize on its anti-Catholic sentiments and ribaldry. Conceivably, bigotry seemed a very salable commodity in the mid 1590's, when fear of Catholic plots and subversives ran high. Whatever the motives were for the revamping of the old play, Shakespeare lacked the temperament to exploit religious prejudices and hysterias. So thoroughly does he expunge the anti-Catholic bombast and bawdry of his source that the religious issue very nearly disappears in *King John,* and John completely loses his stature as a "Reformation" hero.[6]

6. Although the John of *The Troublesome Reign* thinks himself cursed for yielding to the Pope, he also prophesies that from his loins a king will come who will trample on the

It would be easier to think of *King John* as a hack assignment reluctantly undertaken by Shakespeare if substantial portions of the dialogue of *The Troublesome Reign* were preserved in Shakespeare's text, or if he had been content to touch up the verse here and there and add new speeches and scenes. It is possible, however, that he rewrote the play line by line because he found it easier to refashion the dialogue as he went along than to transcribe the original lines of *The Troublesome Reign* and then edit and revamp them. Although willing to rewrite the entire dialogue, Shakespeare did not seriously attempt to make his new version of the play an artistic whole. The style is not of a piece. More important, the dramatic action is awkwardly articulated, not because Shakespeare followed his source too closely, but because he made changes in characterization and plotting which seriously damaged the coherence and unity of plot that exists in *The Troublesome Reign.*

There is at least no doubt who is the protagonist of the old play, because John towers over the other characters in strength, intelligence, and will. He is the only one whose speech is memorable, the only one whose personality is vivid, the only one with some stamp of individuality. There is real doubt, however, about the protagonist of *King John,* because even at the beginning of the play when John seems strong and decisive, he is a less vivid and interesting character than the Bastard, who absorbs the audience's attention from his first entrance on stage. John's soliloquies and asides, his storms of passion and agonies of conscience, are the focuses of the moral drama of *The Troublesome Reign,* but it is the Bastard's speeches which define and interpret the moral issues of *King John.* Cunning and resourceful even in calamity, John never falters as a politician in the old play. He dissembles his submission to the Pope and remains, despite his vices, a symbol of England's heroic defiance of the papacy. By the fourth act of Shakespeare's play, however, John has become a cringing, contemptible figure incapable of defending his realm against his enemies and all too ready to save himself by enslaving England to the Pope.

A protagonist need not be heroic or remain heroic to hold the attention and the sympathy of an audience. But if he is to lose his strength and purpose as the play goes on, his weakness must be, like Richard II's, more engrossing than the forcefulness of other characters. He cannot like John so lose command of himself that he ceases to be a functioning character in the plot. Where Richard III becomes more interesting psychologically as he begins to lose his nerve,

---

Whore of Babylon. No such prophecy is granted to Shakespeare's King John, who does not even remember as he dies his willingness to hand over England to the Pope. Moreover, if Hubert did not mention that John was poisoned by a monk, we would not connect his death with his earlier conflict with the Church and his plundering of the monasteries.

John remains in decline as two-dimensional as he was in the opening scenes of the play; as a result, the very process of his disintegration is somewhat bewildering. Seeing no trace of indecision in the John of the first acts, an audience will not recognize his vacillation over the murder of Arthur as a symptom of anxiety, nor will it grasp the psychological implications of the scene (IV.ii) in which John mumbles about his "reasons" and his "fears" when his barons question his desire for a second coronation.

Dramatic foreshadowing need not rob a play of its essential elements of suspense and surprise. Although the first scenes of *Richard II* intimate that the King's rash blaze of riot cannot last, they do not anticipate the suddenness of his collapse on his return from Ireland. Thus, Act III scene ii of *Richard II* seems to offer a new revelation of Richard's character at the same time that it fulfills the expectation of his tragic failure. There is no analagous foreshadowing of John's tragic failure in *King John;* worse still, his characterization is so opaque that one does not recognize his failure of will as such until it becomes grossly apparent in Act V scene i. In retrospect, the pattern of John's behavior seems absolutely logical and coherent. Once we have seen his collapse, we can recognize his willingness to compromise his title at Angiers and his desire for a second coronation as symptoms of a deeply rooted insecurity about his royal place. But such retrospective understanding comes too late in the theater, where the apprehension of character and action must be fairly immediate.

Although one cannot anticipate from one scene to the next which way the action of *The Troublesome Reign* will turn, the plot is lucid at every moment. One understands precisely why John does what he does, because his motives and intentions are always made explicit. He explains to his barons his reasons for wanting to be crowned again, and he prepares an audience for the reappearance of Pandulph late in the play by explaining in a soliloquy how he intends to make use of Pandulph even as he pretends to submit to him. We cannot say that for reasons of dramatic economy Shakespeare was compelled to omit essential information about John's motives, because not many additional passages would have been needed to elucidate John's behavior and anticipate his plans.[7] Two or three dozen lines added at the proper places in the dialogue would have dissolved the opaquity of crucial scenes and lent fluidity to the plot.

7. Since *King John* is only about two-thirds as long as *Richard III*, it cannot be said that its muddles of plot stem from Shakespeare's need to condense the dramatic action of *The Troublesome Reign*. Wilson notes that *The Troublesome Reign* is only about three hundred lines longer than Shakespeare's play and was probably printed in two parts merely to secure a double profit for the publisher (*King John*, pp. xvii-xviii).

Part of the problem in *King John* may result from Shakespeare's attempt to use an uninteresting assignment for artistic experiments. That is to say, he revises the old play in such a way that John's failure is more subtly ironic than Richard III's. Richard cannot commit the penultimate crime his ambition requires and remain a superman. He quails before a terrible political necessity: he must kill the Princes, who are the rightful heirs to the throne. John, in contrast, gratuitously makes Arthur his "living fear" when no Englishman acknowledges Arthur as the rightful heir to the throne. John's possession of the throne may be, as Elinor remarks, stronger than his right, but Arthur's claim is never made to seem substantial. Only England's enemies, France and Austria, and they for politic reasons, accept it. The English barons and people never question John's right and rise against him only when it appears that he has murdered Arthur.[8] Far from being the true inheritor of the crown, Arthur seems an innocent pawn in the hands of opportunistic allies, one who is as much the victim of Constance's and the Dauphin's ambitions as of John's insecurity.

Prey to needless anxieties about his royal state, Shakespeare's John should seem a more complex psychological characterization than the hero of *The Troublesome Reign*. If he does not, it is because Shakespeare flattens and externalizes the portrayal of John by eliminating the soliloquies and asides which expose his private thoughts and feelings in the source play.[9] Allowing his audience to see John only as the other characters in the play see him, Shakespeare would have it grasp the element of bravado which is supposedly present in John's manner from the beginning. It is doubtful, however, that the most skilled actor could successfully communicate the underlying "truth" of John's nature to an audience before the fourth act, when John begins to turn from confident leader to cringing coward.

The scene in which John suborns Hubert to the murder of Arthur was probably intended to be a crucial moment of psychological revelation. It

8. Although many scholars have claimed that in *The Troublesome Reign*, John has a "just title," whereas in *King John* he is branded as a usurper, the English barons in the old play desert John to plant Lewis "in the Usurpers roome" (II.429), whereas no Englishman in *King John* ever accuses John of being a usurper or ever questions his title. But see Wilson, *King John*, pp. xliii-xliv; Ribner, *English History Play*, p. 121; Gupta, *Historical Plays*, p. 101. All quotations from *The Troublesome Reign* in my text are from the edition of the play in *Narrative and Dramatic Sources of Shakespeare*, ed. Bullough (New York: Columbia Univ. Press, 1962), vol. IV.

9. This is very apparent in the scene of the second coronation, where Shakespeare obscures John's motives for the act (which are explicit in the old play) and makes him unwilling to specify his motives.

turned out instead an occasion for melodramatic posturing, because Shakespeare was content merely to repeat himself. He stages the wooing of Hubert as an uninspired imitation of the brilliant coronation scene in which Richard woos Buckingham to the murder of the Princes. No dramatic tension exists in this second wooing scene because, unlike Buckingham, Hubert is a dramatic cipher at this point in the plot. And there is no fascinating game of wits, because Hubert agrees to commit the horrid deed without the slightest hesitation. The scene belongs completely to John, who reveals little about himself except that he is a melodramatist with a flair for tragic clichés:

> I had a thing to say; but let it go.
> The sun is in the heaven, and the proud day,
> Attended with the pleasures of the world,
> Is all too wanton and too full of gauds
> To give me audience. If the midnight bell
> Did with his iron tongue and brazen mouth
> Sound on into the drowsy ear of night;
> If this same were a churchyard where we stand,
> And thou possessed with a thousand wrongs;
> Or if that surly spirit, melancholy,
> Had bak'd thy blood and made it heavy, thick . . .   (III.iv. 33-43)

What a fall is there from the superb drama of Richard's encounter with Buckingham to this monologue of rhetorical vacillation!

There is much else in *King John* besides the wooing of Hubert that creates a sense of *déjà vu* for those familiar with the plays of the first tetralogy. The high-sounding martial rhetoric and the heralds' brags and challenges at Angiers are the stuff that *Henry VI Part I* is made of. The politic maneuverings, debates, and hypocrisies at Angiers summon up remembrance of *Henry VI Part III*. Although some critics find in *King John* signs of political disillusionment,[10] I think it reveals nothing about the role of Commodity and self-interest in politics that was not apparent in the first tetralogy. What are the machinations of Elinor, John, Pandulph, and the Dauphin compared to those of Margaret, Suffolk, York, and Richard? Just as France is drawn from Arthur's cause by the prospect of an advantageous marriage arrangement, Lewis was drawn from Margaret's cause in *Henry VI Part III* by Warwick's proposal of a marriage

10. Danby sees in *King John* Shakespeare's turning away from a belief in the providential view of history supposedly incarnate in the first tetralogy; he also sees in the play a new cynicism about the nature of politics and a new acceptance of pragmatic political ethics (*Shakespeare's Doctrine of Nature*, pp. 69-74). Reese declares *King John* "the most cynical and disillusioned of the histories" (*Cease of Majesty*, p. 280).

between his daughter and Edward. As a matter of fact, Philip is somewhat nobler than Lewis because he does have scruples; although he first seeks his political advantage, he later sacrifices it to religious principle. Those horrified by the cynicism of the citizens of Angiers, who refuse to choose a king until he wins the battle, should recall that Lewis accepts Edward as the true monarch of England because he has defeated the Lancastrians. The cynicism of Angiers is the expedience of Tudor doctrine turned to the advantage of commoners rather than kings. Like the Tudors, Angiers believes that whatever is—or whoever wins—is right.

It is evident enough in both tetralogies that the world is not inhabited by saints and that men act out of self-interest in politices. What *King John* offers is not a uniquely cynical view of political conduct but rather a uniquely crude representation of political casuistries and hypocrisies. Where *Henry VI Part III* and *Richard III* at times present the farce of politics, the first three acts of *King John,* like the first part of *The Troublesome Reign,* present the politics of farce: history staged as a marionette show in which every political posture is absurdly exaggerated and every political gesture blatantly hypocritical. If some of the great figures of *The Troublesome Reign* are slightly ludicrous, it is not because its author thought of rulers as clowns or intended to satirize them. He portrays kings as fustian-spouting vulgarians because he is unable to depict true majesty. His John and Elinor are rough and ready. They bring the habits and colloquialisms of the village marketplace into the throne room. Armed with such noble expressions as "spit in your hand," the Dowager Queen casually explains the biological facts of pregnancy, even as the King resolves a difficult problem of inheritance by a homely analogy of a farmer and his cow. Coarser still is the feuding of Elinor and Constance, who rail like fishwives over Arthur's right. More circumspect and deliberately satirical, Shakespeare allows his kings their glittering words and gestures at the same time that he exposes their baser motives so that there seems to be as little honesty in royal affections as in royal policies. Richard the Lionhearted is remembered as a relentless seducer; Elinor believes that Constance's campaign on behalf of Arthur might have been prevented by "easy arguments of love," and the Dauphin develops a sudden overwhelming Petrarchan passion for Blanch when John offers an advantageous treaty to France.

No doubt Shakespeare could have made the political maneuverings at Angiers more convincing if he had wished. By preserving the naive plotting of his source play, however, he provides apt subject matter for the Bastard's choric commentaries and makes possible the wide-eyed astonishment and satiric delight of the Bastard's discovery of political Commodity. But though Shakespeare allows the political speeches and turnabouts at Angiers their farcical aspect, he makes no joke of the price that ordinary men pay for the greed and vanity of kings. On the contrary, he makes us more conscious of the moral issue of war in the supposedly cynical scenes of *King John* than in the high-minded scenes of *Henry VI Part I*, where war appears to be the sport of English heroes and there is no accounting of the cost of English victories—no acknowledgment of the massacres, burnings of cities, plundering, and enslaving of innocent civilians which the Chroniclers casually record. At Angiers the French Herald brags that

> the hand of France this day hath made
> Much work for tears in many an English mother
> Whose sons lie scattered on the bleeding ground.
> Many a widow's husband grovelling lies,
> Coldly embracing the discoloured earth.   (II.i.302-6)

In like vein the English Herald speaks of the gallant appearance of English soldiers "that marched hence so silver-bright" and hither return "all gilt with Frenchmen's blood." The continuing reminders of bloodshed and of death will not allow us to see war as a chivalric sport. Even in the heralds' obtuse descriptions it appears as a ghastly hunt:

> .... like a jolly troop of huntsmen come
> Our lusty English, all with purpled hands,
> Dy'd in the dying slaughter of their foes.   (II.i.321-3)

And what the heralds, blinded by patriotic enthusiasms, cannot see is evident to the Bastard, who envisions the battlefield as a place of grisly human sacrifices:

> Ha, majesty! how high thy glory tow'rs
> When the rich blood of kings is set on fire!
> O, now doth Death line his dead chaps with steel;
> The swords of soldiers are his teeth, his fangs;
> And now he feasts, mousing the flesh of men,
> In undetermin'd differences of kings.   (II.i.350-5)

The Bastard lacks the true cynic's callousness and pleasure in mocking human aspiration. Although he inherits Richard III's gift of ironic insight and his role of satiric commentator, he does not, like Richard, delight in parodying religious and moral ideals. Not instinctively political, he is drawn into the arena of politics only because his brother lays claim to his inheritance; and he follows the King because he is relatively indifferent to lands and title, not because he hungers for them. Incapable of deviousness and sham, he is not, as John Danby would have it, the Machiavel legitimized[11] but rather the anti-Machiavel of the play—the antagonist of Pandulph and the Dauphin, who are the direct descendants of Suffolk, York, and Richard. He is a creature of romance, not of policy, a picaresque hero who has no illusions but is optimistic about the possibilities of experience. Imbued with the energy and shrewdness of the Elizabethan merchant-adventurer, he knows the tricks of the trade, the gambit of Commodity and the usurer's knack to catch the unsuspecting gudgeon. The tavern and the marketplace are his milieu, and his natural targets are the tooth-picking affectations and social scrambling of an increasingly mobile Elizabethan society. A man o' the times, he declares his intention to mount and gain advancement, but his fundamental innocence appears even in his opportunistic declarations; just as he would not be gulled, he has no intention of gulling others:

> For he is but a bastard to the time
> That doth not smack of observation—
> And so am I, whether I smack or no;
> And not alone in habit and device,
> Exterior form, outward accoutrement,
> But from the inward motion to deliver
> Sweet, sweet, sweet poison for the age's tooth;
> Which, though I will not practise to deceive,
> Yet, to avoid deceit, I mean to learn;
> For it shall strew the footsteps of my rising.   (I.i.207-16)

Quick-witted, the Bastard is ready to counter a ploy with a ploy. When the citizens of Angiers artfully dodge the question of their loyalty, he suggests that England and France combine their forces against the city. His politic proposal inspires from Angiers the equally politic proposal of a marriage between the Dauphin and Blanch, and in a dizzy moment, the Dauphin turns amorist, France forgets his zeal for Arthur's right, and John, champion of England, offers to part with some of England's possessions to muffle Arthur's claim. Astonished by the rank hypocrisy of kings, the Bastard begins to question his own scruples and wonders whether he is honest only because he has not been sufficiently tempted:

> And why rail I on this Commodity?
> But for because he hath not woo'd me yet:

11. *Shakespeare's Doctrine of Nature,* pp. 73-77.

Not that I have the power to clutch my hand
When his fair angels would salute my palm,
But for my hand, as unattempted yet,
Like a poor beggar, raileth on the rich.
Well, whiles I am a beggar, I will rail
And say there is no sin but to be rich;
And being rich, my virtue then shall be
To say there is no vice but beggary.
Since kings break faith upon commodity,
Gain, be my lord, for I will worship thee!   (II.i.587-98)

Where before the Bastard would learn the ways of "observation" (that is, flattery) to avoid deceit, now, with the example of kings before him, he declares that he would yield to the seduction of Commodity. Happily, he is rescued from this coldblooded purpose by a sudden warming trend in the moral weather of the play which begins in the first scenes of the fourth act when, first, Hubert's better instincts prevail and he spares Arthur's life, and, next, the English barons plead for Arthur's safety to John.

The superficiality of the moral action in the first three acts of *King John* can be traced back to the superficiality of characterization and plotting in *The Troublesome Reign*. The ethical muddles of the last two acts of *King John*, however, must be attributed entirely to Shakespeare because they stem from his revisions of the old play. On the one hand, he makes the moral issue of Arthur's fate seem far more important than in *The Troublesome Reign* by focusing attention upon it in scene after scene. First he invents the scene in which John and Hubert plan Arthur's death. Next he elaborates Constance's laments for the captured Arthur so that they become a prophetic dirge for murdered innocence. Immediately afterward, he has Pandulph predict that John will have Arthur murdered, and when that scene ends, Hubert enters with the executioners to carry out the deed. But though we are led to expect that John's responsibility for Arthur's death will be as crucial an issue as Richard's responsibility for the death of his nephews, we discover that Arthur's fate has no bearing on John's ultimate destiny and no effect on the judgment of John as a tragic hero.

To be sure, Arthur's fate is far more ambiguous than that of the Princes murdered in the Tower, for John's plot against his nephew does not succeed as planned. Spared by Hubert, Arthur falls to his death attempting to escape from imprisonment and the threat of death. The English barons, assuming that Arthur has been murdered, vow revenge against John and desert to the Dauphin. The Bastard is more circumspect. "It is a damned and a bloody work, /

The graceless action of a heavy hand," he says, "*If* that it be the work of any hand" (italics mine). Taking our cue from the Bastard, we might decide that Arthur's death is an unfortunate accident, not "the work of any hand"; but this kind of literalism will not serve, for though John does not push Arthur from the wall, his murderous intent forces him to a desperate effort to escape. As Arthur leaps from the wall, he remarks that it is "as good to die and go, as die and stay," and his broken body feels his "uncle's spirit . . . in these stones." If John is not responsible for Arthur's death, then Creon is not responsible for the death of Antigone, who killed herself after he had sentenced her to be walled up alive. Had John genuinely repented of his plot to murder the boy and yearned to free him, Arthur's death might appear a pathetic mischance. At no time is John remorseful, however; at no time does he think of Arthur's welfare. He laments only that "there is no sure foundation set on blood." At first he tries to make Hubert his scapegoat; then, learning that Hubert has spared the boy, he sends him running—not to free Arthur but to tell the barons that Arthur still lives.

Because the Bastard is the clearest-eyed character in the play, we would be inclined to accept his judgment of Arthur's death if we could determine what it is. Incensed by the sight of Arthur's body, he turns like an accusing angel on Hubert:

> Knew you of this fair work?
> Beyond the infinite and boundless reach
> Of mercy, if thou didst this deed of death,
> Art thou damn'd, Hubert. (IV.iii.116-9)

So terrible seems the killing of this innocent to the Bastard that even those who merely consented to it he thinks damned: "If thou didst but consent / To this most cruel act, do but despair" (IV.iii.125-26). Because he suspects that Hubert (as John's agent) has murdered Arthur, he does not know what course of action to take. As before at Angiers, confusion lies on either side:

> I am amaz'd, methinks, and lose my way
> Among the thorns and dangers of this world.
> How easy dost thou take all England up!
> From forth this morsel of deal royalty
> The life, the right, and truth of all this realm
> Is fled to heaven. (IV.iii.140-5)

A dozen lines later, however, the Bastard is off to John and the "thousand businesses" of the time, and never once does he think to question whether

John consented to, or was in any way responsible for, this "damned" crime. More astonishing still, the Bastard's amnesia spreads to the other characters, because the very memory of Arthur's pitiable death seems to vanish from the minds of the English barons, who, in the last act, not only return to their native loyalty but speak of flowing "in obedience / Even to our ocean, to our great King John" (V.iv.56-7).

Is our bewilderment at the apotheosis of John in the concluding scene "too modern" a reaction? Can we assume that the tributes to John would not have bothered Elizabethans, who were accustomed to a double perspective on royalty, who venerated the office of majesty despite the frailty of kings?[12] Perhaps so, but one must then wonder at the absence of this double perspective in other History Plays, where there is no final paean to the glorious majesty of Henry VI and Richard II, who are far less contemptible than John. If Shakespeare felt that rebellion in *King John* must end with renewed dedication to the throne, he did not have to rub the spots off John; he had only to allow the barons to pledge their allegiance to the newly minted royalty of Prince Henry. Even Tudor royalism does not demand that the evil which kings do be ignored. It demands that subjects accept that evil as their cross or punishment and not take arms against wicked kings. As a matter of fact, if it had been Shakespeare's intention to expound the orthodox Tudor view of rebellion in *King John*, he had simply to follow the lead of *The Troublesome Reign*, which makes Tudor doctrine explicit in the Bastard's speech to the barons:

> Why *Salsburie* admit the wrongs are true,
> Yet subjects may not take in hand revenge,
> And rob the heavens of their proper power,
> Where sitteth he to whom revenge belongs.[13]

Because Shakespeare omits this statement of political doctrine from the Bastard's lines, Tillyard must read the Bastard's mind to explain why he is unmoved by the possibility of John's guilt: "What the Bastard has actually decided is that, though bad, John is not a tyrant as was Richard III. And he has decided right. It was better to acquiesce in John's rule, bad though it was,

12. Tillyard suggests as much: "Thus, when Pembroke repents of sedition, it is to the anointed King of England, not to the bad King John that he vows allegiance. The King of England was indeed the ocean, rightfully claiming the tribute of all the rivers flowing into it" (*History Plays*, p. 223).

13. *T.R.*, II.464-67. Both Ribner (*English History Play*, p. 121) and Reese (*Cease of Majesty*, p. 264) believe that Shakespeare worsened John's character to present the Tudor doctrine of obedience to kings in its most orthodox form. If so, it is quite extraordinary that he should omit the explicit statement of royalist doctrine he found in the old play.

hoping that God would turn the king's heart to good and knowing that the sin of sedition would merely cause God to intensify the punishment, already merited, the country was in process of enduring."[14] I see no trace, however, of these pious considerations in the Bastard's lines. He says nothing of God's purposes to himself or to the rebels, whom he accuses of being unnatural sons, "ingrate revolts," "bloody Neroes," who rip up the womb of their "dear Mother England." His return to John is immediate and unreflective; his politics is an instinctive love of country.

It would be easier to accept the Bastard's loyalty to John if it existed "despite all," that is, despite a recognition of John's failings. What is baffling is the fact that the discerning Bastard can see nothing of John's vices: he is not shocked by John's craven weakness, by his duplicities, by his possible responsibility for Arthur's death, or by his readiness to turn the England which the Bastard loves over to the hated rule of the Pope. The English barons in *The Troublesome Reign* see their king more clearly. When they return to him, they do not speak, like Shakespeare's rebels, of "great King John." On discovering the Dauphin's plot to murder them, they decide to "kneele for pardon to our Sovereigne *John*." For Pembroke at least, John is the lesser of two evils: "Lets rather kneele to him, / Than to the French that would confound us all."[15] In *The Troublesome Reign*, moreover, John's vicious acts are not forgotten. As he dies, he despairs of his salvation because he knows that he has been evil and "must be damned for *Arthurs* sodaine death." When he confesses his greed, tyranny, rage, cruelty, and dishonor, the Bastard can only advise him to "call on Christ, who is your lastest friend."

I do not think that the author of *The Troublesome Reign* was more perceptive about moral issues than Shakespeare or that Shakespeare decided in *King John* to sacrifice ethical insight to the claims of royalist doctrine. If he had wished to stoop to propagandistic purposes, he would have made his royalist message at least as clear and explicit as the doctrine in his source play. My impression is that Shakespeare was careless rather than obtuse. Not particularly interested in John as a tragic hero, he shunts him off into a corner and puts him out of the Bastard's (and the audience's) mind, so that the Bastard can devote himself to his patriotic endeavors and display the nobility and steadfastness which John lacks. In the last scenes of the play, however, Shakespeare must somehow piece together his plot into a final semblance of

14. *History Plays*, pp. 225-26.
15. *T.R.*, II.784-85. The rebels' choice, as Salisbury sees it, is either to "stay and dye" or go "home, and kneele unto the King" (*ibid.*, II. 771-72).

dramatic unity, and he must be faithful to his original purpose (stated in his title) of staging "The Life and Death of King John."[16] Thus, the craven John must be puffed up again to heroic size and returned to the center of the stage, while the Bastard must shrink in stature to become once again his retainer—indeed, to play the ludicrous part of faithful Kent to John's tawdry version of the dying Lear.

There is a genuine tragic power in the concluding scene of *The Troublesome Reign*, where death is for John the ultimate crisis of a guilty life. The conclusion of *King John* must necessarily be more factitious, for Shakespeare, having juggled the moral issue of John's guilt, cannot portray his death as a spiritual crisis. He can only ask us to view John's demise as a pathetic accident and have us pity John's physical cramps:

> There is so hot a summer in my bosom
> That all my bowels crumble up to dust.
> I am a scribbled form drawn with a pen
> Upon a parchment, and against this fire
> Do I shrink up . . . .
> The tackle of my heart is crack'd and burnt,
> And all the shrouds wherewith my life should sail
> Are turned to one thread, one little hair.
> My heart hath one poor string to stay it by,
> Which holds but till thy [the Bastard's] news be uttered;
> And then all this thou seest is but a clod,
> And module of confounded royalty.   (V.vii.30-58)

Even *Titus Andronicus* aspires to a somewhat nobler conception of the tragic. When Richard II laments his fate, he transforms the conventional themes of de casibus tragedy into exquisite poetry. When John bemoans his bowels, he reduces the de casibus idea of tragedy to a visceral angst empty of moral significance. Or perhaps, despite the moral amnesia of the characters in *King John*—perhaps despite Shakespeare's conscious purpose—some ethical judgment is passed on the hero. For though everyone seems to forget what John has done, and though no reference is made to Arthur's death, the images of flame

16. If we believe that a dramatist can shift from one protagonist to another in the course of a play, we can agree with Adrien Bonjour that the rise of the Bastard in the last half of *King John* balances the disintegration of John and preserves the unity of the play (see "The Road to Swinstead Abbey," *ELH,* XVIII [1951], 253-74). This kind of balance, however, is precisely what destroys the unity of Jonson's tragedy *Catiline,* whose nominal protagonist shrinks into insignificance while its moral hero, Cicero, rises to heroic stature. See my discussion of the problems of plot in Jonson's tragedies in *The Moral Vision of Jacobean Tragedy* (Madison: Univ. Wisconsin Press, 1960), pp. 89-99.

and heat in John's lines remind us of the white-hot irons that threatened Arthur's eyes; they also remind us that the barons who lament John's passing once "burned" in indignation at Arthur's death.[17]

If we study the last scene of *King John* apart from the rest of the play, we may conclude that Shakespeare found his idea of tragedy in the Monk's Tale. If we take a more comprehensive view of the play, however, we may suspect that the de casibus clichés of the last scene are a makeshift attempt by Shakespeare to disguise his lack of interest in John as a tragic protagonist.[18] But though John leaves much to be desired as a dramatic hero, he is an interesting companion study to Richard III and Richard II and perhaps a connecting link between them. All three kings are portraits of psychological failure; all three fall at the height of their power because they are fearful of those who might rival them or dispute their right. When Richard III loses his nerve, the plot of *Richard III* loses its vitality. When John crumbles into impotence, Shakespeare, at the expense of dramatic unity, abandons him as a protagonist and makes the Bastard the vital center of the dramatic action. He need not resort to this expediency in *Richard II*, because he portrays Richard's failure of will so grippingly that the play rises to new poetic and dramatic heights even as the hero falls. I do not suggest that Shakespeare had to stumble in *King John* to find his artistic way in *Richard II*. In all likelihood, the only artistic problem he could not solve in writing *King John* was his boredom with the assignment.

17. The patterning of imagery in *King John* indicates that artistic unity cannot be mechanically contrived by iterations of theme, motif, or image. By the time he came to *King John*, Shakespeare, it seems, almost instinctively used iterative imagery in his plays. But the mere repetition of imagery of flame, heat, and burning does not deepen the meaning of, or lend coherence to, *King John*. More often than not, it is the plotting, characterizations, and dramatic situations which lend meaning to the clustering of imagery in Shakespearean drama. Rarely if ever do the patterns of imagery in themselves guide us to the essential thought of the plays.

18. Various critics have thought *King John* a potboiler. E. K. Chambers calls it "hack work" in *Shakespeare: A Survey* (London: Sidgwick & Jackson, 1955), pp. 99-100. Reese suggests that it was an obligatory assignment imposed on Shakespeare by his company, and one which seemed to bore him (*Cease of Majesty*, p. 261).

5. RICHARD II

The naturalness and spontaneity of the Bastard's speeches signal Shake-speare's complete mastery of his poetic medium. Thoroughly at ease now with his blank verse line and able to mimic with it the accent and cadence of daily speech, he could have turned his back forever on the formal rhetoric of the *Henry VI* plays and the declamatory style of *Richard III* and *King John*. Instead of moving forward to explore the new horizons of his poetic powers, he chose to fashion *Richard II* in a style so richly textured and conceited as to appear almost mannered, and so orotund and sententious that the dialogue often consists of choric pronouncements. If this choice of poetic style is retrograde, it is intentionally so, because even as the racy idiom of the Bastard's speeches aims at an Elizabethan "contemporaneousness," the ceremonious formality of *Richard II* summons up remembrance of an antique past. Creating through poetic manner the medieval ambiance and setting of his play,[1] Shakespeare is less concerned to individualize the voices of his characters than to project in their sentences the collective consciousness of an age which treasured formality and order, and which found their analogical and symbolic expression everywhere in the universe. More than a dramatic protagonist, Richard is also the poetic voice of his era and the quintessential expression of its sensibility. When he falls, a way of life and a world seem to fall with him.

Whatever scorn Renaissance humanists professed for the monkish supersti-tion of the middle ages, Shakespeare's contemporaries treasured and enjoyed

1. See Tillyard's excellent discussion of the medievalism of *Richard II* in *History Plays*, pp. 244-58.

its artistic legacy. The ancient ballads moved as severe a critic as Sir Philip Sidney, and the chivalric romances, which inspired the sage and serious Spenser, had an enormous vogue with bourgeois as well as aristocratic readers. To be sure, the winds of change were blowing away the last vestiges of medieval feudalism in the sixteenth century. The manorial system was in decay; castles and abbeys were falling into ruin, and the old aristocracy was losing its preeminent place in the life of the nation. But the past lived on in the immemorial customs of town and country, in centuries-old observances and rituals, and in the pageantries and jousts staged by Tudor monarchs, who sought to recreate the magnificence of medieval courts. Because much of the enduring character of the nation was inscribed in its ancient traditions, Elizabethans hoped to find in the past recorded in the Chronicles and recreated by poets and dramatists a mirror for their own times. Where the "great debates" over the royal succession in the first tetralogy merely expose the ironies of political expediency, the speeches of Gaunt and York in *Richard II* defined for Shakespeare's audiences the aristocratic and conservative bias of their society. Here was incarnate the English reverence of tradition and the English conviction that time-honored right descends inviolate from generation to generation. Thus, while *Richard II* described for Elizabethans days that were no more, it also reaffirmed for them the continuity of past and present that made tradition so vital a force in English life.

There is an artistic pleasure in the evocation of a medieval ethos in *Richard II*, not a political nostalgia for an earlier time. There is no intimation that England under Richard was a prelapsarian paradise, a world of order and harmony that was to be destroyed by a primal sin of disobedience. The opening scenes introduce us to a world which already knows violent contention and mortal enmity, in which men have shed the blood of their nearest kin and fear their father's brother's son. Death in the form of political murder has blighted the garden of the state, and serpents' tongues have hissed their temptation of vanity into the ears of the King, whose extravagance threatens to bankrupt the realm. But if Richard's court is "hollow," as Derek Traversi suggests,[2] it is not an *ancien régime* grown oversophisticated and decadent. Although not cast in the heroic mold of his ancestors, Richard is the son and grandson of warriors; his barons are proud, courageous men like Gaunt, York,

2. *Shakespeare from Richard II to Henry V* (Stanford: Stanford Univ. Press, 1957), p. 17. I disagree with Traversi's assumption that the artificiality of the speeches in the opening scene of *Richard II* is an indication of falsity of emotion or decadence. The artificiality of Mowbray's speeches is no greater, after all, than the artificiality of the Gardener's allegorical sentences in the later Garden scene.

Mowbray, and Bolingbroke, for whom honor is a supreme value. Such men are the true representatives of the feudal aristocracy, on which upstarts like Bushy, Bagot, and Green are parasitic growths. Rather than the shuddering destruction of a political order grown effete and impotent, *Richard II* dramatizes the convulsion of a still vigorous political order which turns against the king who wantonly threatens its existence. Paradoxically, it is the would-be preservers of the status quo who become the agents of revolutionary change; it is the defenders of the old regime who become the leaders of the new. Thus, when the old order gives way to the new, there is no radical change in the moral temper of English politics. Northumberland's manner is blunter than Bushy's, but his words and gestures are not more sincere or admirable. The play acting does not end at Court when the rebels triumph, because they also know how to pretend, how to fawn, and how to stage-manage political shows.[3]

The opening scenes of *Richard II*, then, do not establish the harmony or stability of the medieval state. What they express is the importance of the idea of order to the medieval mind. More than an "elaborate game,"[4] the ceremonies of Richard's court project the decorums that order his kingdom. Courtesy is a supreme chivalric value, not simply a refinement of manner; and manner of speech counts because it bespeaks breeding, even as the forms of language count because the feudal oaths of allegiance are the foundation upon which all hierarchy rests. In such a world, height of name has a literal reality, because lowliness must hug the ground, kneeling in supplication to stated majesty. Mowbray flings himself at Richard's feet in the opening scene; Mowbray and Bolingbroke kneel together before Richard as their joust begins, and they must swear together an oath of allegiance before they depart to exile. Richard is amazed to see Northumberland erect before him at Flint Castle, but Bolingbroke is quick to kneel before York and to stoop before Richard, who raises his cousin up to the throne itself. On that throne, Henry later watches Aumerle, York, and his wife kneel to him in supplication. The climactic moments of the play are ceremonies of ascension and declension acted out on

3. Where Tillyard thinks "a greater sincerity of personal emotion" is the hallmark of the new political order in *Richard II* (*History Plays,* p. 259), Traversi suggests that fear is a "sign of the new order," as in York's readiness "to sacrifice his own blood for a usurper who has only used him as an instrument" (p. 45). It is difficult to think of an order of which Northumberland is a chief representative as more sincere in personal emotion than the order represented by Aumerle, Carlisle, and the Queen, who are devoted to Richard.

4. The phrase is Tillyard's, who, I think, exaggerates the aestheticism of Richard's Court: "We are in fact in a world where means matter more than ends, where it is more important to keep strictly the rules of an elaborate game than either to win or to lose it" (p. 252). On the contrary, just beneath the surface of ceremony at Richard's Court is the grim reality of political conflict conducted with ruthless purposes and effects.

the heights and depths of the playhouse stage. It is from the gallery that Richard descends at Flint Castle to the "ground," the base court where kings grow base. It is from the ground that Bolingbroke ("in God's name") ascends the steps to platformed majesty.

Even as the ceremonies of *Richard II* dramatize hierarchical decorums, the poetry sounds a rhetoric of order in elaborate balances, symmetries, and alliterations, and the dialogue returns again and again to the fundamental sanctities of feudal life: blood, name, family, birth, possession, honor, pride, and courage. The thematic images of the first tetralogy refer to the things of this world, to sights and sounds of nature and human activity; they allude to the harvesting of fields, the hunting and slaughtering of animals, the fury of storms, the swarming of insects. The elaborate conceits of *Richard II* are more immediately "philosophical" in that they body forth the world as emblem and idea, as a metaphysical landscape composed of the Ptolemaic elements, earth, water, air, and fire, each theoretically in its proper place in the ascending hierarchical order. If one looks for Hooker's vision of cosmological order, one can find something like it in the speeches of *Richard II*. Yet one must wonder at a play which describes an ideal cosmological scheme in its poetry and mocks it in its dramatic action.[5] To find in the great speeches of *Richard II* an "Elizabethan World Picture" and in its plot a depiction of the brute realities of power politics is to distort Shakespeare's sense of the complex relationship between political ideals and political realities. As a matter of fact, the poetry of *Richard II* does not declare the universality of cosmic harmony; it speaks instead of the universality of contention and change. It suggests that if hierarchy is natural, sovereign place is neither fixed nor immutable. Stars fall and consume themselves; rivers overflow their banks, and clouds dim the radiance of the sun. The sea endlessly challenges the land, the falcon ventures into the eagle's space, and the elements themselves are protean in their qualities. The yielding water can be as forceful as the rage of blood and the swelling tide of oceans; it can drown land and quench fire. Such conceits do not project Shakespeare's belief in analogical order; they express in dramatic verse his awareness of man's will to discover pattern and stability in a universe of disorder and flux. There would be no need for metaphysical conceptions of hierarchy if every king, baron, and commoner were as he should be. It is

5. Where Tillyard stresses the cosmic lore of *Richard II*, Ribner says, "There is a pathetic irony in Richard's proclaiming the commonplaces of Tudor political theory at the very moment when Bolingbroke is making head against him in spite of them" (*English History Play*, p. 164).

precisely because the nature of kings is not always regal that the royal office must be made a religious mystery and the king an image of divine Authority. If enough men believe, as Gaunt does, that it is sacrilegious to lift an arm against anointed majesty, then, whatever gods may be, there is a divinity that hedges a king.

Medieval theologians used the idea of cosmological order to relate the imperfection of human existence to the perfect harmony and purposefulness of God's universe. In medieval feudalism the idea of order served as a restraining influence on political ambitions, because it made all authorities and privileges interrelated and interdependent. In the absence of institutions which could effectively maintain the status quo and equilibrium of power, it was essential that every member of a feudal society accept his place, acknowledge that of his superiors, and respect the rights of those beneath him. As York attempts to remind Richard, all feudal authorities are links of a single chain. All aristocratic privilege is supported by the same mystery of blood inheritance and guaranteed by the same rights of time. While the King's place is greater, his right is no different in kind from that of his lowliest peer. A king could be weak, extravagant, grasping, and capricious, as Richard was, and the feudal hierarchy still survive, but it could not survive if a king were allowed to disregard the rights of his subjects.

Coming to *Richard II* from *Richard III* and *King John,* we may think that its depiction of political conflict is somewhat attenuated or lacks immediacy and intensity. We have to keep in mind, however, that the earlier History Plays deal with extreme and melodramatically conceived political situations—with failures of order that loosed mere anarchy on the world in the rages and plots of Machiavellian conspirators. Because Richard is weak and irresponsible, his kingdom faces a political crisis in the opening scenes of the play, but because of the restraints of tradition, the power struggle is oblique, and the challenges masked by protocols. Capable now of artistic nuance and indirection, Shakespeare did not have to make history a study in blacks and whites, and he had available to him Daniel's poised and analytical account of the politics of Richard's fall in *The Civil Wars*. He found in Holinshed, moreover, a relatively sober chronicle of Richard's catastrophe, one that is untouched by the propagandistic distortions that made Margaret, Suffolk, and Richard III gloating villains. Although Holinshed roundly condemns Bolingbroke and his followers (and all his subjects, for that matter) for their disloyalty to Richard, he does not attempt to vilify them. He does not malign Bolingbroke's character or motives; and he passes no judgment on York, who failed to support Richard as the King's Lord Governor, or on Northumberland, who played a fairly treacherous role in bringing Richard into Bolingbroke's hands.

Of course, Shakespeare might have followed *Woodstock* in making Richard a criminal who brought down a just catastrophe upon himself, or followed the French Chronicles in making him a saintly martyr crucified by malicious traitors.[6] He was not tempted, however, toward these extreme, partisan perspectives, because he saw that there were neither heroes nor villains in the drama of Richard's fall, and neither simple rights nor simple wrongs on either side. Aware that Richard betrayed himself even as he was betrayed, Shakespeare sensed that there was a psychological mystery at the heart of his behavior, for though infatuated with his royalty, Richard surrendered it to Bolingbroke without a real struggle. He never fought against the rebels although there were men ready to bear arms to defend his right; he stole away from an army prepared to fight for him, and he bid his supporters flee. Captured without a struggle, he even consented to participate in the ceremony of his degradation. Daniel can think of very reasonable motives for Richard's acts.[7] Shakespeare more perceptively confronts the illogic of his behavior and the fascinating contradictions of his nature. Here was a king notorious for sensuality and extravagance, who lacked neither physical courage nor political acumen and tenacity. Engaged in bitter political struggles from his earliest days, he wrested control of his realm from powerful relatives, and while very young demonstrated extraordinary valor and coolness in dispersing the Jack Straw rebels, even as he proved his manliness at the last by slaying three of his murderers.[8] Not surprisingly, Shakespeare is unwilling to portray Richard as

6. It seems almost certain that Shakespeare consulted both *La Chronicque de la traison et mort de Richart Deux roy Dengleterre* (edited and translated by B. Williams, *English Historical Society*, IV, 1846) and Jean Creton's *Histoire du Roy d'Angleterre Richard II* (edited and translated by John Webb in *Archaeologia*, XX, 1824). The number of verbal echoes in *Richard II* from *La Chronicque de la traison* is impressive. For example, the *Chronicque* reports that Londoners on hearing of Bolingbroke's return from exile said, "Our lives, our possessions, and all we have are at his service" (p. 187). In Shakespeare's play, Richard responds to Scroop's report of Bolingbroke's triumphal return to England, "Our lands, our lives, and all are Bolingbroke's" (III.ii.151). See note 19 in this chapter for Shakespeare's borrowings from Creton.

7. There is no intimation in Daniel's poem of Richard's will to surrender to Bolingbroke. Sensibly advised by his loyal followers to accept Bolingbroke's terms at Flint Castle, Richard is treacherously captured by Northumberland in Daniel's poem—an incident Shakespeare omits from his play. When asked to surrender his crown, Richard, according to Daniel, first tries to retain the show of majesty, then resolutely says he would sooner die than relinquish the crown, but finally is persuaded to give up the crown to save his life (*Civil Wars*, pp. 108-26).

8. Although Shakespeare begins *Richard II* at the same point at which Hall begins his Chronicle, he must have read Holinshed's account of the earlier years of Richard's reign in

an effeminate Edward II or as the puppet of his sycophants as in *Woodstock*. Although York and others complain that the King is misled, the Richard we see is manipulated by no one. The one time he appears with his coterie, he clearly commands—he decides to farm out the realm, to allow blank charters, and to seize Gaunt's estates. York argues that too many vain tongues have buzzed in Richard's ears, but the Richard we see is too self-absorbed to listen to any words but his own and too shrewd to be easily corrupted. Neither indecisive nor ineffectual, he has lashed out at and murdered a powerful enemy. From the very first scene, however, it is apparent that he cannot meet the particular challenge which Bolingbroke represents, and his fear and hatred of Bolingbroke breeds in Richard something very like a will to disaster.

To see Richard only as a poet-*manqué* or a political fantasist is to see less than half of Shakespeare's portrait. With a poet's taste for language and an actor's hunger to hold the center of the stage, Richard looks forward as the play begins to the spectacle of Mowbray and Bolingbroke "frowning brow to brow." But he knows precisely what their quarrel is about, and he is not taken in by their high sentences and noble postures. He knows that, though they speak the same language of devotion, one of them merely flatters him. Because he is willful and arrogant like Lear, Richard is capable of stupendous folly and, like Lear, has much to learn about his nature and royal state. But he does not, like Lear, doom himself because in a moment of rash anger he forgets who loves him, or because he cannot recognize his enemies. Aware that Bolingbroke's ambition soars to a kingly pitch, he intuits also that Bolingbroke would be his kingdom's heir. His blindness comes, paradoxically, from too much light, from too lucid a recognition of the threat which he cannot admit to himself or to others.

Fully in command of his materials and fully engaged in his artistic task, Shakespeare triumphs in *Richard II* precisely where he failed in *King John*—in the subtle psychological revelation of his protagonist's nature. The portrayal of Richard is necessarily oblique in the opening scenes, because he strikes the conventional postures demanded by ceremonial occasions. We would more quickly grasp his character and more quickly fathom the political situation of the opening scene if, as Holinshed reports, Richard grew furious at Boling-

---

which Richard's manliness and courage were manifest. It is generally assumed that Shakespeare's depiction of the Cade rebellion in *Henry VI Part II* was based on accounts of the Jack Straw uprising, during which the young Richard II acted with great courage. Shakespeare certainly knew Daniel's appraisal of Richard: "though weake he was, / He was not ill; nor yet so weake, but that / He shew'd much Martiall valour in his place, / Adventring oft his person for the State" (*Civil Wars*, p. 150).

broke's mention of the murder of Gloucester.[9] The Richard whom Shakespeare conceives is incapable of meeting Bolingbroke's challenge in this direct fashion. Although he can turn with anger and scorn on those who represent Bolingbroke, he never dares pit either his rage or his authority against his cousin. He is vain and sophisticated enough, moreover, to enjoy the hidden drama of the encounter and the masking of motives; he takes pleasure in declarations of impartiality and gratitude which he edges with subtle and mocking irony. Perhaps Shakespeare demands too much from his audience in expecting them to follow the oblique exposition of the first scene, but a perceptive listener would not miss the curious fact that the King does not wish the issue of treason and murder to be pursued. He would note also that Richard's pretense of negligent indifference and impartiality is not very convincing. For, while Richard warns Bolingbroke that he is not prepared to think ill of Mowbray, he licenses Mowbray to say what he will about Richard's princely cousin, whom he carefully puts in his place as his "father's brother's son."[10] It is also revealing that Richard undertakes to calm Mowbray but calls on Gaunt to pacify Bolingbroke. Mowbray will not obey the King's command to throw down Bolingbroke's gage, but he turns toward Richard and flings himself at his feet in a gesture of submission, declaring: "My life thou shalt command, but not my shame." The obdurate Bolingbroke, in contrast, turns toward his father, unwilling to pick up his gage and unwilling also to make Mowbray's gesture of fealty. He refuses Richard's command because he would not seem crestfallen in his father's sight.

Because he is careless of his own reputation, Richard cannot fathom Mowbray and Bolingbroke's rage, and he cannot quiet it. His clever jests accomplish nothing, his royal commands are disregarded; but he has immense skill in camouflaging his failure. Just as he artfully puts Gaunt between himself and Bolingbroke, he artfully avoids pressing the matter of his subjects' obedience to his commands:

> We were not born to sue, but to command;
> Which since we cannot do to make you friends,
> Be ready, as your lives shall answer it,
> At Coventry upon Saint Lambert's day.   (I.i.196-9)

Every inch a king, he commands Mowbray and Bolingbroke to do that which only a moment before he forbade. With such sleights of hand, a weakling like

9. Holinshed, *Chronicles*, II, 845.
10. See the illuminating discussion of the opening scene of *Richard II* in Palmer, *Political Characters*, pp. 124-28.

Richard can maintain the semblance of authority. He cannot, however, settle issues by evading them. Because he has not met Bolingbroke's challenge, he has merely postponed the direct confrontation which must eventually come.

The first scene of *Richard II* intimates the King's shallowness and weakness; the second documents his unscrupulousness and sets forth the myth of royal authority that shores up his pretense of majesty. Urged by Gloucester's widow to revenge his murder, Gaunt confesses his obligation to act, but stronger than any familial tie is his conviction that Richard's office is sacrosanct. He cannot lift his arm in anger against "God's substitute / His deputy anointed in His sight." Yet even Gaunt's patience has its limits, especially when he is tricked by Richard in the third scene into becoming a partner to the banishing of his son. Precisely why Richard chooses to halt the joust between Bolingbroke and Mowbray at the very last moment we do not know, but we recognize the characteristic theatricality of the gesture: here is the weakling's pleasure in commanding (and humiliating) men stronger than himself. And, though we do not know what happens in the council that precedes the sentences of banishment, we recognize the triumph of Commodity in the inequitable terms: ten years of exile (quickly cut to six) for Bolingbroke; perpetual banishment for Mowbray—the first of the princely favorites to discover the meaning of courtly reward in the second tetralogy. Too politic to confess his obligation to Mowbray, Richard nevertheless hesitates to pronounce his sentence, and Mowbray, who expected better, is stunned by this betrayal of his "dearer merit." Shameful to the last, Richard callously dismisses his appeal—"It boots thee not to be compassionate"—and then seeks to appease Gaunt by cutting the term of Bolingbroke's exile. But he cannot, with sham solicitude, court Gaunt's favor any more than Gaunt can with platitudes teach Bolingbroke to think positively about his years of exile. As Daniel phrased it, Richard has "thought best to lose a friend to rid a foe";[11] he will soon learn that he needs friends, and that his clever words have won him only a security of words. He is safe from the threat of Bolingbroke only so long as Bolingbroke honors his oath of exile.

Where rhetoric had the power in *King John* to turn men and nations about, arguments and appeals seem impotent in *Richard II*. Gaunt's and York's counsel cannot save Richard, because he will not listen, and Richard's sentences cannot reconcile Bolingbroke and Mowbray or appease Gaunt or

11. *Civil Wars*, p. 87. Daniel's shrewd insights into the political implications of the sentences of banishment probably cued Shakespeare's more oblique portrayal of the same events.

move Northumberland or affect the silent earls who witness his anguish in the deposition scene. On the other hand, words are of immense consequence in a feudal world, where so much depends on oaths, titles, and names, and where, for the sake of a name, men will take arms against a king, as Richard learns when he attempts to erase the name of Lancaster. He is not so foolish as to seize Bolingbroke's inheritance against all tradition and established right just to get money for his Irish wars. He strikes a coward's blow at his living fear, and the depth of that fear is momentarily revealed in the shrill fury with which he turns on the loyal Gaunt and in the bitterness of his response to York's defense of Hereford: "Right, you say true! As Hereford's love, so his [Gaunt's]; / As theirs, so mine; and all be as it is!" (II.i.145-6). Unable to outface Bolingbroke, Richard would destroy him in exile. He seeks, as Gaunt understands, to kill the name of Lancaster, but the name survives and becomes the rallying point of opposition to the King. It is the name of Lancaster which Bolingbroke says he comes to seek in England, and he must find that name on everyone's lips before he disbands his armies.

After the unpredictable twists and turns of plot in *King John*, the unfolding of the dramatic action in *Richard II* has a compelling simplicity and authority. Three great "public" scenes in Acts I and II are enough to chronicle Richard's infatuation with disaster. Spacing these "public" scenes are two brief "private" moments: first, when Gaunt speaks with Gloucester's widow, and, second, when Richard and his favorites joke about Bolingbroke's departure to exile. In the former, Gaunt recognizes the threat of Richard's irresponsibility but will not take arms against him; in the latter, Richard notes Bolingbroke's courting of the people but dismisses any fear of his rivalry. Self-indulgent and capricious, Richard seems to act on the spur of the moment, and yet the pattern of his behavior unfolds with an inexorable logic, because each of the public scenes in which he appears is a variation of the one before; each is another step toward, and a rehearsal for, his fateful encounter with Bolingbroke at Flint Castle. In the opening scene and in the tourney scene, Mowbray is Richard's surrogate. Then the dying Gaunt bears the brunt of Richard's hatred of Bolingbroke, while York struggles to remain neutral and Northumberland decides to take Bolingbroke's part.

The scene of Gaunt's death, too often regarded as simply an occasion for memorable sentences, is crucial to the political drama of *Richard II*, because here Richard commits the unpardonable sin against feudal right for which he must pay with his crown and his life. He comes prepared to patronize his uncle again, only to discover that the dying Gaunt cannot be cajoled and will no longer be still. Convinced that Richard will destroy England, Gaunt does not leave the quarrel to God; he is more concerned with saving England than with saving Richard, whom he considers already doomed. It is the "orthodox" Gaunt who speaks contemptuously of Richard's failings, who first declares him unfit to rule and suggests that if Richard's grandsire had known what crimes Richard would commit, he would have deposed Richard before Richard attained the throne. New inspired by his love of England, Gaunt speaks of it as a "blessed plot," another Eden, a "demi-paradise," but he does not imagine a divinity hedging a reckless king or an army of angels mustering to defend incompetent majesty. His advice to Richard is absolutely pragmatic: a king must use his head to save his head, because he cannot degrade the land without degrading himself. He cannot lose the affection and loyalty of his people without growing pale and sickly.

Where Gaunt is willing to risk Richard's ire by speaking bluntly, York would avoid conflict and risk. Knowing that Richard will not listen to good counsel, he urges Gaunt to be silent or at least circumspect. Silent himself while Richard heaps abuse on Gaunt, he then offers a timid plea on Gaunt's behalf and finds his tongue only when Richard seizes Gaunt's estates. Then his words sound a dangerous warning because they intimate the breaking point of loyalty: "How long shall I be patient? Ah, how long / Shall tender duty make me suffer wrong?" (II.i.163-4). York's patriotism, though as sincere as Gaunt's, is less ideal and less disinterested. He does not speak of the mystical entity of England; family, inheritance, and the rights of time are his themes. He sees Richard's lawlessness as a mortal danger to the aristocratic rights which guarantee his own place, for if Richard can take away Hereford's inheritance, no title or estate is safe. Where Gaunt places England above any other cause, York instinctively identifies the nation's well-being with his own, and he attacks Richard as one who, turning on his own blood, jeopardizes the very idea of right. Absolutely frank in expressing his disaffection, he warns Richard against seizing Hereford's lands:

> You pluck a thousand dangers on your head,
> You lose a thousand well-disposed hearts,
> And prick my tender patience to those thoughts
> Which honour and allegiance cannot think.   (II.i.205-8)

Although York could not be blunter, Richard will not hear the threat in these words and foolishly appoints York to be his Lord Governor while he is in Ireland.

Just as York was too timid to speak out when Gaunt did, so the other barons say nothing while York protests Richard's act. Cautious and secretive, Northumberland will not open his discontented thoughts until the King has gone and only after he has heard Ross and Willoughby speak. Then his only concern is to protect his own possessions:

> The King is not himself, but basely led
> By flatterers; and what they will inform,
> Merely in hate, 'gainst any of us all,
> That will the King severely prosecute
> 'Gainst us, our lives, our children, and our heirs.   (II.i.241-5)

These words carry us down from the heights of Gaunt's patriotism to the plains of self-interest. Unlike the outspoken Gaunt, Northumberland, Willoughby, and Ross offer no counsel to the King, and without any struggle of conscience take arms against him. First they blame the favorites, not Richard, but as they warm to their subject, they speak more freely of their "most degenerate king." Even here their plans for reforming the kingdom are ambiguous:

> . . . then we shall shake off our slavish yoke,
> Imp out our drooping country's broken wing,
> Redeem from broking pawn the blemish'd crown,
> Wipe off the dust that hides our sceptre's gilt,
> And make high majesty look like itself.   (II.i.291-95)

Can high majesty look like itself so long as Richard is king? The question is so dangerous that the would-be reformers do not pause to consider it. They are content to speak in figures, though they act swiftly and directly enough. Yet they do not appear either unscrupulous or unconscionable; they rally to Hereford's cause because it is their own—in defending his right, they protect theirs.

So responsible seems Richard for the calamity that befalls him, and so inevitable seems his tragic fall, that one cannot believe Shakespeare wanted to persuade his audience that Richard should have been allowed to continue the rash blaze of riot which threatened to destroy England. According to Tillyard, the doctrine of *Richard II* is "entirely orthodox. Shakespeare knows that Richard's crimes never amounted to tyranny and hence that outright rebellion against him was a crime."[12] Yet in fact Richard was guilty of the lawlessness which medieval and Renaissance theorists defined as tyranny. Accused of tyranny by his contemporaries, he is called a "wanton Tirant" in *Woodstock*, whose author makes much of the corruption of the law by Richard's rapacious

---

12. *History Plays*, p. 261.

favorites.[13] Shakespeare grasps the more important issue of Richard's political lawlessness and leaves no doubt that at his worst he was, as *The Mirror for Magistrates* declares, a monarch who "ruled all by lust."[14]

When a king recklessly endangers the foundations of law and plunders his country, what is an honorable subject to do? He can remain loyal despite all; he can rebel; or he can like York try to avoid having to commit himself in either way. One can sympathize with York's hesitation because one can see as he does that Bolingbroke is wronged but not innocent. Where Hall relates that Bolingbroke came back to England only after the greatest men in the country sued for his return, Shakespeare has the report of Bolingbroke's return come at the very close of the scene in which Richard seizes Gaunt's estates. Perhaps Shakespeare telescopes time only to achieve a striking effect: no sooner does Richard overreach himself, than nemesis in the form of Bolingbroke appears. Yet this handling of events leaves open the possibility that Bolingbroke led an army to England and then discovered that Richard had given him a perfect excuse for rebellion.

Daniel more explicitly questions the motives of Bolingbroke, who swore on landing in England that he came back only to gain his ducal estates. Shunning the easy wisdom of hindsight, he refuses, however, to find Bolingbroke guilty of calculated ambition. Perhaps, he suggests, Fortune conspired with Pride and Time,

> To make so easie an ascent to wrong,
> That he who had no thought so hie to clime
> (With favouring comfort still allur'd along)
> Was with occasion thrust into the crime;
> Seeing others weakenes and his part so strong,
> "And who is there, in such a case that will
> "Do good, and feare, that may live free with ill?[15]

Like Daniel, Shakespeare sees Bolingbroke as a "man of destiny," or, rather, as a man who gives himself to his destiny by refusing to think about the consequences of his acts. John Palmer describes him as "that most dangerous of all climbing politicians, the man who will go further than his rivals because

13. Although Hall and other Chroniclers note that the accusations made against Richard at the time of his deposition strained credulity, they leave no doubt that Richard, who was accused by his contemporaries of tyranny, did trample on legality and justice. In *Woodstock*, Richard is called "wanton Tirant" by John of Gaunt, who takes the murdered Woodstock's place as defender of the common weal.

14. So evident is Richard's vicious disregard of law and his rapacity in *The Mirror* that he need not be called a tyrant: he is tyranny personified.

15. *Civil Wars*, pp. 94-95.

RICHARD II   115

he never allows himself to know where he is going."[16] Leading an army against the King, he declares himself obedient to the will of heaven; and heaven or fortune plays its part in events. Even as winds and tides delay Richard's return from Ireland, portents of disaster dismay those faithful to him. Had Bolingbroke met determined opposition, the height of his ambition would have been measured by his willingness to press on. Because there is no opposition and commoners and nobles flock to him, his return from exile becomes a triumphant crusade. Declaring the hopelessness of resistance, the King's favorites scatter to save themselves. York, Richard's Lord Governor, is determined to do "somewhat," but not very much in Richard's behalf. Using his age as an excuse for hesitation, he contents himself with such feeble gestures as gathering carts of armor, and even before he meets Bolingbroke his decision to be "neuter" is made.

Meeting no obstacles, Bolingbroke does not have to decide consciously how far he will go. He can allow himself to be carried toward greatness on the tide of events. Even when he faces Richard at Flint Castle, he need not scale forbidden heights of power because Richard descends to his own abasement. Prey to hysteria as he lands again in England, Richard is incapable of dealing with the crisis of the rebellion. One moment he loses himself in fantasies about the earth which he has despoiled. The next moment he dreams that his dazzling radiance will dissolve the clouds of rebellion. This sense of omnipotence quickly fades, however, as reports of calamity, crowding one upon the other, drag his high thoughts down to the earth which is their resting place. It is not enough to say that Richard luxuriates in his sorrow or finds pleasure in the prospect of his degradation. When he substitutes the self-pity of imagined martyrdom for the fantasy of omnipotence, he surrenders to a destiny which has an unimpeachable authority because it has been so long dreaded—a destiny which seems unavoidable because his very attempts to prevent it have only brought it into being. He would like to imagine the self-affrighted Bolingbroke trembling at his sunlike radiance, but in fact it is he who trembles at the prospect of the meeting, and who is prepared beforetime to give all—his lands, his name, his life—to Bolingbroke. This abject surrender is an emotional relief as well as a torment because it ends Richard's need to pretend and to fear; it resolves the terrible contradiction between his imperious arrogance and his knowledge of his weakness.

Where Richard, despite the promptings of his followers, submits too readily

16. *Political Characters*, p. 134.

to "destiny," his opponents avoid any mention of the future. Leading an army against sacred majesty, Bolingbroke and Northumberland discuss neither plans nor goals: they chat about the countryside and the pleasure of companionship during a journey. Despite the bland triviality of their conversation, however, they obviously understand each other. Out to rid the nation of sycophants, Northumberland fawns on Bolingbroke, deferring to him as if he were an heir apparent. Bolingbroke, in turn, as Hotspur will recall, is a very king of smiles and courtesy who graciously accepts proferred services even as he writes out verbal promissory notes that will fall due when his infant fortunes come of age. Quick to kneel before York and suave in his apologies for his actions, Bolingbroke, like his supporters, assumes the customary patriotic stance of rebels. What York knows to be "gross rebellion and detested treason," Bolingbroke, with some justification, describes as a challenging of law. Determined to rid the nation of its leeches, he does not hesitate to revenge himself on the hated sycophants, whom he accuses of misleading the King. Yet he is deferential of York's pose of neutrality and very cautious in moving against Richard. He swears devotion while he threatens devastation. He parades his army but does not hurl it against the defenseless king, because he knows that Richard is still armed with the mystery of his kingship. When in his fantasy Richard called on his name to arm, we smiled; yet twenty thousand men were ready to die for Richard, and if Bolingbroke proceeds too callously, or even too obviously, twice twenty thousand men may arm themselves again for Richard's sake. Before the magic potency of Richard's title, Bolingbroke and his followers must make the ancient gestures of fealty; they must insist to York and to Richard (and to themselves) that they come only for Boling-broke's inheritance. Those who support Bolingbroke do not claim the right to put aside oaths of allegiance; on the contrary, they declare that they have taken solemn oaths to support his cause.

Although Bolingbroke is apprehensive about his meeting with Richard, the issue is never really in doubt. For, despite their protestations and their gestures of fealty, Bolingbroke's supporters no longer think of Richard as king. Northumberland, to be brief, omits Richard's title; the more loyal York is astonished that Richard "yet looks" like a king. The rebels' plans, moreover, reach beyond the meeting at Flint Castle; as Richard guesses, he must return with them to London whether he wishes to or not. Had Richard proved himself in this crisis to be as regal as the sun, Bolingbroke might possibly have been "the yielding water." Had he maintained his authority with unshakable confidence, Bolingbroke might have been trapped by his protestations of loyalty and forced to settle for his ducal estate. But, though Richard can outface the lackey Northumberland, his nerve fails at Bolingbroke's approach. Plunging toward calamity, he utters the thoughts that Bolingbroke cannot; he unkings himself even while his opponents speak of duty and devotion:

> What must the King do now? Must he submit?
> The King shall do it. Must he be depos'd?
> The King shall be contented. Must he lose
> The name of king? A God's name, let it go!
> I'll give my jewels for a set of beads,
> My gorgeous palace for a hermitage,
> My gay apparel for an almsman's gown,
> My figured goblets for a dish of wood,
> My sceptre for a palmer's walking staff,
> My subjects for a pair of carved saints,
> And my large kingdom for a little grave,
> A little little grave, an obscure grave.   (III.iii.143-54)

Advised by Aumerle to temporize, Richard, overwhelmed by a sense of impotence, seeks refuge in religious fantasies; when he must prove his kingliness, he proves unable to command his own nature: he wantons with his woes.

There is no indication in later scenes that Richard recovers from his failure at Flint Castle. He finds no fortitude in resignation and no strength to endure because his renunciation of the world is an aesthetic attitude self-pityingly struck. Yet he does begin to face the bitter truth about himself that he has so long known and denied. Too intelligent to delude himself, he realized as he landed in England that his tears were futile, his words idle, and his conjurations of earth and heaven senseless. A less intelligent man might have clung to the last tattered shreds of his royalty at Flint Castle, but Richard is no more deceived by the regal gestures he makes than by the kneelings and scrapings of his enemies. He flings away the pretense of rule because he is too humiliated by its feebleness; and although he would escape into fantasy, he also would confess the reality of his state to followers who have mistook him all the while. He is not the sun-king who can dissolve the clouds of rebellion; he is a glistering Phaethon, a mock-Phoebus who could not control the coursers of the sun. In earlier scenes Gaunt, York, and Northumberland served as choruses to the King's wantonness. Now that his princely education has begun, Richard can act as his own tragic chorus. Anatomizing his follies even while he exposes the shams of his enemies, he discovers too late what he is and needs, and he cherishes the tender feelings of York, who weeps for Richard but supports Bolingbroke.

As he falls from power, Richard rises in our sympathies, for calamity makes him wiser and more gracious though less kingly and less capable of rule than before. His days of folly ended, he is in the mighty hold of the Bolingbroke he tried to beggar. Once he alone betrayed his responsibilities; now he is surrounded by men who have betrayed their oaths of allegiance but who continue their sham of obedience. Where Richard callously dismissed the loyal Mowbray, Bolingbroke facilely wipes the blood of Bushy and Green from his hands. Where Richard made a mockery of his princely obligations, his enemies throw away respect, form, and ceremonious duty. To preserve ancient right, they violate the sacred bond between subject and king, and would then judge the King guilty of all the disorder in the land.

At his deposition Richard will be asked to confess his political crimes. The Garden scene, which comes before, offers a more compassionate judgment in which the Gardener's indictment of Richard's failures is countered by the Queen's loving devotion.[17] Isabella speaks of Richard's degradation as a second fall of man. One scene later, Richard compares himself to Christ, and after the deposition, York speaks of Richard's entry into London as if it were a second journey to Calvary. How shall we interpret these religious allusions? We might say that Shakespeare "balances" the English view of Richard's lawlessness with the French view of his Christlike martyrdom, except that Richard's capriciousness and narcissism are nothing like Adam's innocence or Christ's selflessness. Like Christ, however, Richard stands for sacrifice. Like Christ's, his trial is a sham of justice that deposes a mockery king. He has a Judaslike Bagot to accuse him and for judges a host of "Pilates" who wash their hands of any complicity in the degradation of a king by listening to Richard's "willing" abdication.

York's announcement that Richard "with willing soul" adopts Bolingbroke as his heir is the cue for the ritual drama of the deposition to begin. Called forth to surrender his tired majesty in open view, Richard refuses, however, to play the role as it was cast, because though dazed and defeated, he will not, like the pliant Bagot, speak freely of his guilt. Outraged by the prospect of a public humiliation, he decides to expose the sham of his willing abdication and

17. For the last time in the Garden scene, the medieval world of *Richard II* is presented to view before the deposition of Richard ushers in the new regime. Here the political allegory of the garden of the state commingles with the literary allegory of the garden as the setting for love. Thus, the poetic language of flowers speaks of political realities even as it creates a mood of lyric pathos; it defines both Richard's incompetence and the tenderness of the Queen's feeling for her "fair rose."

to change his part from defendant to prosecutor. Yet he cannot alter the script very much; nor can he escape the damning exposure of himself. We do not know what private reasons he had for agreeing to abdicate; all we know is that he consents to the mockery of his "willing" abdication, and that consent is damning, for a true king would have refused to collaborate in his degradation. Although it was probably not in Richard's power to save his crown, he alone could determine how he would lose it—what show of legitimacy he would lend to the proceedings against him. He appears at the deposition because he cannot resist the opportunity to be once more at the center of the political stage, and to make the emotional appeals which he knows will be futile.

Henry VI could lose a crown to find himself. Richard is too vain and self-absorbed to experience this kind of spiritual growth. Although he would wrap himself in the purple mantle of Christ, he knows the shamefulness of his conduct. Even as he calls his barons Judases, he admits that he is the greatest traitor of all, one who betrays his royalty by pretending, however badly, that he is willing to renounce it. Tormented by contradictory impulses, he would cast off the pretense of majesty, and he would also cling to it for a last few moments. He cannot sustain his part, however, before the tenacious Bolingbroke; intending to "expose" the fraudulence of the deposition, he ends by confessing his incompetence to rule and by acknowledging Bolingbroke's royalty.[18]

A purely impartial proceeding would have weighed Richard's crimes against those of his revolted followers. Here only the King is found guilty, and he must accept the verdict, for if he allows men to consider him a god on earth, he must be willing also to serve as their scapegoat. If in prosperous times the strength of twenty thousand loyal men flourishes in his cheeks, then he must accept as his own the guilt of the twenty thousand men who were driven to rebellion by his shameful conduct. If his carelessness must be their affliction, their disloyalty must be his princely "failure." The Mayor who acted as audience to Richard and Buckingham's posturing in rotten armor was a pliant hypocrite ready to believe anything he was told about Hastings' guilt. The earls who stand silent and shamefaced at Richard's deposition are another breed. They see what they want to believe: the orderly continuation of royal authority and the preservation of ancient ceremony, tradition, and form.

18. In Daniel's judgment, despite Bolingbroke's noble qualities and capacity to rule, the deposition of Richard was a grave error because it led to the civil wars of later years. Shakespeare's profounder psychological study of Richard's collapse and failure of will

Among the silent witnesses is York, who later describes to his wife the shameful scene of Richard's return to London as Bolingbroke's prisoner:

> No man cried "God save him!"
> No joyful tongue gave him his welcome home.
> But dust was thrown upon his sacred head;
> Which with such gentle sorrow he shook off,
> His face still combating with tears and smiles
> (The badges of his grief and patience),
> That had not God for some strong purpose steel'd
> The hearts of men, they must perforce have melted
> And barbarism itself have pitied him.
> But heaven hath a hand in these events,
> To whose high will we bound our calm contents.
> To Bolingbroke are we sworn subjects now,
> Whose state and honour I for aye allow.   (V.ii.28-40)

This is no hypocrite who sentimentalizes the man he betrayed. His heart grieves for the callous mistreatment of the King, but he is content to have Richard deposed and to attribute to God's will the course of events in which he played a significant role. Coming after the deposition scene, York's description of Richard's "Calvary" makes the rude jeering populace a larger audience to the preceding spectacle.[19] We know now that the ritual of deposition was not a politic fraud contrived to hoodwink a gullible commons. Thousands played their parts in the humiliation of the King, and though it was stage-managed by Bolingbroke, the ritual expressed the will of a nation.

The elegiac tone of York's speech makes events that have just occurred seem distant and "remembered." No longer the main actor in the drama of history, Richard faces a personal destiny that is more pathetic than tragic. Unable to win the crown of heaven, he also cannot accept his fate on earth, because without a crown he does not know what part to play or even who he is:

> I have no name, no title—
> No, not that name was given me at the font—

---

does not allow an audience to reach Daniel's conclusion, because the man who betrays himself the way that Richard does at Flint Castle and at the deposition is hardly fit to rule. In Shakespeare's play, Richard does not learn too late how to be king; he confesses too late his unkingliness.

19. York's description of Richard's entry into London is one of the most striking evidences of the influence of Creton, who on one page speaks of the Pilate role of the English in Richard's fall and of Richard and Bolingbroke's entry into London. The Londoners in Creton speak of the event in precisely York's manner: "And they most devoutly gave laud and thanks to our Lord for it, saying that it was his will, and that otherwise he could not have done" (*Archaeologia*, XX, 179).

But 'tis usurp'd. Alack the heavy day,
That I have worn so many winters out
And know not now what name to call myself!
O that I were a mockery king of snow,
Standing before the sun of Bolingbroke
To melt myself away in water drops!   (IV.i.255-62)

Like the dying Faustus, whose despairing speeches he echoes, Richard is
tormented by a realization of loss and emptiness, for in giving up his kingship,
he finds nothing except the nothingness of his existence. When he looks in a
mirror for proof of his existence, he sees only shadows and mocking images.
Once he talked of the dazzling radiance of his majesty; now he knows that if
men winked at him, it was only in contempt. No sun-god, not even a glistering
Phaethon, he sees himself at the deposition as a mockery king of snow melting
before the brightness of Henry's regality, and he can find no escape from this
sense of his unreality. Lacking, as Isabella sees, the will to resist his fate, he is
too shallow in his religious convictions and too accustomed to the presence of
an audience to bear the solitude of imprisonment. His attempts at philosophy
and theology are no more than facile, and though he tries to avoid the pain of
self-realization by spinning out conceits, he cannot keep his thoughts from
returning to the dead center of his nihilism:

                    Sometimes am I king:
        Then treasons make me wish myself a beggar,
        And so I am. Then crushing penury
        Persuades me I was better when a king;
        Then am I king'd again; and by-and-by
        Think that I am unking'd by Bolingbroke,
        And straight am nothing. But whate'er I be,
        Nor I, nor any man that but man is,
        With nothing shall be pleas'd till he be eas'd
        With being nothing.   (V.v.32-41)

One last moment of heroism and Richard is spared the mockery of his
existence.

The crisis of Richard's incompetence ends with his deposition. The crisis of
Henry's reign begins as soon as he is enthroned, because he can more easily
seize the crown from Richard than possess it in peace and safety. Having made
the crown stoop to armed might, he cannot quickly raise it again above the
arena of political contention, for he has deposed a myth of authority in
degrading Richard. If one king can be set aside, so can another; and if force can
determine who wears the crown, there is no longer any limitation on the height

of ambition. York may transfer to Henry the emotional loyalty he once felt for Richard, but other men will not acknowledge the new king, and Henry's authority cannot rest on his opportunistic alliance with the Percies—an alliance which Richard prophesies will not last. To strengthen his position Henry must, like Richard before him, manipulate the forms of judgment. Wringing all the political advantage he can out of Gloucester's murder, he stages a hearing before the deposition scene in which Bagot is called forth to speak of Richard's part in the murder of Gloucester. True to his kind, Bagot implicates Aumerle; other peers, eager for Bolingbroke's favor, add their accusations; and, as in the opening scene of the play, gages are flung down and charges of treason and murder hurled. The situation is tightly controlled, however, by Bolingbroke, who halts the show after Bagot has done his part in accusing Richard and the peers have tripped over one another in their desire to challenge Aumerle. Now the stage is set for the announcement of Richard's abdication, and when Carlisle tries to interfere, he is immediately arrested by the henchman Northumberland, who proves that it is as dangerous to speak honestly to the new King as to the old.

By the time the deposition scene has ended, there is no doubt of Henry's political qualities—he is strong, determined, shrewd, and ruthless, not particularly attractive but eminently capable. What he is like as a man is hidden until the fifth act, where something of his personal nature is revealed. We discover, almost with surprise, that this silent, skilled politician is a father disturbed by the waywardness of his son. We learn too that he has enough humor to appreciate the comedy of York's quarrel with his wife over the judgment of Aumerle. Tillyard would have us admire the conduct and the statements of York, who supposedly "utters the most correct sentiments."[20] At best, however, York is an odd specimen of Tudor orthodoxy—very slack in supporting the existing government when Richard was king and in defending Richard's right as his Lord Governor. Uttering the most correct sentiments, York warned Bolingbroke not to take too much and then helped him take the crown. Rather than a standard-bearer of Tudor royalism, York seems more accurately described by Palmer as a pragmatist,

a sturdy, honest, well-meaning man, prompt with sensible advice but easily flustered, shrewd enough to see what's coming but not clever or resolute enough to prevent it. He stands for the average gentleman amateur in public life, as true to his friends and as firm in his principles as the times allow. Normally he makes the best of a bad business—which is usually not so bad after

20. *History Plays*, p. 261.

all, either for himself or for the nation. Such men are loyal to a government as long as it has legal or traditional status and the means to enforce it. With every appearance of probity and devotion—by no means wholly assumed—they contrive to find themselves in the long run sturdily swimming with the tide.[21]

True enough, and yet this sensible, adaptable creature is astonishingly adamant in condemning his only child. Unlike the callous Northumberland, who can pursue his advantage and advancement without qualm ("my sins on my head"), York would be true to the feudal values he cherishes. Having equivocated his loyalty to Richard, he is determined to prove a liegeman to Henry, if necessary by sacrificing an Isaac at the altar of loyalty.

Shakespeare did not enlarge the role and develop the character of York, who is a very minor and sketchy figure in the Chronicles, simply to make him a mouthpiece for pieties or to add him to the list of trimmers in the History Plays. Like More's Hythlodaye,[22] York lives under a political system which offers no satisfactory course for the subject of an arrogant, heedless king. He can offer counsel, which will be disregarded. He can flee the court and the problem of political action (which is York's first instinct), but if he is drawn back against his will into the toils of political crisis, he can only justify to himself the choice that he thinks right—or tell himself, as York does, that he really has no choice at all. Where characters like Blanch and France in *King John* debate their dilemmas, York lives his; and where the Bastard brushes aside his perplexity, York finds escape first in "inaction" and then in commitment. To recognize York's integrity, however, is not to agree with Bolingbroke that he is a "sheer, immaculate, and silver fountain" of truth, and Aumerle a muddy, defiled stream of treason. There can be no simple judgment of loyalties in a time of change when fidelity to the past becomes treason to the present. Although compared to the pragmatic and opportunistic alliances which support the new regime, Aumerle's devotion to Richard seems precious, it does not make the conspiracy to murder Henry any less vile. A futile attempt to call back yesterday, the plot dooms Richard and sacrifices the peace of England.

Instead of providing an ideological solution to the problem of political loyalty in *Richard II*, Shakespeare makes us aware of its enormous difficulty. We realize that men bow to circumstances in bowing to kings. Since there is no

---

21. *Political Characters,* p. 142-43.
22. Although earnest medieval and Renaissance moralists wrote books of sage and serious advice for princes, the futility of such counseling is vividly expressed by Hythlodaye in the dialogue of Book One of More's *Utopia.*

alternative to the rule of Henry, it is "right" for Aumerle to kneel before him; and if Henry is not the rightful heir to the throne, he is nevertheless the true king. Like Aumerle, Henry must bow to necessity. The barons rebelled to redeem the crown from "broking pawn," but the new king comes to power owing debts of gratitude that cannot be paid without cheapening his majesty. Because his claim to the throne is questionable, Henry must leave no doubt of his authority or his will to rule. Although he can forgive his not-very-dangerous cousin Aumerle, and be generous to Carlisle, whose courage he admires, he must hound the other conspirators and rebels to their destruction. And whether he wishes to or not, he must be rid of Richard, because Richard is his living fear, the excuse for if not the cause of murderous plots and bloody rebellion.

After the peaks of dramatic intensity reached in the fourth act, the plot of *Richard II* almost inevitably descends to an anticlimax in the fifth, in which Shakespeare's artistic interest or energy apparently wanes. The tone of the York-Henry-Aumerle episode is uncertain, and the rhyming couplets here and in the last scene are astonishingly pedestrian. In V.ii the unnamed Exton and his accomplices are thrust out on the stage, by the prompter's hand, it seems, not the playwright's. More awkward still—especially for the King—is Exton's intrusion on the royal council in the concluding scene, where he defies all rules of ceremony and decorum in his haste to exhibit the corpse of Richard. Nevertheless, the tableau of mourning that concludes *Richard II* has an artistic power and rightness lacking in the de casibus clichés that embroider the last scene of *King John*. Like Richard in the opening scene, Henry in the closing scene must pretend to judge a henchman for a crime in which he is complicit. At the same time that he makes Exton his scapegoat, he is honest enough to admit that he needed the poison of Exton's act. Bowed with sorrow over Richard's corpse, as the nation will bow with sorrow for years to come, he feels the weight of the kingly cares he took with the crown. Like Richard he has shed a kinsman's blood; like Richard he fears rebellious subjects; and like Richard he banishes the follower who was his hangman. Wretched once because he was sentenced to exile, Henry now has reason to envy Mowbray's pilgrimage to the Holy Land, and he will die still longing for the clearness he might win by leading a Crusade against the Turk.

6. HENRY IV PART I

After the deliberate formality of *Richard II,* the spontaneity of *Henry IV Part I* seems all the more miraculous. It is as if the problem of dramatic structure, so carefully worked out in *Richard II,* suddenly ceased to exist for Shakespeare because his genius had repealed the laws of artistic gravity and discipline. The more we study *Henry IV,* the more we are impressed by the artfulness of its design: the parallelisms of its scenes, the echoings of motif and theme, and the juxtapositions and contrasts of character and attitude. Still, there is no sense of contrivance as the action unfolds, because the plot seems to be created moment by moment by the characters without the author's intervention. The tavern scenes are literally extempore; the clashes of personalities in the palace or in the rebels' councils have the immediacy and unpredictability of life. Thus, even though we know that the spontaneity of *Henry IV* is a virtuosic contrivance, the sleight of hand is so masterful that the artistic patterns seem marvelous coincidences, not continuing reminders of the author's shaping intelligence.

One pays a price, however, for the illusion of spontaneity, because casualness cannot be hurried or cut to measure. "Improvisation" must have scope to mirror the random quality of experience, the odd turns of conversation and mood. Either the plot must lengthen to include the holiday of the tavern scenes or the audience must settle for less of the serious matter of politics and history. Four-fifths as long as *Richard III, Henry IV Part I* contains but a fraction of its Chronicle material; and its account of the past seems a trifle sketchy compared to the vast panorama of history that unfolds in each of the *Henry VI* plays. The Percy rebellion is all that we know of the early years of

125

Henry's reign, and even that momentous political event remains until the last act in the background rather than the foreground of the plot. Before Shrewsbury, most of the drama of the uprising occurs offstage, not behind the scenes but rather between them, so that we catch only oblique reflections of the developing pattern of events as Hotspur reads a letter from a reluctant ally or as reports of the rebellion reach the tavern. Such important figures as Northumberland, Mortimer, and Glendower appear only once and then not in scenes that reveal them as political leaders. We see how passionately Mortimer loves his Welsh wife and how Glendower's sorcery irritates Hotspur, but we do not know the political motives which keep Mortimer and Glendower from fighting by Hotspur's side at Shrewsbury.[1]

I do not mean to suggest that the portrayal of history in *Part I* is meager or perplexing. On the contrary, there is a greater depth of insight into political motives and relationships in *Part I* than in the earlier History Plays, and there is a more inclusive view of the drama of politics than before, not despite the presence of the tavern scenes but because of them. It is easier, however, to appreciate Falstaff than to explain how the comic scenes join with the "serious action" of the play to make up a larger artistic whole. When we see a fine performance of *Part I*, we have no doubt of the unity of its plot and its conception; when we try to analyze this unity, it proves ineffable. Either we find ourselves documenting subtle parallels and elusive echoes that no audience would apprehend, or we create the impression that the play has a "double" rather than single plot which creates one dramatic world in the tavern scenes, another in those of the palace. We can, of course, hold the plot together by making the tavern scenes nothing more than a conventional setting for the drama of Hal's escape from the temptation to vanity and riot. But to conventionalize the tavern scenes, we must close our eyes to all that is subversive of homiletic earnestness in the dialogue and play-acting in the Boar's Head, and if we ignore the subversive charm and ironic perspective of the comic scenes, we cannot then justify their disproportionate share of the dramatic action. Who, moreover, can take seriously the "Morality drama" of the tavern scenes in which the prodigal is not very prodigal or susceptible to temptation, but the audience is so easily enchanted by the figure of Riot that only the warnings of scholarship guard it from seduction?

It is one thing to speak of the "dramatic balance" of *Henry IV Part I*, as do Brooks and Heilman, who see in it a "view which scants nothing, which covers

1. It is only by the way that we hear that Glendower was "overrul'd by prophecies" (IV.iv.16-18). Mortimer's absence is never explained.

up nothing, and which takes into account in making its affirmations the most searching criticism of that which is affirmed."[2] It is another thing to dwell on the ironic poise, tensions, ambivalences, and ambiguities of Shakespeare's art as if there were an irreducible parallax in his vision of reality. The amplitude of Shakespearean drama does not depend upon the presence of dialectical oppositions, for the comprehensiveness and "balance" of his vision is evident in every scene, in every line of his plays. It is very doubtful, for example, that Hal's caricaturing of Hotspur in the tavern really qualifies an audience's perception of Percy; and it is even more doubtful that this mockery is required to balance or correct an audience's admiration for Hotspur's youthful heroism. The scenes of Hotspur with his family, his wife, and his allies tell all we need to know about the egotism of his motives and the rashness of his enthusiasms. Conversely, we do not need the scenes of Hotspur to recognize that the saturnalia of the Boar's Head is not an ideal representation of good cheer and fellowship, because Hal is restless at times and bored, and always condescending to his companions, whom he promises to cast off.

What is remarkable in *Part I* is not its balancing of contrarieties but its unity of vision and of plot which embraces and demands the interplay of comedy and history. For, though the issues of state are decided in council chambers and on battlefields, it is in the tavern scenes that the central themes of courage and cowardice, of lying and truth, and of honor and instinct are made explicit and held up to ironic scrutiny. It is in the jests, practical jokes, and sallies of wit in the Boar's Head that the play grows "philosophical." In the first tetralogy there seemed to be no connection between the public drama of politics and the private lives of politicians, because the great figures in history apparently lived out their lives in council chambers and had no thoughts or desires that were not connected to the struggle for power. The perspective of the *Henry IV* plays is wider in that it includes the intimacy of Hotspur's relationship with his wife and Falstaff's relationship with Hal—and with Doll. Shakespeare does not simply leaven the drama of history with comic interludes or use those interludes to comment ironically on great events. Rather he presents history in a different light by portraying its makers at their ease as well as in the toils of politics—as husbands, lovers, drinkers, comedians, fathers, sons, and comrades as well as political allies and enemies. We realize that the apparent impersonality of the power struggle as reported by the Chronicles is

2. Introduction to *Henry IV Part I, Understanding Drama,* ed. Cleanth Brooks and R. B. Heilman (New York: Holt, Rinehart & Winston, 1948), reprinted in the Norton Critical edition of the play, edited by James L. Sanderson (New York: Norton, 1962), p. 171.

an illusion, for behind the logic of events in *Henry IV* is always the illogic of human motive, and woven into the grand design of history are the many strands of petty spite and malice. We realize too that however coldblooded men may seem in pursuing their goals, they are rarely coldblooded or detached about their goals. Where Hotspur is obviously too rash and impulsive, too personal in his quarrel with the "ungrateful" King, Worcester seems wholly rational and calculating. But Worcester's quarrel with the King is no less personal than Hotspur's. He does not want land, titles, or any of the conventional prizes of power for which the politicians of the first tetralogy contend; he wants the King to remember at all times what he was before the Percies helped him to the throne. Worcester's dispassionate strategic calculations, moreover, are little more than a game of blindman's buff in which plans and preparations for war are based on conjectures about the enemy's intentions:

> And 'tis no little reason bids us speed,
> To save our heads by raising of a head;
> For, bear ourselves as even as we can,
> The King will always think him in our debt,
> And think we think ourselves unsatisfied,
> Till he hath found a time to pay us home.   (I.iii.283-88)

So long as policy is determined by "realists" like Worcester, so long will nations continue to arm against inevitable conflicts. Strategic planners have not advanced beyond his calculations—they have simply programmed them for the "objective" decisionmaking of computers.

In *Part I* men like Henry and Worcester quarrel about the past because they remember it differently. Just as Hal's recollection of Gadshill and Shrewsbury is at odds with Falstaff's, so Henry's recollection of his ascent to the throne is very different from that of the Percies'. None can dispute that Richard was deposed and murdered, and that Henry, aided by the Percies, assumed the throne. But where the Percies claim that they were innocents duped by a vile politician who lied to them about his motives, Henry will confess only that he plucked allegiance out of men's hearts in Richard's very presence. And his memory of Richard's shameful misconduct as king is far more vivid than his memory of any personal wrongdoing. The longer Henry lives, the more his thoughts revert to the past, and the more communicative becomes the "silent King" of *Richard II*. It is doubtful, however, that he ever reveals to the audience the truth about his motives that he so tenaciously hid during his climb to the throne. For whether he speaks to others or to himself he is always acutely aware of what he "betrays" about himself. His confessions of ruthlessness to Hal are calculated lessons in statecraft just as his laments over the past in *Henry IV Part II* are public apologias.

Because he is forever guarded in his relationships with others, Henry seems more of an "actor" than do the other characters in *Part II*. But then all the world's a stage in the second tetralogy, and all the men and women players of the roles which personality and circumstance dictate. Although some are more conscious than others of their acting, none is without some part which he acts out for himself and for the audience of the world. Some pretend to courage, others to loyalty, neutrality, or prodigality. Some are eternally cheerful, others eternally suspicious or perpetually disappointed with the bad faith and mendacity of those they loved and trusted. Injured innocence and moral indignation are among the most popular roles in *Part I*. Falstaff assumes them with Hal, Hal with Falstaff, Henry with the Percies, and the Percies with Henry. Falstaff mimics the King, as do Hal and Blunt; and Henry plays the reluctant chastizer of rebels, while Worcester plays the reluctant rebel, one who did not look for Shrewsbury but found rebellion in his "path."

Few of the parts which men conceive for themselves are solo, because even the greatest of egotists requires supporting players. Every hero needs his villains and every martyred innocent his betrayers—men who can be cast as liars, cheats, ingrates, cowards, vile politicians, or gray iniquities. If one could believe the debauched Falstaff, before he knew Hal, he knew nothing. If one could believe the Percies, before they knew Bolingbroke, they knew nothing of policy and disloyalty. The tavern poses are, for the most part, jokingly assumed, but the accusations of falsehood and ingratitude in the palace are very earnest. Henry contends in I.iii that his patience has been abused by the disrespectful Percies, who have mistaken his mildness for weakness. Perhaps so, but it is hard to believe that Henry has been "smooth as oil" and "soft as young down" when every word he utters is a steely threat. To be fair, one has to recognize that Worcester's manner is intolerably provoking if not actually insolent. Instead of justifying the withholding of the Scottish prisoners, Worcester accuses the King of ingratitude and reminds him of the obligations owed to the Percies which derogate his majesty. How astonishing that a politician as astute and cautious as Worcester, one who thinks first and always of his own safety, should bait the King in this way—unless he has been goaded to the point of defiance by Henry's words and acts. Since the scene opens with the quarrel very near its climax, we cannot judge who provoked whom; but there is no doubt about the nature of the challenge which the Percy recalcitrance poses to the King's authority, and there is no doubt about Henry's willingness to face it. He does not, like Richard II, hide behind regal gestures and ironic pleasantries. He does not urge his former allies to forgive and forget. He sends Worcester away to restudy his obedience and refuses to be diverted by Hotspur's charming apology from the main issue of the Percy disobedience. Whatever the reasons for Hotspur's conduct at Holmedon, the fact remains that he refuses a royal command—"yet he doth deny his prisoners." Instead of obeying the King as his subjects, the Percies would bargain with him as his equal.

Admirably direct in his clash with the Percies over their prisoners, Henry is more devious about the question of ransoming Mortimer. There is, in fact, a shrillness in his rage at the "foolish Mortimer" which betrays his fear of the man who was acknowledged by Richard as his "next of blood." Unwilling to hear any defense of Mortimer, whom he brands a traitor, Henry would bully the Percies into submission by threatening

> . . . I shall never hold that man my friend
> Whose tongue shall ask me for one penny cost
> To ransom home revolted Mortimer.   (I.iii.90-92)

Hotspur will not be intimidated. Frank in his own apology, he leaps immediately to the defense of Mortimer in the very teeth of Henry's threat by denying that Mortimer ever "fell off" but by the chance of war. Here is truth and simplicity incarnate; yet we would not swear that Hotspur relates the true story of Mortimer's encounter with Glendower:

> Three times they breath'd, and three times did they drink,
> Upon agreement, of swift Severn's flood;
> Who then, affrighted with their bloody looks,
> Ran fearfully among the trembling reeds
> And hid his crisp head in the hollow bank,
> Bloodstained with these valiant combatants.   (I.iii.102-7)

Where the report of Holmedon spills forth artlessly and frankly, the account of Mortimer's battle with Glendower seems a varnished tale, made up if not actually memorized. What Hotspur describes is not a scene from the annals of war but an illustration from a book of fairy tales so naively drawn that Henry turns on him as if he were a fibbing boy:

> Thou dost belie him, Percy, thou dost belie him!
> He never did encounter with Glendower.
> I tell thee

He durst as well have met the devil alone
As Owen Glendower for an enemy.   (I.iii.113-17)

What is the truth about Mortimer? The audience should be able to judge for itself because Mortimer later appears on the stage, but all that one can tell about him is that he seems blandly amiable and more eager to stay with his Welsh bride than to ride off to war. This slight acquaintance with Mortimer suffices, however, because he is obviously the occasion rather than the cause of the break between Henry and the Percies. Neither Worcester nor Northumberland makes a plea for Mortimer to the King. And, though Hotspur swears that he will empty all his veins on Mortimer's behalf, he is enraged more by Henry's ingratitude to the Percies than by his neglect of Mortimer. What Hotspur cannot bear is the thought that his family was "fool'd, discarded, and shook off" by the man whom they made king, and what Hotspur wants is personal vengeance, not justice for Mortimer.

Whatever is opaque and indirect in the opening scene of *Richard II*, there is no doubt that treason, honor, and blood are central themes, formally announced and rhetorically underlined in the dialogue. The themes of *Henry IV Part I* are more casually introduced and more subtly and elusively woven into the dialogue and action. No choric sentences about Truth occur during Henry's heated dialogue with the Percies, though truth and falsehood are the central issues of the quarrel. First Henry warns Worcester against the falseness of disobedience; then he condemns Mortimer's lack of truth and accuses Hotspur of lying for Mortimer's sake. When the King exits, it is the Percies' turn to condemn the treacherous Bolingbroke who promised more than he paid to those who helped him become king. Later in the play the theme of truth returns in comic variations as Falstaff and Hal accuse each other of lying and as an exasperated Hotspur challenges Glendower to "tell truth, and shame the Devil."

Despite these lighter moments, the plot of *Part I* keeps demanding serious answers to the question of truth, which it poses in tripartite form: Is Henry (as the Percies doubt) the true king? Is Hal (as Henry doubts) the true prince? Can thieves or politicians be true to one another? And when we return to the Chronicles after reading *Part I*, we recognize (as Shakespeare did) that truth was the central issue of Henry's quarrel with the Percies. According to Holinshed, the King suspected the Percies' motive in demanding the ransom of Mortimer and gave a fraudulent excuse for refusing the demand. When the Percies rebelled, Holinshed reports, they declared that Henry swore falsely to them on his return from exile that he came only to claim his ducal inheritance.

They also broadcast a number of slanders and lies, not the least of which was that Richard II was still alive. But, though expert at spreading falsehoods, the Percies were unprepared for the falsehood of the noblemen who swore to support their cause yet never came to Shrewsbury. Betrayed by others, the Percies ended by betraying each other; in fact, the battle of Shrewsbury might not have been fought except that Worcester, Holinshed reports, lied to Hotspur about the King's offer of terms.[3]

Despite Falstaff's complaints about the mendacity of others, the world of *Henry IV Part I* is not really given to lying. If truth seems a scarce commodity in taverns and in throne rooms, it is not because deep-dyed hypocrites abound but because the characters in the play are suspicious and self-absorbed, unable to recognize their equivocations and unwilling to countenance any version of the truth other than their own. The problem of truth is further compounded by the cleverness with which men can bend and twist language. Often the problem of truth is one of semantics as well as of moral character. Falstaff prays that Hal, the true prince, will prove a false thief "for recreation sake." And if Hall agrees to take purses, he may prove as true to his heritage as he is false to his princely position, because he is the son of a man who boasts of plucking allegiance out of men's hearts and stealing courtesy from heaven. One can play the false thief, moreover, in contrary ways—either by being "as false as a thief" or by being "false in one's thievery," a mock criminal. We could say that Hal is a false thief in that he does not rob honest men, and that he is falser still in that he robs his fellow thieves. Or we could say that Hal proves at Gadshill true to his thieving kind, if not to his thieving companions. Is he a man of his word? He promises to repay Francis' gift of a pennyworth of sugar with a thousand pounds, and he promises to reward Falstaff by giving him "the hanging of the thieves," a prospect which turns the fat old knight a trifle melancholy. The counterfeit thief can be endured because he returns the stolen money. The counterfeit prince is intolerable because his false impression of kingliness debases the coinage of majesty.[4] When Henry's right to rule is being challenged, it is not enough for Hal to claim to be Henry's heir; he must win his birthright at Shrewsbury and he must prove himself legitimate by being true to

3. See Holinshed's account of the fraudulent excuses, "cloaked drifts," contrived forgeries, slanderous reports, and outright lies bruited during the Percy conflict with the King, *Chronicles*, III, 22-25.

4. The motif of counterfeiting recurs in the dialogue and action of the play. Hotspur, for example, would have "crack'd crowns / And pass them current too." Falstaff counterfeits dying at Shrewsbury and proves thereby that he is "the true and perfect image of life indeed."

the father he ignores and faithful to the responsibilities he neglects. To outward appearances, however, truth and loyalty are not Hal's primary qualities. He is first mentioned in *Richard II* as a truant to the chivalry of his ancestors, and no sooner does he appear in *Henry IV Part I* than he threatens to be as dubious a companion as he is a prince, no readier to second Falstaff at Gadshill than to aid his father against the Percies.

Even as the robbery at Gadshill is a comic counterpart to the Percy conspiracy, Falstaff, who would tempt Hal to highway robbery, is the comic counterpart to Worcester, who would draw his nephew into a plot against the King. Sir John would tutor a prince in the ways of thievery; Worcester would teach a chivalric hero the manners of a rebel. Even as Hal's reference to the hanging of thieves promises a dubious reward for his favorite, Hotspur complains that the Percies have served as Bolingbroke's hangmen and not received their reward. More suspicious still of Henry's purposes, Worcester fears that they will find their reward on the gallows unless they save their heads "by raising of a head." We cannot take seriously the drama of temptation in the tavern when it is the innocent Hal who first suggests taking purses and the reprobate Falstaff who complains of Hal's corrupting influence. But we must take seriously the drama of temptation that unfolds in the palace, where the lure to anarchy and misrule comes, not from a debauched Falstaff, but from a politic Worcester who is, to all outward appearances, a model of sobriety. If prudence and moderation are the chief lessons of *Part I*, then Worcester, who warns Hotspur against "defect of manners, want of government, / Pride, haughtiness, opinion, and disdain" (III.i.184-85), can qualify as Shakespeare's moral chorus. Yet what is Falstaff's lawlessness compared to Worcester's? What is the danger to the state of a fat, old, broken-winded, somewhat cowardly highway robber compared to that of the judicious Worcester, whose plots drench the soil of England in blood? One may learn how to waste time in the tavern, but to know the true meaning of vanity and riot one must go to the halls of state, where pride, wrath, and envy are literally deadly sins.

The reckless Falstaff lives as if every day were holiday and the future crowded with companionship and good cheer. The careful Worcester is forever planning against tomorrow, but his prudential wisdom is a counsel of despair. Convinced that conflict with Henry is inevitable, Worcester makes it so, and it never occurs to him—not even on the way to the scaffold—that there might have been an alternative to the fate he in large measure chose. He is not moved by Hotspur's appeals to honor nor is he amused by Hotspur's outburst against the cankered Bolingbroke. With his brother Northumberland, he coolly observes Hotspur's outrage in I.iii even as he plans to exploit it. It is a poignant irony that Hotspur should lecture his politic relatives on the meaning of familial honor. It is more ironic still that he cannot see in his uncle and father the duplicity he despises in the King. Ready to hurl his defiance openly against Henry, he is led into a secret plot that Worcester has already set down. Demanding truth from Henry and then again from Glendower, he finds only falsehood and treachery in his own kin.

I do not think that it is "sentimental" to enjoy Hotspur's openness and good humor, so long as we recognize the conceit and infatuation with risk that sully his noblest impulse. Hungering for reputation in the way other men hunger for power, he will let another sit on the throne, but he must wear the dignities of great renown "without corrival." Generous in spirit, he would open his veins in a "good cause," but he will not think of the misery of the thousands of other men who will unwillingly bleed because of the rebellion. Too narrow in his devotion to family and too trusting of his kin, he cannot admit the egotism of his motives or realize the contradictions of his outrage. On the one hand, he would see his family as innocent dupes of the vile politician Bolingbroke, who deceived them by pledging that he came back only for his ducal rights. On the other hand, he fumes at the ingratitude of Henry, who reneged on his promises and now orders the Percies about as if he owed them nothing. Thus, Hotspur would be innocent of the "crime" of having aided Henry to the throne even as he is furious that his family was not sufficiently rewarded for their aid to Bolingbroke. In Hotspur's view, the Percies acted as Henry's hangman but did not receive the hangman's perquisite. They helped to kill a king but did not receive the king's clothes, for it is the cankered Bolingbroke who wears the robes of majesty and denies their present suit for Mortimer.

The richness and delight of Hotspur's personality makes one wonder at the desire of some critics to treat him as a clown or as the sullen ground on which Hal's princely brilliance glitters. The actors who play Hotspur will not demean him in this way. They make us aware of his warmth, exuberance, and poetry, qualities somewhat lacking in Hal; and they almost convince us that the rebel is more attractive than the prince. For if Hal's poise accentuates Hotspur's recklessness, Hotspur's frankness calls attention to what is calculating and disingenuous in Hal's relations with others. When Hotspur teases his adoring wife, the humor is tender and intimate; when Hal, slightly bored and drunk, teases Francis, the joke smacks of contempt and casual cruelty.

We can say that Hotspur is the better companion, Hal the better prince. The one is more engaging as a man, the other far better suited to great responsibility. To grant Hal the fullest measure of his princely talents is not, however, to agree that he is Shakespeare's ideal of rule—a character whose personal defects are a part of his princely perfection, whose coldness and calculation are seen by Shakespeare as necessary virtues in a leader. If Shakespeare gave us the Hal of the folk legend, a youth who loved the low company which he ultimately turned away, we might speak of his aloofness in the tavern scenes as a schooling of self for the impersonal demands of office. But what shall we say of the Prince who in his first appearance speaks contemptuously of his tavern companions, whom he intends to use to line his princely enterprise? Just as Falstaff keeps his eye on the main chance and expects to profit in times to come from his friendship with Hal, Hal confesses in soliloquy that he intends to turn a small investment in seeming prodigality into a handsome profit of reputation. Although he obviously enjoys Falstaff's company, Hal tells us that he plays at comradeship as well as at prodigality and not only plans to discard his cronies but even now considers them the base contagion that momentarily obscures his princely radiance.

To be sure, Hal is not, as some have pictured him, a Machiavellian prince who craftily deceives his tavern cronies even as he will later "dupe" his English subjects into supporting his claim to the throne of France. He never pretends deep feeling for Falstaff and Poins, and, if anything, he is more ingenious in his self-justifications than cunning in his dissimulations. He is more candid in his conversations with other men than in his colloquies with himself in which he labors to rationalize his behavior. When Hotspur embroiders the truth about Mortimer's soldiership, his artificiality of manner betrays him; when he tries to argue before Shrewsbury that rashness is caution, his illogic is transparent. More conscious of, and subtle in, his casuistries, Hal is more difficult to "see through." Though we know him better than does Falstaff, who claims to know him "like the Lord that made ye," we cannot say that we fully understand the prince who plays a limited engagement as tavern roisterer and who explains his tavern holiday as a clever public relations stunt. This is a man whose reasons and rationalizations so finely commingle that they cannot be sorted out, but whose bent of mind is consistent in conversation and soliloquy. Shrewd in his appraisals and thoroughly pragmatic, he studies other men so that he may learn to master them; and because his moral attitudes are attuned to those of the practical world, he sees no reason to justify his manipulation of others, though he feels compelled to justify his seeming dissipation. It would not occur to him that drinking sack and sugar may be less of a fault than falsifying men's hopes, and he could not imagine that his tavern holiday might seem to others more attractive than his utilitarian justification of it.[5]

Although we cannot allow one soliloquy to determine our view of a character as fully developed as Hal is in dialogue and dramatic action, neither can we ignore the fact that in each play in which Hal appears, he is allowed only one soliloquy, and in each instance that soliloquy is a crucial revelation of character and motive.[6] The alternative to viewing Hal's soliloquy in I.ii as a disclosure of self is to regard it, as many critics have done, as a choric device by which Shakespeare communicates essential narrative information to his audience, assuring them that Hal "will exhibit all the proper regal virtues" when the time comes.[7] One must wonder, however, why an Elizabethan audience needed reassurance about the princely character or destiny of the greatest of England's heroic kings, whose exploits at Agincourt were celebrated in poems and ballads, in the Chronicles, and in the source play *The Famous Victories*. If, as Professor Tillyard argues, Shakespeare was compelled to make Hal a "copybook paragon" in *Henry V* because his audience knew the legend of Harry's perfection by heart,[8] surely there was no need to dispel any doubts about Hal's future greatness in scene ii of *Henry IV Part I*, especially when, as Tillyard notes, there is not the slightest intimation that Hal can be seduced by Falstaff. Describing Hal as "aloof and Olympian from the start," Tillyard remarks that he "never treats Falstaff any better than his dog, with whom he condescends once in a way to have a game."[9]

Even if we grant that Shakespeare may have thought his audience too gross to see what Tillyard and others do in the Hal of the first tavern scene, we must still wonder why he did not just allow the groundlings to enjoy their superficial view of Hal as the prodigal of the legend. Unless Shakespeare's audience was

5. John Palmer shrewdly notes that if Hal "is merely looking for a reason to be merry with his friends, surely he might have found a better one. To plead that he is permitting their base contagious clouds to smother up his beauty in order that he may shine all the more brightly when they have served his turn is not the sort of excuse which would have suggested itself to a really good companion" (*Political Characters*, p. 185).

6. Compare the soliloquy at the end of the first tavern scene with the one soliloquy which Hal speaks in *Henry IV Part II*, when he takes the crown from his father's pillow (IV.v.21-47); and with his one soliloquy in *Henry V*, which occurs after his encounter with his soldiers about the campfire on the eve of Agincourt (IV.i.247-301).

7. Tillyard, *History Plays*, p. 300. J. Dover Wilson also insists that the soliloquy has a conventional function of conveying "information to the audience about the general drift of the play" (*The Fortunes of Falstaff* [Cambridge: Cambridge Univ. Press, 1964], p. 41).

8. *History Plays*, p. 305.

9. *History Plays*, pp. 271-72.

made up of prigs and Puritans, they could not really have trembled for Hal's future because, like thousands of theatergoers, he enjoyed Falstaff. After all, we never see Hal in the throes of debauchery and we find his capacity for holiday reassuring; we like and trust a man who can drink and joke, unbend and stoop to the level of our own tastes. To have our confidence and good will, a youthful profligate need not apologize for his casual "vices." If he appears generous, frank in his affections, and fundamentally innocent in spirit, we are perfectly ready to grant that having sowed his wild oats, he deserves—as do all the youthful profligates of seventeenth-century comedy—a good wife, a handsome fortune, and a noble future.[10] In other words, Hal needs no choric soliloquy to warn us that he is the Cinderella prince of the legend. He needs the soliloquy to underline the fact that he is not prodigal in temperament at all, and certainly not a happy-go-lucky youth indifferent to his royal future. Rather than a Huck Finn who prefers the freedom of the tavern to the restrictions imposed by his noble destiny, he is a Tom Sawyer who enjoys his moment of raffishness but by inclination is one of the respectable and perhaps even one of the Elect. Very conscious of the way that men respond to the image of royalty, and no less instinctive a politician than his father, Hal is the creator as well as the creature of political mythology, the author as well as the hero of his legend.

It seems to me preferable to interpret the soliloquy as soliloquy rather than to turn Shakespeare into a blunderer who did not realize the chilling effect of Hal's contemptuous lines about his comrades and who failed to see how Hal's diction and metaphors associate his calculated redemption with the crassness of commodity and sharp business practices:

> So, when this loose behaviour I throw off
> And pay the debt I never promised,
> By how much better than my word I am,
> By so much shall I falsify men's hopes;
> And, like bright metal on a sullen ground,
> My reformation, glitt'ring o'er my fault,
> Shall show more goodly and attract more eyes
> Than that which hath no foil to set it off.
> I'll so offend to make offence a skill,
> Redeeming time when men think least I will.   (I.ii.232-41)

10. The generous rake enjoys a happy career also in Restoration comedy. Indeed, his type can be seen in any number of Hollywood movies in which a slightly ribald, reckless, and warmhearted young hero wins the heroine away from the proper, respectable, young banker whom the parents prefer.

Like a clever Elizabethan shopkeeper, Hal knows how to display the merchandise of his behavior in such a light that it appears richer than it is. He knows,
too, how to play the princely bankrupt—how to conceal his princely assets
until they bring a double profit. We may not like this element of calculation in
him, but it is one of his fundamental traits. The Hal who will "use" his tavern
companions is the same Hal who will make Percy his factor and who promises
to tear the reckoning of honor out of Hotspur's heart. He is also the same Hal
who in soliloquy in *Part II* will promise to "pay plenteously" with tears for the
crown he takes from his father's pillow, and who in soliloquy in *Henry V* will
ask what are the "rents" and "comings-in" of Ceremony and promise God to
pay more fully the debt of conscience.

Far from being a neutral choric announcement, Hal's soliloquy in the tavern
strikes the keynote of his characterization in succeeding plays. For just as he
explains to the audience why he wastes his time with low companions in *Part I*,
he will explain to Poins in *Part II* why he cannot weep for his dying father, and
to the traitors in *Henry V* why he cannot be merciful to them.[11] We can take
Hal's part in Hal's casuistic way and explain that it is Francis' fault that Hal
plays nasty jokes on him—because the "subhuman" deserve subhuman treatment. Or we can accept Hal for what he is: fascinating but not endearing; not
quite the paragon some would have him nor the heartless prig others see.
Although quick-witted, he is rarely a match for Falstaff because he cannot
anticipate the sudden dazzling reversals and agile leaps of Falstaff's thought
and mood. Thus, even though he holds the trump cards after Gadshill, he does
not win the game of wits, because Falstaff makes the very questions of
cowardice and truth seem ridiculous. In these encounters Hal has a grave
disadvantage in that he cannot, like Falstaff, ridicule everything. Although he
jokes coarsely about cheapening maidenheads, he will not cheapen courage or
princeliness; he will not pretend to be a good fellow at the price of his royal
dignity.

The time will come when Henry V will look back with shame on the "riots"
of his tavern days. Even now there is a faint tinge of disgust in his reference to
the base contagion that smothers up his beauty from the world. He can take
Falstaff's bulk as a subject for his wit, but he does not share Falstaff's pleasure
in the flesh. When Sir John plays at being king, corpulence is rhapsodized as
well as licensed. When Hal becomes the kingly homilist, Falstaff's great belly
becomes an emblem of surfeited appetite as well as of festive indulgence:

11. Palmer writes very penetratingly of the need for self-justification which character-
izes Harry in each play in which he appears (*Political Characters*, pp. 185-87).

Why dost thou converse with that trunk of humours, that bolting hutch of beastliness, that swoll'n parcel of dropsies, that huge bombard of sack, that stuff'd cloakbag of guts, that roasted Manningtree ox with the pudding in his belly, that reverend vice, that grey iniquity, that father ruffian, that vanity in years?

                                                                    (II.iv.494-500)

For Falstaff the urge to repentance is a fleeting impulse or a comic pose. For Hal the thought of redemption is no laughing matter. Earnest even in holiday, he scrupulously examines his conduct and finds it good; he explains to us and to himself that he labors in the tavern in his vocation as a prince just as Falstaff explains that he labors in his vocation as a highway robber. Knowing how men merchandize their reputations and hope for bargain redemptions, Falstaff jokes about finding a commodity of good names. Hal, on the other hand, seriously intends to gain that commodity even as he seriously intends to reject Falstaff as the "tutor and feeder" of his "riots." After all, it is not Shakespeare who casts Hal as the hero of a Morality drama of temptation and redemption. It is Hal who casts himself in the role even as he casts Falstaff in the role of reverend Vice and gray iniquity. I do not mean to suggest that beneath the loose behavior of the pseudo-libertine is the tight-lipped manner of the Precisian to be. I do suggest that Shakespeare's conception of Harry, as it unfolds in the second tetralogy, is all of one piece, a marvelously unified and sustained study of a personality that develops in Aristotelian fashion from potentiality to essence—from seeming roisterer to devout conqueror. The more we see of Hal in the tavern, the less we fear that he will grow too attached to Falstaff. We wonder, however, whether this poised, ironic, self-absorbed prince will ever be capable of intimacy or of emotional attachment to another person. We sense, even in *Part I*, that Hal needs Falstaff even as he needs ultimately to banish him.

Compared to the cartoonlike figure of the Prince in *The Famous Victories*, Shakespeare's portrait of Hal may seem astonishingly sophisticated and modern. Yet Shakespeare's skepticism about Hal's prodigality has the authority of the Chronicles. Holinshed says of the Prince:

Indeed he was youthfullie given, growne to audacitie, and had chosen him companions agreeable to his age; with whome he spent the time in such recreations, exercises, and delights as he fansied. But yet (it should seeme by the report of some writers) that his behaviour was not offensive or at least tending to the damage of anie bodie, sith he had a care to avoid dooing of wrong, and to tender his affections within the tract of vertue, whereby he opened unto himselfe a redie passage of good liking among the prudent sort.[12]

12. *Chronicles*, III, 54.

These sentences very nearly strip away the embellishments of myth from the reality of Hal's earlier years. Neither tavern brawler nor purse-snatcher, Hal had spent his youth in the serious business of politics and war. Trained early to royal responsibilities, he had led armies against his father's enemies and had even assumed command of the government during one of his father's illnesses. Such sobriety is very admirable in its way, but it is not the stuff of epic and legend. We would have our heroes dashing and a bit rakehelly rather than earnest and virtuous: we prefer to sing of the outlaw Robin Hood than to ballad the Sheriff of Nottingham. And as Richard III understood, we want to believe that our leaders are reluctant to be chosen, that they are so humble and disinterested in power that they must have greatness thrust upon them. We rejoice in the thought that the greatest of monarchs had a misspent youth, and much prefer this fictional prince to the real one, who apparently schemed with his allies to wrest the throne from his ailing father.[13] We would rather believe that Hal boxed the ear of Authority than that he lusted for the crown.

The mythologizing of Hal's life is fascinating, however, because the legend of his youthful wildness hints directly at what it conceals. While Holinshed and most other Chroniclers make no mention of the actual struggle for power between Henry and Hal, they report that slanderous tales of Hal's ambition "brought no small suspicion into the kings head, least his sonne would presume to usurpe the crowne."[14] And though the legend tells that Hal was so careless of his royal future that he lost his place in the royal Council, it also tells that he had so large a retinue of followers that he had to seek an audience with his father to deny his ambition—a denial again required, according to the legend, when he took the crown from his father's pillow while Henry lay dying. Shakespeare does not imagine a Hal whose ambition threatened his father's place, but he makes much of Henry's suspicion of his son and suggests the engrained antagonism that colored their relationship. The first word we have of Hal, in the fifth act of *Richard II*, is that he threatens to insult his father's newly minted majesty by wearing a whore's token at the jousts that are to celebrate Henry's coronation. Henry's anger and disappointment with his son are evident in the first scene of *Henry IV*, where he disowns Hal in thought; soon afterward Hotspur jokingly remarks that he would have Hal poisoned with a pot of ale, "But that I think his father loves him not / And would be

13. See C. L. Kingsford's introduction to *The First English Life of King Henry the Fifth* (Oxford: Clarendon Press, 1911), p. xxi.
14. Holinshed, III, 53.

glad he met with some mischance."[15] What feeling Hal has for his father at the beginning of *Part I* we do not know, because Hal never mentions him; and that lack of reference is in itself significant, for obviously Hal feels no guilt in shirking his royal responsibilities. His excuses are wholly self-regarding; he has to explain to himself why he wastes his time with base companions, but he has no need to justify to himself his absence from his father's side. At the outbreak of rebellion, he does not immediately and remorsefully leap to his father's aid. He jokes with Falstaff about a commodity of maidenheads and then prepares leisurely with the play extempore for his return to the palace and his meeting with his father. When he does face the King, he is not particularly repentant. Coolly he admits to some "wandering," for which he would be pardoned; and though ready enough to falsify men's hopes, he complains that he has been slandered by rumor mongers.

When Glendower and Hotspur meet, fireworks go off and electricity crackles between these opposite poles of personality. When Henry and his son face each other, it is as matched adversaries, very alike in their wariness, their political shrewdness and practicality. No coward at least in his tavern jests, Falstaff pretended to see the characteristic stupidity of Lancastrians in Hal's face. We recognize in Hal more significant familial traits. The man who doffed his bonnet to an oyster wench has a son who carouses with drawers. The father, according to Hotspur, is a king of smiles; the son, according to the drawers, is a king of courtesy. The father banished Exton and then Worcester from the court; the son promises in the play extempore to banish all his tavern comrades. Like his father, Hal knows what majesty is and what it requires. Although he can stoop (or seem to stoop) to lowness, he is as contemptuous of Falstaff's counterfeiting of royalty as Henry is contemptuous of Richard's feeble pretense of kingliness. Father and son are so alike in temperament that the same words come naturally to their lips. When Henry (as Falstaff anticipated) makes a sentimental appeal, Hal answers with his father's words to the Percies: he promises to be more himself. And when Hal returns to the tavern, he rebukes the fibbing Falstaff exactly as Henry had rebuked the fibbing Hotspur: "Art thou not ashamed?"[16] But though Hal can resemble his

15. The linking of poison and Hal's antagonism with his father occurs again in Hal's speech when he rescues his father at Shrewsbury. If he wanted his father dead, Hal says, he could have "let alone / The insulting hand of Douglas over you, / Which would have been as speedy in your end / As all the treacherous potions in the world" (V.iv.53-56).

16. III.ii.184. In this last tavern scene, Hal is already detached from his thieving comrades, a spectator rather than participant in the comedy, which centers on Falstaff's

father in word and manner, he is distant from him as a person. If, as Dover Wilson remarks, "the Prince's attitude is perfect, as it ever is with his father,"[17] it is also chill. He pledges to be a true prince, not a loving son, and he shows little sign of the filial devotion which made Bolingbroke immediately exclaim in *Richard II* that he would not be dishonored in his father's sight.

To be sure, Henry does not win our sympathy as a neglected parent, because he is pitiless in his hectoring, and so deliberate in his attack on Hal that we can scarcely believe the tender emotion that suddenly fills his eyes with tears. His first words are a scathing rebuke, and each line that follows adds insulting accusations. Treating his son as if he were an enemy, he closes with him as he did with the Percies and pursues the theme of Hal's delinquency as tenaciously as he pursued the theme of Mortimer's treachery. Although Henry adopts, as always, a high moral tone and seems genuinely to fear for England's future, his lecture is hardly edifying. He is no Gaunt pleading with Richard to love and cherish his nation. He is a shrewd politician warning the heir apparent how loose behavior lets slip the knots of loyalty. His subject is the getting and keeping of power, the cultivation of political images, and the manipulation of popular emotion. Even as Henry condemns Hal's derelictions, he confesses his own unfealties: how he plucked allegiances, how he stole courtesy from heaven and wrested opinion from the crown. Henry's obtuseness is fascinating in that, on the one hand, he denies that he deliberately sought the crown; on the other hand, he holds up his politic cunning as a model for his son, whom he sees as a scourge that breeds revengement out of his blood. But if Henry will not admit much sense of guilt—he speaks of a "displeasing service" to God—his memory of the past is more honest than that of the Percies, who lament the "sweet rose" Richard and who would forget their eagerness to wipe off the dust that hid the sceptre's gilt. As scornful as ever of the inept king he overthrew, Henry recalls his rise from banished outcast to king as the supreme experience of a life burdened afterward with illness and care, and it is almost with regret that he returns again to the present circumstances of the Percy rebellion and Hal's irresponsibility.

As his father admonishes and reminisces, Hal plays the almost silent prince, confessing little and promising less. He finds it difficult, however, to listen to his father's praise of the glorious Hotspur, and he is unprepared for the

---

relationship with the Hostess. He seems already "older" than Falstaff, whose childishness he humors, as again at Shrewsbury.

17. *Fortunes of Falstaff,* p. 64.

crowning accusation that he is a coward and probable traitor, who "through vassal fear, / Base inclination, and the start of spleen," might fight against the King

>   under Percy's pay,
> To dog his heels and curtsy at his frowns,
> To show how much thou art degenerate.   (III.ii.124-28)

Does Henry mistake his son? Or does he know precisely how to test Hal's mettle and how to expose the princely self hid behind the cloak of loose behavior? Although Hal wanted to incur no debts of obligation, he responds to his father's words with a furious and boasting pledge:

> Do not think so. You shall not find it so.
> And God forgive them that so much have sway'd
> Your Majesty's good thoughts away from me!
> I will redeem all this on Percy's head
> And, in the closing of some glorious day,
> Be bold to tell you that I am your son,
> When I will wear a garment all of blood,
> And stain my favours in a bloody mask, . . .
> Percy is but my factor, good my lord,
> To engross up glorious deeds on my behalf;
> And I will call him to so strict account
> That he shall render every glory up,
> Yea, even the slightest worship of his time,
> Or I will tear the reckoning from his heart.
> This in the name of God I promise here,
> The which if he be pleas'd I shall perform.   (III.ii.129-54)

Whatever doubts Henry may have about Hal's filial affection, he no longer doubts his princeliness, for he hears in Hal's lines an echo of his own youthful pride and will. The father who would not be dishonored in his father's sight hears his son promise that he will prove his right "to tell you that I am your son." The father who spoke of tearing out the "slavish motion" of his tongue hears his son promise to tear the reckoning of honor out of Hotspur's heart. Satisfied with what he has found in Hal, Henry grants him a princely role in the struggle against the rebels.

What an extraordinary version this scene is of the prodigal's return. There is no tender emotion, no warm embraces, no tears—or at least, none that are wholly above suspicion. The father does not welcome his son back into the bosom of the family; the king forms a political alliance and strikes a grim bargain with his heir: "A hundred thousand rebels die in this." We might, I suppose, rejoice in Hal's noble anger or in his choice of duty, except that what we hear in his words is the cry of enraged ego, not the voice of princely dedication. Or rather what we hear is a primitive and furious determination to bathe his wounded reputation in Hotspur's lifeblood. Just as Hotspur would make Henry his scapegoat, Hal would make Hotspur a bleeding sacrifice to his good name and find his "clearness" in a grisly baptism. There is not one thought more of England's good in Hal's lines than in Hotspur's; his only concern is his stained reputation, which he intends to redeem in the most expeditious way possible. Like a clever speculator, he will not labor in the vineyards of glory, but by using Hotspur as his factor, he expects to win a commodity of good names—to make a killing at Shrewsbury.

When Hotspur dreams of plucking honor from the pale-faced moon, and Hal promises to tear its reckoning out of Hotspur's heart, one agrees with Falstaff that it is madness to jeopardize life or limb for mere scutcheons or for the bubble reputation. Sensible and urbane like Falstaff, we prefer an inglorious life to a glorious death, and we share his skepticism about the mindless and fanatical dedications for which thousands have bled. At the same time, however, we are not inclined to take his catechism to heart, for even as we enjoy Falstaff's frankness, we know that his cynicism cheapens every thing it touches. We know that once we accept the legitimacy of the question, "What good will it do you after you are dead?" we must be prepared to abandon all that we value—love, friendship, truth, honesty, and justice. And if we must choose, we may prefer the risk of fanaticism to the safety of so coarse and mean-spirited an assessment of values.

Far more devastating than Falstaff's catechism is the critique of honor implied by Shakespeare's portrayal of characters like Hotspur, Tybalt, Mercutio, Laertes, Troilus, and Coriolanus. But, while Shakespeare exposes in play after play the rashness and blindness of "honorable" acts, he returns again and again to the theme of honor, not ready to deny its meaning or its importance as a guide to conduct. Knowing how often cautious self-interest is the rule of our lives, he could appreciate the beauty of quixotic dedications, and though unwilling to make the service of honor greater than the god, he could see the necessity for standing on principle, for finding a quarrel in a straw when honor's at stake. To Falstaff it would be absurd for a man to sacrifice his life, his dearest possession, for any cause; but the characters we most cherish in Shakespeare's plays are those who do not think their life their dearest possession. In life as in literature, sublimity and moderation rarely touch hands. We treasure the legend of the dying Sidney, who in extreme thirst gave

up a precious cup of water to a common soldier. We find less admirable the
gesture he made of removing his leg armor that cost him his life. But the legend
of his death is all of a piece: it speaks of the chivalric carelessness of self that
makes possible a supreme generosity.

While Shakespeare no doubt believed in moderation, he was not ready to
reason out the need for love and devotion or to measure the proper amounts of
each in the conduct of a Desdemona or a Kent or a Hal. Thus, attempts to
square Shakespeare's moral imagination with an Aristotelian rule produce
interpretations that are simplistic as well as overly schematic. It is not the
reasonableness of Hal's behavior at Shrewsbury we admire but the absoluteness
of his commitment to his father's cause and his willingness to risk all for it.
And though Hotspur needed a greater measure of reason in his life, he needed
even more a cause worthy of his nobility. It is as inadequate to say that
Hotspur is "too zealous" in his pursuit of honor as it is to say that Angelo is "too
zealous" in his pursuit of rectitude.[18] Where Angelo is too coldly self-righteous
and too legalistic in his thinking to know what virtue really is, Hotspur is too
self-absorbed and immature to know what honor truly requires. A Mars in
swaddling clothes, an infant warrior, a child of honor, he is from first to last
tutored by Worcester in the manners of a rebel, and what he learns does not
prepare him for the testing at Shrewsbury. He fails to meet the challenge of
leadership, not because he is less at the end of the play than he was at the
beginning, but because he is too much the same. When the times call for
self-discipline and caution, he is still willful, impetuous, and overconfident—as
ready to bait his ally Glendower as he was to slight the popinjay who came to
demand his prisoners after Holmedon. He must express his irritation at
Glendower's fantasies and insist upon his "plainness" even though it endangers
his cause. One delights in a man so indifferent to the spoils of civil war that he
forgets the map on which they are marked. Yet Hotspur is indifferent also to the
crass motives of his allies, who publish their patriotic motives while they secretly
prepare to dismember England. Or perhaps Hotspur is conscious enough of the
ugliness of their purpose to call attention to the purity of his own motive by
joking about altering the channel of the Trent. Thus, while Hotspur is nobler than
his allies, he stoops to their purposes; and it is hard to say who is more dangerous:
the opportunists who strictly calculate the profit of rebellion or the hot-tempered
idealist who will sacrifice thousands at the altar of his reputation?

If we do not see how honor, truth, and courage are weighed in the balance at

18. Shakespeare realized that men who are "excessive" in their virtue are very likely
deficient in human sympathy and self-knowledge. His psychological insights consistently
carry him beyond schematic moral formulations.

Shrewsbury, we may complain that the ending of *Part I* reduces complex issues to brute simplicities: How do we know the true prince? by his strong right arm and death-dealing sword. How do we measure honor? the winner, as Hal predicted, takes all. We have only to think back to the representation of Bosworth Field in *Richard III* to realize how much the emphasis seems to be placed on the superficial excitement of war in the scenes of Shrewsbury. Instead of the spiritual and psychological drama of Richard's ghost-haunted dreams, Shakespeare allows us in the last scenes of *Part I* a series of excursions and alarums embellished with the comedy of Falstaff's encounter with Douglas. We know what is decided at Bosworth because the moral oppositions there are absolute: hope stands against despair; compassion and brotherhood triumph over enmity and divisive hatreds. The moral oppositions at Shrews-bury are less clearly defined because Henry and his antagonist Worcester seem matched in temperaments and postures. Both protest their care for England and their reluctance to fight. Just as Henry forever insists that he did not seek the crown, Worcester insists that he did not seek rebellion, and though his pose of injured innocence is not convincing, neither is Henry's pose of sorrowing disappointment. When Worcester and Hotspur declare the wrongs that the Percies have suffered, they remind us yet again of the dubieties of Henry's motives and character. Like Falstaff, Henry knows when to promise and when to pay—he even knows, like Falstaff, when to forgive those who remind him of his unpaid debts.[19]

One does not have to be as politic as Worcester to doubt that Henry, who would not ransom Mortimer, would not honor the fair terms of peace he offers the rebels. The judicious Daniel, for example, was convinced that Henry could not possibly have kept his word.[20] But it is one thing to speculate about Henry's possible duplicity; it is another thing to see Worcester's betrayal of Hotspur at Shrewsbury. Sick though the King may be in body (and in soul), the rebel cause is sicker still, infected with opportunistic motives, vainglory, and falsehood. Thousands more are willing to defend Henry's right than to oppose him, and his cause is, in a very literal sense, the nation's, for a rebel

19. There is an amusing parallel between Falstaff's handling of the Hostess in the last tavern scene (III.iii) and Henry's handling of Worcester at Shrewsbury. Falstaff never denies that he owes money to the Hostess, which he will not pay, but he forgives her for allowing his pocket to be picked in the tavern. In somewhat the same manner, Henry is willing to forgive Worcester for mentioning the debt of gratitude that he owes the Percies, though he never admits that the debt is real.

20. According to Daniel (*Civil Wars,* p. 163), Henry's fears prompted him to propose terms to the rebels: "Yet, sure, hee could not meane t'have peace with those, / Who did in that supreame degree offend."

victory will mean the dismemberment of England. Although Hotspur lends to his side the glow of his personal chivalry, he does not rise above the baser element of his allies' treachery; and though he is robbed by Worcester of a last opportunity to choose an honorable peace, he has no inclination to make terms with the King he bitterly mistrusts. Betrayed by scheming politicians as Talbot was, he is no Talbot at the last, for though he speaks facilely of dying before the battle, his dying words reveal that he was not prepared to sacrifice all—his youth and his life—for his cause.

Naively overconfident, Hotspur had fumed at a dish of skim milk who warned him by letter that his purpose was dangerous and his friends uncertain. At Shrewsbury, however, he finds, not the promised allies, but letters and expressions of regret from the kinsmen who should be at his side. Lied to by Worcester, who fears Henry's motives, Hotspur also lies to himself about the odds of battle because he will not confess the hopelessness of his cause. Even as Worcester is untrue to him, he is untrue to the soldiers he leads into battle to line the enterprise of his personal glory. For one moment Hotspur, who demands truth from everyone else, admits the truth to himself: that his father's "sickness" infects the lifeblood of their enterprise. Immediately afterward this candor gives way to specious arguments. Before, he would not hear one word of caution; now, parodying Worcester's passion for security, he pretends to find safety in the very recklessness of the venture:

> Were it good
> To set the exact wealth of all our states
> All at one cast? to set so rich a main
> On the nice hazard of one doubtful hour?
> It were not good; for therein should we read
> The very bottom and the soul of hope,
> The very list, the very utmost bound
> Of all our fortunes.   (IV.i.45-52)

This sham of sober discretion turns inside out Hotspur's earlier hyperbole of daring. At first he wished to rescue drowned honor from unfathomable oceans; now he dares not plumb the bottom of hope. Thus, as Hal reaches up toward the ideal of courtesy, Hotspur stoops to the idiom of the tavern gambler; he talks glibly of the cast and the hazard of "our states," forgetting that the real stakes are the lives of thousands of men.

Of course, chance plays its part in men's affairs. Had Hotspur won at Shrewsbury the kind of victory against enormous odds that Harry will win at Agincourt, history would have recorded his "folly" as magnificent soldiership.

Yet it is not chance that determines the victory at Agincourt or the defeat at Shrewsbury. Harry triumphs because he can inspire his band of brothers. Hotspur loses because he views the battlefield as an arena of personal glory. The "happy few" at Shrewsbury are Blunt, Stafford, Hal, and John, not Hotspur, Douglas, Worcester, and Vernon. And, where Hal fights for the sake of his family, Hotspur, deserted by his father and his brother-in-law Mortimer, can find no dedication except to the primitive excitement of war:

> They come like sacrifices in their trim,
> And to the fire-ey'd maid of smoky war
> All hot and bleeding will we offer them;
> The mailed Mars shall on his altar sit
> Up to the ears in blood.   (IV.i.113-17)

Where Hotspur cannot wait to fight, Falstaff would be content to make the tavern his drum. Is he a coward? The answer depends upon how heroic we think fat old men ought to be. Knowing that he could not possibly stand up to the mighty Douglas, Falstaff plays dead at Shrewsbury even as he ran from Hal and Poins at Gadshill. But Douglas too believes that discretion can be the better part of valor, because he runs from the field after Hotspur is killed. To see how courage and honor are defined at Shrewsbury, we must look beyond deceptive appearances, for men prove their truth as well as their falseness there by lying. Several die because they pretend to be the King, and one survives as a sham hero because he successfully mimics a corpse. Despite his gross impostures, Falstaff is less counterfeit a hero than is Worcester, who betrays Hotspur because he fears Henry and who dares battle at hopeless odds because he cannot accept the risk of peace.

It is often suggested that Falstaff has to die because his presence and ironic wit would have mocked the famous victory celebrated in *Henry V*. Yet Falstaff can be allowed his full say at Shrewsbury because nothing that he says can persuade us that Blunt's truth and courage are meaningless. If men fought only for personal glory, Falstaff's cynicism would be the only reasonable view of honor. But when loyal men like Blunt lay down their lives for the sake of their country, we must agree with Falstaff that there *is* honor for you. We can cheapen Blunt's sacrifice by imagining him the dupe of a politic king who dresses many decoys "in his coats" at Shrewsbury.[21] To do so, however, we

---

21. Holinshed reports without comment the fact that Douglas killed Blunt and three others "apparelled in the kings sute and clothing" (III, 26). He does, however, stress the "high manhood" of the King, who "did that daie manie a noble feat of armes, for as it is

have to ignore the scenes which Shakespeare wrote in which Blunt's disguise is an emblem of his truth, not of Henry's policy. Quite obviously the King does not seek to avoid the danger of battle and he readily admits his identity to Douglas.[22] Blunt, moreover, speaks a figurative truth when he says that he is the King, because his loyalty, multiplied a thousandfold, makes the King's Body a mighty host which Douglas and Hotspur cannot kill. It is because the King and his subjects are one—because the blood of thousands like Blunt and Stafford flourishes in Henry's cheeks—that he can crush the rebel army. Thus, even though Shrewsbury does not bring an end to civil war, it leaves no doubt of Henry's right as king. For if Worcester cannot tell the present from the past, the royal Henry from the outlawed Bolingbroke, we can see the difference between the man who, with Worcester's aid, seized Richard's crown and the aging monarch, burdened with kingly cares, who preserves the unity of England at Shrewsbury. More important still, we can see the difference between the Henry who allows the son he mistrusts to prove his loyalty in battle and the Worcester who cannot trust or keep faith with friend or foe. Having doomed himself and his allies by his politic scheming, he patiently embraces his "unavoidable" fortune and goes to the block oblivious to the irony of his excuse that he did all for his safety.

Like Worcester, Falstaff can learn nothing from his experience at Shrewsbury. He may feel a certain contemptuous pity for the poor wretches he led to be peppered, but he can not be moved by the anguish or the nobility of men's deaths on the battlefield. We know Falstaff too well by this time to be surprised by his self-concern, and we do not expect (or demand) any act of heroism from him. We do not anticipate, however, the ugliness of his encounter with Hotspur's corpse, where for the first time in the play he becomes something of a buffoon, an object of uncomfortable and unpleasant laughter. In the tavern he was an honest liar who made a joke out of heroism by his preposterous brags. On the battlefield, however, he would counterfeit the hero in earnest; and, by robbing Hal of his glory, he would turn Hotspur's corpse into a commodity of good names. Like a greedy, fibbing child he demands his

---

written, he slue that daie with his owne hands, six and thirtie persons of his enimies." What a perversion of recorded fact it would have been for Shakespeare to have made Henry's conduct at Shrewsbury seem cowardly! Daniel, with his usual circumspection, judges that Henry "divided" his person into four parts at Shrewsbury, "to be lesse knowne, and yet known every where," intending thereby "His safetie, and his subiects better care" (*Civil Wars*, p. 166).

22. Interpreting the symbolism of Blunt's disguise differently, Traversi reaches an opposite conclusion: "A royalty that needs to disguise itself behind a 'wardrobe' is something less than truly royal" (*From Richard II to Henry V*, p. 101).

reward, and like a greedy child he is humored by Hal, who will lie for him—if a lie will do Falstaff grace.

It is such gracious lies which leave no doubt of Hal's truth and nobility. Determined to cleanse his stained reputation in Hotspur's blood, he finds instead the baptism of his own streaming wounds and refuses to leave the field, not because he hungers for glory but because he feels an overwhelming debt of obligation to the brave men who have died for his father's sake. He does not simply prove himself a better warrior than Hotspur. He triumphs for a time over the passion for honor which made him akin to Hotspur. After Shrewsbury, as again after Agincourt, he is supremely at ease with himself, freed from the need to prove and to justify himself. The honor he has won cannot be robbed from him by Falstaff because it does not depend on the world's opinion or on such scutcheons as the body of his enemy.

At Shrewsbury (as in sixteenth-century England) the national interest prevails over lesser alliances, the power of the state over feudal attachments and regional antagonisms. In fact, before long in the tetralogy, Welshmen and Scots, England's enemies in *Part I*, will take their place among the happy few who win a magnificent "English" victory at Agincourt. But, even as Shrewsbury presages a new political era, it also reaffirms a very ancient code of values, for Hal's courage and devotion and his willingness to share the glory of the day exemplify what is noblest in the traditions of chivalry. Once he threatened to wear a whore's token in a joust; now he respectfully performs the rites of courtesy. He covers Hotspur's mangled face with his own favor, and he asks for the release of Douglas, not as Worcester did to gain a political ally, but to honor a valiant foe.

In acknowledging the beauty of the chivalric ideal, Shakespeare does not ignore the cost of the honor won at Shrewsbury. He shows the deaths of Blunt and Hotspur and he tells through Falstaff of the "peppering" of ordinary soldiers who either fill the pits at Shrewsbury or will be found begging for alms at town's end. The mingling of moods in the last scene of *Part I* recalls the closing of *Richard II*, in which Henry also gives harsh sentence and generous pardon. Like the henchman Exton, the accomplice Worcester is condemned; like the courageous Carlisle, the heroic Douglas is set free. Never again will rebellion pose so great a threat to Henry's rule, but one suspects at this point that he will more easily destroy his enemies than come to terms with his own flesh and blood. For while the battlefield has brought the royal family together, it has also exposed the depths of Henry's suspicion of his son. When Hal rescued his father from Douglas, Henry seemed almost surprised that Hal placed some value ("some tender") on his life. Hal, in turn, exclaimed that "they did me too much injury / That ever said I heark'ned for your death" (V.iv.51-52). Even though he proves his loyalty by saving his father's life at Shrewsbury, Hal will not long remain by his father's side, and because of his behavior he will have to prove again in *Part II* that he does not wish his father's death.

7. HENRY IV PART II

If *Henry IV Part I* did not exist it would be easy enough to appreciate the artistic achievement of *Henry IV Part II*. But when *Part II* is placed alongside *Part I,* it seems a lackluster sequel, one that repeats the material of its predecessor and that amplifies Falstaff's part to satisfy the appetite of Elizabethan audiences for "fat meat." Even those, like Dover Wilson and Tillyard, who defend *Part II* as essential to the historical and moral design of the second tetralogy, are not ready to grant its individual artistic character and integrity, because they insist that it is a continuation of *Part I*—the second half of the drama of Hal's redemption supposedly left uncompleted at the close of the earlier play. Tillyard writes:

> The structure of the two parts is indeed very similar. In the first part the Prince (who, one knows, will soon be king) is tested in the military or chivalric vitues. He has to choose, Morality-fashion, between Sloth or Vanity, to which he is drawn by his bad companions, and Chivalry, to which he is drawn by his father and his brothers. . . . [In *Part II*] again he is tested, but in the civil virtues. He has to choose, Morality-fashion, between disorder or misrule, to which he is drawn by his bad companions, and Order or Justice (the supreme kingly virtue) to which he is drawn by his father and by his father's deputy the Lord Chief Justice.[1]

It is difficult, however, to understand how Hal's acceptance of Justice can be a central concern in *Part II,* when his part in the plot is minimal before the fourth act and when there is not the slightest intimation in his character of any

---

1. *History Plays,* p. 265. See also Dover Wilson's argument that the two parts of *Henry IV* are one play in his introduction to the new Cambridge edition of *Henry IV Part I* (Cambridge: Cambridge Univ. Press, 1964), pp. vii-xiii.

bent toward lawlessness. Not once does it seem even remotely possible that he might be misled by his bad companions, for he openly expresses his disgust for Poins and treats Falstaff in about the same way he had treated Francis. However "unfinished" the characterization of Hal may be in *Part I*, all doubts about his princeliness are erased at Shrewsbury; and even before Shrewsbury there are hints that his relation with Falstaff will not long continue. Pleading that *Part I* is incomplete because it does not present the whole story of Hal's "redemption" is rather like arguing that *Richard III* is incomplete because it does not document the redemption of England under Henry Tudor. Although Shakespeare's art is long, English history is longer still, and there is little advantage in defending *Part II* by compromising the artistic unity of *Part I*.

Much of the scholarly argument over the relation of *Part II* to *Part I* is merely theoretical because it depends upon conjectures about Shakespeare's "original" intentions and methods of composition.[2] Although again and again lines in one History Play seem clearly to anticipate or foreshadow events in succeeding plays, we cannot really distinguish after the fact between Shakespeare's deliberate calculations and his brilliant improvisations. It is reasonable to assume that after the success of the first tetralogy, he had sketched out in his mind a plan for the second tetralogy even before he began to compose *Richard II*. But it is also obvious that he did not follow a wholly preconceived design in the second tetralogy, because though he promises in the Epilogue to *Part II* that there will be more of Falstaff, the fat old knight does not appear in *Henry V*. How many other changes of plan and intention he made in the second tetralogy is not known, but one may guess that his artistic ideas and purposes altered as his powers matured, as he capitalized on the happy accidents of his inspiration or responded to the enthusiasms of his audiences. To the extent that the second tetralogy appears an artistic unity, it also seems to unfold a premeditated design; yet its plays do not fit together in a perfectly coherent and seamless way, because there are abrupt and unanticipated shifts of mood from one play to the next. The final sorrowful moments of *Richard II* lead us to expect that the calamities prophesied by Richard and Carlisle will be the subject matter of succeeding plays, but despite these ominous forebodings, comedy prevails and chivalry triumphs in *Henry IV Part I*. As *Part I* ends, the future of England seems secure and the spirit of tragedy exorcised, but there is a sudden darkening of mood as *Part II* begins.

Those who wish to prove that Shakespeare, for want of new material or

2. See, for example, Harold Jenkins, *The Structural Problem in Shakespeare's Henry the Fourth* (London: Methuen, 1956).

inspiration, imitates *Part I* in *Part II* can cite many similarities in the comic scenes, characterizations, plotting, and themes of the two plays.[3] If *Part II* fails to delight us, however, it is not because Shakespeare attempts unsuccessfully to recapture in it the gaiety and exuberance of *Part I*. The Prologue to *Part II,* delivered by Rumor "painted full of tongues," invites us to behold an anxiety-ridden scene, and as soon as Falstaff enters without Hal, it is evident that he has "changed" and that the comic spirit of the Boar's Head now depends more on hostility and denigration than on the pleasure of good company. Is it not curious that Shakespeare, seeking to exploit the popularity of Falstaff with his audiences, should make him less attractive than before? And is it not more puzzling still that he should try to please the groundlings with a play which even committed professional scholars declare "unpleasant" in tone and subject matter? Where *Part I* is a brilliant and vigorous composition, rich in contrasts and glowing in color, *Part II* is a study in sepia, a pervasively somber and shadowed monochrome. Where *Part I* is alive with youthful energy, idealism, and optimism, *Part II* is heavy with the disillusion and debilitation of age, and it lays bare in scene after scene the ugly erosion of principle in the latter years of Henry's reign. At Shrewsbury men of honor and chivalry beat back the rebel cause, but it is politic fraud and sanctimony that secure the King's victory at Gaultree Forest. Once the doors of the tavern could be clapped home and the sheriff put off; now Fang and Snare enter with a warrant for Falstaff's arrest, even as later beadles will seize on Mistress Quickly and Doll Tearsheet. Once the tavern was a refuge from a time-ridden world, but now an aging Falstaff brings into the Boar's Head the mercenary instincts and cynical calculations of the rebel leaders. Only the bitter dregs remain of the wine of friendship that flowed in *Part I*. Falstaff speaks contemptuously of his Page, Bardolf, and Shallow; Hal insults Falstaff and Poins, and the one time that Hal and Falstaff meet in the tavern does not make us wish they were together more often.

Since Falstaff is seen with Hal only once before he is cast off, it is extraordinary that the rejection scene should be the penultimate moment of the plot. It is no less extraordinary that Henry's deathbed quarrel and reconciliation with Hal should be a climactic moment of the dramatic action when father and son never meet before that moment. The isolation of characters from one another is very deliberate in the plotting of *Part II.*

3. See, for example, the comparison of the order of historical and comic scenes in the two parts of *Henry IV* by M. A. Shaaber in "The Unity of *Henry IV*," *Joseph Quincy Adams Memorial Studies* (Washington, D.C.: Folger Library, 1948), pp. 217-27.

Although the first scene suggests that Northumberland will play a major role in the historical action, his path turns out to be an oblique tangent from the main course of events. The Lord Chief Justice wends an even more solitary way through the play until he is "adopted" by Hal in the last act. He bumps into Falstaff and the Hostess here, John and King Harry there, but until the last scene he does not so much enter the plot as move through its interstitial spaces. For the first three acts, Hal's role runs parallel to the main course of events but is not a part of it; Henry, though the nominal protagonist, does not enter the play until the third act, and, like Hal, he has no part in the action against the rebels. Thus, while the dramatic action of *Part II* moves across a large geographical landscape, the roles which the characters play seem more confined in scope and significance and more self-enclosed than in *Part I*.[4]

Because the characterizations of *Part I* are closely interrelated—paired, opposed, and juxtaposed to one another—it is almost impossible to isolate our impression of Hal from our impression of Falstaff, Henry, and Hotspur. In *Part II*, however, Hal and most of the other characters are presented as solitary figures. Despising the company they keep, Falstaff and Hal are alone even when they are with Bardolf, Poins, or Shallow. Similarly, Northumberland is isolated in the bosom of his family because he finds there the scorn of his daughter-in-law Kate, who accuses him of deserting Hotspur at Shrewsbury. The dying Henry is lonely in a different way, absorbed in thoughts of his past and oppressed by the unending turmoil of his reign. Although treachery and falsehood soiled the rebel enterprise in *Part I*, the King's men proved their loyalty and devotion at Shrewsbury and there were delightful moments of camaraderie in the Boar's Head. In *Part II*, however, the disintegration of relationships seems universal: in the comic scenes Falstaff preys on old acquaintances; on the battlefield the rebels, deserted once again by Northumberland, are deceived by John's pledges of amity; and in the palace the King awakens to find his crown stolen from his pillow by his son and heir. The final scene of *Part I* showed the royal family united by the crisis of the rebellion. The last scene of *Part II* portrays the final dissolution of the bond between the King and his former companions.

A play in which the central characters rarely meet and interact may well strike an audience as a series of episodes and vignettes rather than as a unified dramatic action. Indeed, it is difficult to say just what the dramatic action of

4. This is true even of Falstaff, whose speaking part is enlarged in *Part II* but who plays a less significant role in the historical drama because he is no longer the confidant and "surrogate father" of the Prince.

Part II is, because there is no strongly marked direction in the unfolding events and no point like Shrewsbury toward which all lines of plot inevitably converge. The shape of history in *Part I* was determined by the actions of Henry, Worcester, Hal, and Hotspur. In *Part II*, however, the dynamic force of history is not the human will to action but rather the relentless movement of time which carries men onward to their ultimate destiny. Because again and again the hopes and plans of the characters are frustrated, they seem unable to control their destinities. They belong to history but they do not "make it."

Of course, the end of a regime is not a time for bold new enterprises. It is a time for waiting, a period of anxious transition and uncertainty. While the King lies deathly ill, rumors multiply and men ruminate about the past or ponder what lies ahead under the untried heir. But the somber mood of *Part II*, which is created by the pervasive thematic emphasis on weariness, age, and illness, seems not so much an expression of the unsettled political situation of England as an expression of the malaise of the characters' lives. It is curious that the motif of illness predominates only in *Part II*, when the body politic was more diseased under Richard II and his plundering sycophants, and more fevered when the Percy alliance with Glendower and Douglas threatened its very continuance. It may be that in *Part II* Shakespeare speaks not about a particular historical situation, but about unchanging human realities; yet I do not think that *Part II* expresses a disillusioned awareness of human shallowness and helplessness. What it expresses is the opportunistic cynicism and the facile rationalizations of men who prefer to think themselves the subjects of time. When Gaunt spoke of Richard lying in the deathbed of his land, he spoke in figures; he employed a traditional metaphor to prophesy the probable consequences of Richard's misconduct as king. When York, Westmoreland, Henry, and Warwick speak in *Part II* of the sickness of the state or of the times, their "conceit" is more literally intended, for they would have us believe that nations are subject to distempers that must be physicked by purges and bleedings. They speak of the physiology of the body politic as if it were an entity apart from those who comprise it and subject to necessities which men can merely acknowledge and accept.

If we assume that Warwick and York speak for Shakespeare, and that the iterated imagery and the recurrent themes and motifs of *Part II* communicate an authorial vision, then we may, like Traversi, speak of Shakespeare's portrait of anarchy and impotence or his sense of the "corruption of human values by time and ill living."[5] But this is to ignore the dramatic circumstances and ironic

5. *From Richard II to Henry V*, pp. 108, 129, 135-36.

tonalities of the speeches in *Part II;* worse still, it is to take the characters of the plays at their own very dubious word. After all, much of the sickness of the times is as feigned as Bullcalf's cold or as psychosomatic as Northumberland's "crafty-sickness." Shall we take seriously Northumberland's invocation of apocalyptic disorder in the opening scene (which Traversi calls a "vision of universal chaos")[6] when Northumberland's own follower comments on the "strained" quality of his passion? Hearing Northumberland rant, we strongly suspect that his rage for disorder will come to nought because he is the Pistol of rebellion, histrionic in his gestures, melodramatic in his language, and cowardly in his purposes—no more a threat to the security of England than is the drunken Falstaff who proclaims to his followers in Act V that the laws of England are at his commandment.

Instead of seeing the characters of *Part II* as so many choric spokesmen for Shakespeare's vision of our human predicament, we should see them as men o' the times who are either determined to make a commodity out of the political diseases they lament or determined to counter such cynicism with fraud and ruthlessness. None are so helpless in *Part II* as those who will not act; none are so blind as those who will not see; none are so disillusioned as those who refused in earlier years to anticipate the consequences of their deeds. Just as the hunger for spoils is the father to the rebels' thought that their demands must be met at Gaultree Forest, so also the need for money is father to Falstaff's delusion that King Harry is sick with longing to see him. What is appalling is not the shallowness and blindness of the characters in *Part II* but rather the clarity of their pitiless calculations. Although rumors multiply in uncertain times, men as clever as Northumberland are not duped by them. He will not credit the false reports of Hotspur's triumph at Shrewsbury, because he knows all too well what the outcome of that battle had to be. He had, as Morton remarks, summed the account of chance; he had weighed the possibilities for profit and loss before he bade his son, his only child, "go forth" to fight against impossible odds. Men must accept the circumstances of their existence: they must grow old, they cannot choose but grow old. But must they also grow false to one another? Must Northumberland speculate with Hotspur's life? Must Falstaff prey on the Hostess and Shallow, and must York exploit the misery of a strife-torn age? Must rebellion be put down by treachery and massacre? The necessities of Gaultree Forest lie in the natures of John, Westmoreland, and York, not in the circumstances of Henry's reign or in the "human condition."

6. *From Richard II to Henry V,* p. 111.

Rebellion is not a desperate disease in *Part II* that requires desperate cures. Once again Northumberland proves more dangerous to his allies than to the King; and the rebels who do come to Gaultree Forest can be hoodwinked because they have no will to fight: they would much rather scrape Richard's blood off Pomfret's stones than risk their own. Sensible businessmen who plan to gain a handsome profit without dangerous speculation, they want to blackmail the King, not dethrone him, and they are certain that he will bargain with them because they calculate that he is too weak to do otherwise. Despising Hotspur's recklessness, they would construct the edifice of rebellion soundly, using the double surety of York's religious position as their foundation, but they meet their match in a prince who is capable of greater sanctimony and sharper practice. The opposing generals at Gaultree Forest are not heroic leaders. They are the anti-heroes of a time when gallantry exists only in memory,[7] when the only magnanimous view is Feeble's—that a man can die but once—and the only moment of chivalry is Falstaff's spirited defense of Doll's honor against the base insinuations and threats of Pistol.

Feeble's heroism and Falstaff's gallantry are touching as well as absurd and important to the sense in the play of the poignancy of individual lives. We know in *Part II* how difficult the problem of political order is because we see how fragile human relations are—how sons disregard fathers or fathers betray sons, and how friends use one another. The generations passed in the earlier History Plays—men lived and died—but only in the second tetralogy do men actually grow old, and only in *Henry IV Part II* is there the poignancy of age with its attendant loss of vitality, optimism, and personal ties. Only in *Part II* do we witness the loneliness of men who find themselves at the last without love or friendship, honor or trust. Even as the scenes of *Part I* demonstrate that great men have personal lives, the scenes of *Part II* reveal that ultimately all lives are "personal"—that the King is but a man who, despite his high estate, lives day by day, sleepless night by sleepless night.

Like Northumberland, who urges Kate to cease lamenting "ancient oversights," Henry would find himself not guilty of wrongdoing, but he is forced to admit that he has frighted sleep. Once he could hold up his political success as a model for Hal to follow, and he could relive in memory the excitement of his triumph over the incompetent Richard, but now he shudders at the memory of the past. Although he lives to see rebellion cooled and the crown safely in the possession of his heir, he has the taste of ashes in his mouth. He

7. That memory, interestingly enough, is not of Hal's gests at Shrewsbury but of Hotspur's shining gallantry, which is lovingly recalled by his wife (II.iii.18-32).

knows the vanity of his ambition and the failure of his relationships with his nearest kin and closest allies. But though experience has lengthened Henry's perspective and sorrow has lent him poetic eloquence, he is too biased to serve as Shakespeare's chorus. Amply warned by York, Carlisle, and Richard II of the disorders that would follow his assumption of the throne, Henry now protests in his memorable speech about the "revolution of the times" that he could not anticipate the consequences of his acts. Refusing still to admit that his ambition reached above his head, he recalls that necessity so bowed the state that he and greatness were compelled to kiss. But who can accept Henry's disclaimers when his every thought is focused on the exercise of power? Just as Warwick can demonstrate the logic of Northumberland's career of treachery, an audience can trace the consistency of Henry's conduct up to and including his dying advice to Hal to busy giddy minds with foreign wars.

While Shakespeare gives full scope in the History Plays to the workings of chance and accident, he does not, like the authors of *The Mirror for Magistrates*, exclaim against Fortune or Mutability. Knowing that life is process and history a panorama of endless change, he does not envision the quest for order as a search for an unchanging status quo; he suggests in *Henry IV Part II* that renewal can be as necessary in the lives of nations as in the lives of men, and that change may be needed to erase embittered memories and to allow men to free themselves from the past that threatens to repeat itself in endlessly recurring spasms of bloodshed. Although Shrewsbury destroyed one rebel army, another waits at Gaultree Forest; and if the rebels fail again, Mowbray predicts, there will be others to take their place. Once again at Gaultree Forest as at Shrewsbury, the rebels find cold letters from Northumberland, and once again the opposing sides parlay before the battle. As suave in his justification of the oversights of the regime as York is in his justification of revolt, Westmoreland is seconded by John, who sneers at York's show of sincerity—his "counterfeited zeal of God"— and then adopts his own sanctimonious pose. Although bound by Christian principle to condemn the sin and not the sinner, John allows the rebels their extorted terms and then hangs them. It does not bother him that he promised the rebels amity and love "upon my soul," because he looks on his offer of peace as an ingeniously equivocal business contract which the rebels have foolishly accepted at face value. And when this chicane enables him to massacre them, he offers up the victory to God.

What can men count on when princes' vows are cheap as dicers' oaths? What can men build on when trust is laughed at as shallowness and folly? The answer is that the land abides, the countryside and its people endure, uncorrupted by the struggle for power that makes necessities of treachery. Immediately after Henry protests against the "revolution of the times" that mocks men's purposes, Shallow appears to speak of the unchanging certainties of rural life in Gloucestershire, where all is predictable except the price of bullocks and a score of ewes at Stamford Fair. There must be more to life than Shallow's reckonings, more to strive for than a good harvest or a shrewd bargain, because such security allows men to grow dull and complacent. Yet when a cup of wine is a signal for treachery at Gaultree Forest, there is something to be said for Shallow's conviviality; and when withered applejohns are the props in the Boar's Head for heartless jokes, one thinks fondly of the pippins that Shallow serves with a dish of carraways in his orchard.

Like Iden's soliloquy in *Henry VI Part II* and Richmond's prayer at the close of *Richard III*, the scenes in Shallow's orchard recall the peaceful activities that men abandon to engage in the destructive hunt of war. A more ironic employment of the pastoral motif in *Henry IV Part II* are the poetic allusions to the sickening agriculture of war in which women and children are mowed, foes rooted out or harvested, and populations weeded. The allegorical sentences of the Gardeners in *Richard II* made the problem of the state seem simple enough. To preserve order in England, the King had only to "keep all even" by judicious pruning, and to eliminate noisome weeds and parasites. But it is not easy to translate these allegorical sentences into practical policy in *Henry IV Part II* because, as York points out, the King cannot "precisely weed this land," his foes being so "enrooted with his friends" that every act of rigor merely increases the likelihood of future strife. It is not clear, moreover, whether the soil of England must be bled because it is overfertile (too fat with discord) or whether it must be manured because it is too thin and cold—too depleted of hope and idealism.[8] If Falstaff were still the Falstaff of *Part I*, there would be no doubt that his fatness is to be preferred to John's thinness, his indulgence to Lancaster's rigor. But no longer is fatness identified with expansive humor and festive cheer. Now it has a grosser corpulent reality; now it is identified with diseases of oversurfeited appetite which require purging. Although Falstaff's waist (and waste) is as large as ever, it has as little to do with fecundity as does Doll's goodly bulk, which is delivered of a cushion by

8. The thematic antithesis of thinness and fatness is much more complex in *Part II* than in *Part I,* where it defined the difference in temper of Hal and Falstaff. In *Part II,* thinness and fatness, associated also with coldness and heat, allude not only to human temperaments but also to rigor in law, the thin edge of justice, to hardness and mercy, fertility and sterility.

starveling beadles. And though Falstaff dwells contemptuously on Shallow's gauntness, Shallow has fruitful lands and full purses, while Sir John is barren of hope and consumed by the need for money.

Except in his encounters with the Lord Chief Justice, Falstaff is as quick-witted as ever; his humor is less attractive, however, because the glorious self-satisfaction that once splashed over his moments of melancholy has evaporated. Before he was always virtuous enough for his world and envious of no one: even when they abused him, his companions were stout lads, hearts of gold. Now there is a constant edge of irritation and exasperation in his sallies against his Page, Bardolf, Hal, and Shallow. We are not greatly shocked when he again abuses the King's press by extorting money from the likes of Bullcalf. What pains us is that this time Falstaff takes no pleasure in the swindle and shows no sympathy for the wretches he recruits. Once an irrepressible jokester, now he is touchy, resentful of tricks and slights, and as petty in his reckonings and appetites as the next man. Once the nonpareil satirist of the respectable, now he frets about his standing as a gentleman and about the clothes proper to his station.[9]

Perhaps Shakespeare prepares us for the rejection of Falstaff by exposing the seamier side of his life—by dramatizing the whoring and the cheating that before were only alluded to. But I do not think that Shakespeare alters his characterization of Falstaff as an expedient of plot. He presents in *Part II* the old Falstaff degraded by the new circumstances of his life. Even in *Part I* Falstaff's holiday depended on Hal. Even then his freedom from the exigencies of life was conditional, for his saturnalia was financed by Hal, who met all the reckonings, put off the sheriff, and repaid the stolen money. It was Hal's presence that made a hanging offence a harmless prank, even as it was Hal's boyishness that lent credence to Falstaff's charade of eternal youth. Now that the Boar's Head revels are ended, Falstaff's occupation is gone. Without a royal audience to perform for, he turns monologist, and for want of better companions, he confides his schemes and desperations to the audience. Like most unemployed actors, he is something of a rogue and vagabond—someone

9. Wilson notes that Falstaff becomes in *Part II* a ludicrously foppish man-about-town, who worries about his social position and the cut of his clothes (*Fortunes of Falstaff*, pp. 91-2). Wilson does not note, however, that the Hal of *Part II* is no less concerned about his position and about matters of clothing. In the first scene in which Hal appears, he comments at length about Poins's lack of clothing: his several silk stockings, his paucity of shirts, and his "low ebb of linen" (II.ii.18-30). Hal's care for clothing and appearances is equally evident when he comments on his brothers' suits of mourning in V.ii.

who lives as he can without too much concern for the sources of his income. Long before he is officially banished, he is quite literally a social outcast, badly out of pocket, pursued by bailiffs, and harangued by the respectable.

The shabbiness of Falstaff's way of life in *Part II* is emphasized by his encounters with the Lord Chief Justice, who has the dignity of his office and an honorable age. A model of propriety, the Chief Justice would be perfectly suited to lecture Falstaff were it not for the self-righteousness of his manner. He would have Falstaff confess his age and prepare for his end; but though he objects to old men like Falstaff drinking and whoring, he does not object to old men like Falstaff fighting at Gaultree Forest so that the respectable can kiss "my Lady Peace" safely at home. When Falstaff fondles Doll in the Boar's Head tavern, we can laugh at the joke of an aging lecher whose whore unpacks her stock of professional endearments. Or we can hear in Doll's words a touch of affection and sympathy lacking in the homilies of her betters, and we can recognize that she speaks the truth when she tells Falstaff that he is "going to the wars; and whether I shall ever see thee again or no, there is nobody cares" (II.iv.71-3). Although cautioned by the Chief Justice, Prince John, and King Henry the Fifth to prepare for his end, it is only with Doll that Falstaff can face the truth about himself: "I am old, I am old." And it is only from the Hostess that he will receive any measure of Christian charity.

As Falstaff confesses his weariness and age to Doll, Hal and Poins eavesdrop. In *Part I* they disguised themselves in buckram suits to play the jest on Falstaff at Gadshill. Now they disguise themselves as drawers to catch Falstaff in an unguarded moment with Doll. This time, however, Hal's trip to the Boar's Head is a bit of slumming; he does not go to spend an evening with his old companion but to "see Falstaff bestow himself to-night in his true colours," and not be seen. For only a moment does Hal seem willing to match wits with Falstaff as in the old days. What he enjoys now is making Falstaff cringe and plead, "No abuse, Hal o' mine honour! no abuse . . . . No abuse, Hal . . . . No abuse Hal. None, Ned, none."

To see Hal with Poins and Falstaff is not to wonder whether he will be able to reject them but to wonder why (to use his own phrase) he profanes a moment with them when he is so bored by and ashamed of their company. Making no effort to seem the good comrade, he tells Poins that it disgraces him to know his face or remember his name, and he is harsher still with Falstaff, whom he humiliates with words and (so we hear) with blows. Since the tavern has lost its charm for Hal, why does he not return to the palace? Tillyard offers the sentimental hypothesis that Hal avoids the Court because he sees the terrible price the crown has exacted from his father.[10] No evidence in the play, however, suggests that Hal shrinks from the prospect of royal responsibility. His first thoughts in *Part II* are of his princely greatness and he never puts his high destiny far out of mind. No longer will he tolerate any jokes about his royal lineage and so conscious is he of his royal height that he compares his "descension" from prince to prentice to Jove's transformation "from a god to a bull." The Hal who meditates on his majesty in this fashion and without a moment's hesitation plucks the crown from his father's pillow is not overawed by the prospect of rule. What he shrinks from is his father's presence; what he shrugs off is the obligation of filial duty. When Poins asks how he can speak so idly, his father being so sick, Hal replies that his "heart bleeds inwardly" that his father is sick and if it were "meet," he "could be sad, and sad indeed too." To take Hal at his word, is to agree with Traversi that he is "caught in circumstances formerly accepted in levity which oblige him to keep his deepest emotions to himself, making them lie as an undivulged burden at his heart."[11] But to accept Hal's explanation that he hides his inner sorrow lest vulgar men like Poins think him a princely hypocrite is to credit him with an extraordinary sensitivity to base opinion. For he would rather bow before the cynicism of men he despises than comfort the father he loves. He would prefer that his father think him callous than that the rabble sneer at his true affection. He says that he could be sad, but he is not. He could also go directly to his father's side after being reminded that his father is so sick, but he chooses instead to spy on Falstaff at the tavern.

Does the true prince love his father any better than he loves Poins and Falstaff? The dying Henry asserts that Hal loves him not, and nothing in Hal's behavior would lead an audience to disagree. Henry's other sons attend his last hours; Hal manages to arrive at the palace just in time to see his father alive, and no sooner does he sit by his father's bed than his attention is drawn to the crown. When he is convinced immediately afterward that his father is dead, he takes the crown and leaves the stage. Of course an actor playing Hal can with a suppressed sob or two and gestures of silent grief present a Prince overwhelmed with sorrow. But nothing in the text of the scene provides a cue for such pantomimed emotionality. Indeed, to compare the deathbed scene in *Part II* with its analogue in *The Famous Victories* is to see how deliberately

10. *History Plays,* p. 281.
11. *From Richard II to Henry V,* p. 127.

Shakespeare has omitted from Hal's lines the grief and the deeply felt remorse which the Prince expresses in the old play:

Now thrice accursed *Harry*, that hath offended thy father so much, and could not I crave pardon for all. Oh my dying father, curst be the day wherin I was borne, and accursed be the houre wherin I was begotten, but what shal I do? if weeping teares which come too late may suffice the negligence neglected too soone, I wil weepe day and night until the fountaine be drie with weeping.[12]

Although Warwick, who, in the preceding scene was also Hal's apologist, speaks to the awakened Henry of Hal's offstage tears, in Hal's soliloquy there is only the promise that he shall pay for the crown with tears and heavy sorrows of the blood:

> Thy due from me
> Is tears and heavy sorrows of the blood,
> Which nature, love, and filial tenderness
> Shall, O dear father, pay thee plenteously.
> My due from thee is this imperial crown,
> Which, as immediate from thy place and blood,
> Derives itself to me. Lo, where it sits—[*Puts it on.*]
> Which God shall guard; and put the world's whole strength
> Into one giant arm, it shall not force
> This lineal honor from me. This from thee
> Will I to mine leave, as 'tis left to me. [*Exit.*]   (IV.v.37-47)

This is not the outcry of deep sorrow. This is the speech of one deeply aware of the propriety of grief, of the debt of sorrow that must be conscientiously paid. Where the wastrel of *The Famous Victories* knows that belated tears cannot make up for the neglect of his father, Hal thinks the account can be satisfactorily closed. He knows very well how he should feel even as he is acutely aware of how his display of emotion should appear in the eyes of others. Thus, when, dressed in his kingly robes, he meets his brothers, he notes immediately their looks of sorrow, and again promises to grieve: he "will deeply put the fashion on / And wear it in my heart." To say that the fashion of sorrow is another of Hal's disguises would be unfair. One cannot escape the conclusion, however, that grief for Hal is not spontaneous; it is a public gesture and response. If sorrow looks royally, he will wear it. If, on the other hand, a heavy look would make him seem a princely hypocrite to vulgar eyes, he will weep only inwardly.

12. *Famous Victories,* 623-28, in *Narrative and Dramatic Sources of Shakespeare,* IV, 317.

Four times in seven lines of soliloquy in the deathbed scene, the Prince of *The Famous Victories* speaks of his "father." Similarly, Clarence and John in *Part II* speak to the King as "father." Only once in both parts of *Henry IV* does Hal address Henry as "father," and even then he thinks the King may be dead: "My gracious lord! my father!" When Hal is summoned back to the bedchamber to face the King, he resumes his official aloofness. Once again he addresses his father as "my liege" and "your Majesty," declaring himself a loyal subject rather than a loving son. When he kneels before Henry, it is not as a child asking blessing, but as a faithful retainer protesting his "obedience" and "true and duteous spirit." Too much in the sun at court, Hal has preferred the shelter of base contagious clouds in the tavern, and though ready enough to grasp his royal future when his father dies, he hesitates even then to acknowledge his bloodstained ancestry. The first time he appears after the deathbed scene, he adopts the Lord Chief Justice as his foster parent, "as a father to my youth." A self-made prince, he would have the future without the past, the crown without its attendant guilt. Making a scapegoat of Henry who, he declares, has "gone wild into his grave" with Hal's affections, he contrives to be born again with a new mythic paternity—the son of Justice and Good Government.

If Hal is not quite born again when he becomes king, he is artful at dissociating himself from the past which is onmipresent in the lines and scenes of *Part II* and in the thoughts of its characters. The battle of Shrewsbury, which is recapitulated in the opening scene, is called to mind again by events at Gaultree Forest and by Kate's and Lord Bardolph's allusions to Hotspur's daring in battle. Mowbray's son recalls the interrupted joust between his father and Bolingbroke; Henry thinks also of the days of Richard II when he returned from exile to claim his inheritance; and Shallow and Falstaff reminisce about their service under John of Gaunt. More subtle poetic and dramatic echoes of *Richard II* also appear in *Part II*. The music sounds at Henry's deathbed as it sounded before Richard was murdered, and the lamentations of the dying Henry rephrase Richard's meditations on the hollow crown. Despairing of his state, Richard had urged his followers to "throw away respect, / Tradition, form, and ceremonious duty." Now Henry, convinced so it seems of Hal's depravity, urges him to "pluck down my officers, break my decrees; / For now a time is come to mock at form." Finding himself literally in Richard's place, "deposed" by the son who seized the crown and whose thoughts "stab" at a half an hour of his life, Henry, like Richard, thinks of dust, graves, and worms, of the dimness of his day, and the melting of his state:

Stay but a little; for my cloud of dignity
Is held from falling with so weak a wind
That it will quickly drop; my day is dim.
Thou hast stol'n that which, after some few hours,
Were thine without offence; and at my death
Thou hast seal'd up my expectation. . . .
What, canst thou not forbear me half an hour?
Then get thee gone and dig my grave thyself,
And bid the merry bells ring to thine ear,
That thou art crowned, not that I am dead.
Let all the tears that should bedew my hearse
Be drops of balm to sanctify thy head.
Only compound me with forgotten dust;
Give that which gave thee life unto the worms.   (IV.v.99-117)

All this is deeply felt, but somewhat dramatized. As in *Part I*, Henry's outrage with his son swells histrionically and subsides abruptly. One moment he is convinced that Hal is an abandoned profligate; the next moment he congratulates him on his clever way with words and invites him to sit on the bed to hear his latest counsel. No less an actor than his father, Hal plays again the maligned innocent while Henry plays again the martyred king, but this time Hal is quick to kneel and plead his undying loyalty. Forgetting in a moment the actual words he spoke as he took the crown, he invents a stilted colloquy with the crown that begins: "The care on thee depending / Hath fed upon the body of my father," and he earnestly explains that he put on the crown to "try with it (as with an enemy)." Who could remain angry with so quick-witted a boy? Perhaps Hal does bend the truth a trifle, but it does not matter because his ingenious explanation falls on appreciative ears. The son who took the crown vowing that the world's whole strength would not force it from him now protests that God should ever keep the crown from him if he in the slightest welcomed it. His admiring father exclaims that God put it in Hal's mind to take the crown so that he could win his father's love "pleading so wisely in excuse of it." Thus, if Henry does not find a loving son, he sees in Hal his true inheritor, one who is as nimble at kneeling and as quick at seizing a crown as he was in his youth—one to whom he can confide his innermost thoughts. For a moment with Hal, Henry stands at the very brink of revelation, ready to confess before he dies his guilty ambition for the crown, which he speaks of as an honor "snatch'd with boist'rous hand." But when the words must be spoken, Henry steps back from the precipice:

God knows, my son,
By what bypaths and indirect crook'd ways
I met this crown.   (IV.v.184-86)

Who but Henry Bolingbroke could describe his career in this way? He will not admit that he stole the crown or even reached for it. He *met* it. Just as rebellion lay in Worcester's path and he found it, so too royalty lay somewhat crookedly in Henry's path and he picked it up. One moment he complains bitterly that like the industrious bee he will be murdered for his pains. The next moment he confides that he "cut off" those who advanced him and speaks of taking out the "stings and teeth" of his friends. When Henry describes how he treated his "friends," Hal's treatment of his tavern cronies does not seem harsh at all; but Henry could have made terms with the Percies, and he might have lived at peace with them if he had allowed them to demean his prerogative. Because he refused to compromise, he had to fight, and because he won, he left his heir a throne redeemed from broking pawn and politic obligations.

In Daniel's *Civil Wars*, Henry advises his son to prove his royal mettle with princely accomplishments.[13] Shakespeare's Henry offers the more Machiavellian advice that Hal "busy giddy minds with foreign quarrels," even as he had planned a Crusade to distract his subjects from looking "too near into [his] state." Henry's obtuseness is remarkable because he does genuinely long for the expiation a Crusade might bring; and Hal's response is also remarkable because he is neither startled nor shocked by his father's words. If anything, he seems unable to comprehend his father's sense of guilt. When Henry says, "How I came by the crown, O God forgive," Hal answers matter-of-factly:

> My gracious liege,
> You won it, wore it, kept it, gave it me;
> Then plain and right must my possession be;
> Which I with more than with a common pain
> 'Gainst all the world will rightfully maintain.   (IV.v.221-25)

Like his brother John, Hal has the knack of reducing problems of conscience to questions of legality. Since he inherits the crown by due succession, he admits to no qualm about his right to wear it, though on the eve of Agincourt he will beg God not to think of the "fault" his father committed in "compassing the crown."

Contrasting Hal and Henry, John Palmer remarks that

The character of the man who intends to succeed with the approval of his conscience is unfolded beside that of the man who has succeeded in despite of his conscience and is dying of a broken spirit. Henry of Monmouth is the son

---

13. The dying Henry warns Hal in Daniel's poem that "unlesse thy worth confirme the thing, / Thou never shalt be father to a King" (*Civil Wars*, p. 177).

of his father. Conscience, in Bolingbroke, is sick; in his heir it is merely sensitive.[14]

I would refine this distinction a trifle. Henry has the strength (or callousness) to commit acts which he knows are guilty. Hal's conscience is more precise. He cannot, like his father, allow "destiny" to carry him to his desired ends. Examining his behavior at every turn, he must justify his conduct to himself whether he is in the tavern, the palace, or the vasty fields of France. He must prove to his moral satisfaction that his cause is good—that he has the right, or no choice but, to do what he intends, and that it is always someone else's fault that he cannot be merciful or charitable. His father can speak of the luxurious pleasures of the palace—the perfumed chambers, the canopies of costly state, the sound of sweetest melody—which fail to bring him the rest he needs. Hal can no more admit the satisfactions of power and estate, however, than his father could admit his royal ambition. Even as he reaches for the crown, Hal describes it as a "golden care," a rich armor that scalds with safety. In a similar vein, he must protest that the new and gorgeous garment of majesty does not sit easy on him, even though he looked forward in his soliloquy in *Part I* to the glittering image his royalty would have. And when he kneels before Henry to deny his eagerness for the crown, his thoughts dwell on its exalted power to which the poorest vassal "doth with awe and terror kneel." Henry IV can speak with some conviction of loving his people well, just as he can reach out imaginatively to share the experience of the wet ship boy who sleeps on the high and giddy mast during the storm. But Hal, who acquires the common touch in the tavern, even there despises the baseness of Poins, and finds it difficult to recognize the humanity of the Francises of the world. When at Agincourt he too has "frighted" sleep, he speaks contemptuously of ordinary men who with gross vacant minds snore out the night.

Watching Hal amuse himself with Falstaff in the tavern, and listening to Falstaff's scornful references to Hal, we know that their final break is close at hand. So little remains of their original relationship as *Part II* begins, that there need be no rejection scene except that the desperate Falstaff must believe that Hal is still his "sweet boy." We know that Hal will be as good as his word—he will banish Falstaff and add his sermon to those addressed to Falstaff by the Lord Chief Justice and Prince John. Falstaff is unprepared for what is to come, however; and he is so pathetically vulnerable in his sweating eagerness and so hypocritical in his babblings about devotion and affection that we are tempted

14. *Political Characters*, p. 187.

to avert our eyes even before Harry begins his rebuke. Those who complain that Harry's reply is unkind[15] are sometimes accused of a sentimental unwillingness to accept the necessity for the rejection of Falstaff. But sentimentalists do not really want the tavern holiday to continue forever; they want only to smile through their tears as Harry and Falstaff part. We do not wince because Hal rejects Falstaff; we wince because he rejects him without any trace of regret, because in giving up Falstaff Harry gives up nothing which he cherishes—not even a memory, for in retrospect the holiday of the tavern seems a nightmare of riot from which Harry awakens with a shudder. Would that the Prince had a better companion! Or any companion for whom he could feel a lasting affection.

Once Hal had justified his acquaintance with Falstaff and Poins by saying, "I know you all." At the close of *Part II* he shrugs off all propinquity with "I know you not." Though he will privately soften the blow of imprisonment with the promise of an ample pension, he publicly allows his old companion only measure for measure: a rebuke answerable to Falstaff's folly. Where the new King of *The Famous Victories* bids Jockey mind his manners and turns him away with a sigh, "Ah, Tom, your former life greeves me," Shakespeare's Harry turns upon Falstaff with the distaste of the righteous for the fallen. More priggish at this moment than John, he offers a Christian admonition that has no trace of Christian charity or human sympathy:

> Fall to thy prayers.
> How ill white hairs become a fool and jester!
> I have long dreamt of such a kind of man,
> So surfeit-swell'd, so old, and so profane;
> But being awak'd, I do despise my dream.
> Make less thy body, hence, and more thy grace;
> Leave gormandizing. Know the grave doth gape
> For thee thrice wider than for other men.   (V.v.51-8)

No doubt Harry is aware of the public effect of this sermon as he was aware of the public effect of his earlier lecture to the Lord Chief Justice. Both speeches are in their way official pronouncements, declarations of policy, seals placed on the fact of Harry's miraculous redemption. Nevertheless, his sermon to Falstaff sounds absolutely sincere, for by now there can be no doubt that the homiletic stance is more native to his disposition that was his impulse to

15. The list of those who think Harry's words are unkind is very long, and includes even Tillyard, who speaks of the "unkind" things which Harry says to Falstaff (*History Plays,* p. 268).

holiday, which always required a sober justification and which had long before proved somewhat tedious.

Those who find Hal the Prince much more attractive than Harry the King argue that Shakespeare lapses into conventionality in depicting the full flowering of Harry's royal perfection. Perhaps it is more correct to say that it is Harry who lapses into conventionality when once he assumes his adult responsibilities—a fate which few youthful rebels avoid, especially when their youthful rebellion was less than met the eye. Some men are corrupted by power, others are dehumanized by it. Some grow pompous and self-important in office; others grow insensitive and begin to enjoy the manipulation of their inferiors. Such is not Harry's fate. He does not become cold and self-important as he begins to wield power; rather he is attracted to power and finds his fulfillment in its exercise because he is from the beginning incapable of fellow feeling, of intimacy, and spontaneity. In donning the gorgeous garment of majesty and assuming the destiny which he has long anticipated, he remains very much himself. Except for his official gravity, the King who rebukes Falstaff in the last scene is no different from the Prince who made Falstaff cringe and plead no offense in the tavern. Nor is the Prince who amuses himself with Falstaff, Poins, and Francis in the tavern very different from the King who plays a game of cat and mouse with the Lord Chief Justice before embracing him and who entraps the traitors at Southampton with their own words in *Henry V*.

Although the Lord Chief Justice and others are astonished by Harry's grave demeanor in the last act of *Part II*, the audience does not see a sudden or radical change at that point in Harry's deportment or manner of speech. And if we take a longer view of the characterization of Hal, we realize that a sobriety of attitude and deliberateness of statement were traits that set him apart from Hotspur and Falstaff in *Part I*. Willing enough to appear profligate in his behavior, he was always respectful of the conventionalities of syntax and rhetoric which his father overstepped in moments of poetic excitement. We cannot imagine Hal dealing as freely and as imaginatively with language and metaphor as Henry does in describing Richard II:

> The skipping King, he ambled up and down
> With shallow jesters and rash bavin wits,
> Soon kindled and soon burnt; carded his state;
> Mingled his royalty with cap'ring fools;
> Had his great name profaned with their scorns
> And gave his countenance, against his name,

To laugh at gibing boys and stand the push
Of every beardless vain comparative.   (*1HIV*,III.ii.60-7)

Although Hal's wit is quick and ingenious, his imagination never soars and his poetic fancy is tied to the prosaic facts of commerce, factoring, merchandizing, debt, and payment. This fundamental conventionality of mind and temperament is the very cornerstone of his later successes, for he never has to search for the appropriate word or gesture; he never has to stoop down in thought to communicate with the mass of men. Although too conscious of his greatness to be a comrade to his soldiers, he can superbly express their thought and feelings, because he shares their view of war and glory. Though he is aloof from others, he is thoroughly a part of the world which hails his triumphs. It is a grievous mistake, therefore, to see his behavior in the rejection scene as the revelation of a singular hypocrisy or heartlessness. Rather than "an attempt to buy the praise of the respectable at the cost of honour and truth,"[16] Harry's admonition to Falstaff is his pledge of allegiance to the respectable world which applauds his rejection of his old companions even as it will cheer on his imperial ambition in *Henry V* and praise his judiciousness at Agincourt. Just as John admires Harry's "fair proceeding" with Falstaff, Canterbury and Ely will admire his statesmanship and piety, and Gower will admire his sound judgment at Agincourt: "the King most worthily hath caus'd every soldier to cut his prisoner's throat. O, 'tis a gallant king!" (IV.vii.9-11).

The kind of man who must have and who will win the applause of multitudes, Hal is gracious, his father observes,

> if he be observ'd;
> He hath a tear for pity, and a hand
> Open as day for melting charity.
> Yet notwithstanding, being incens'd, he's flint;
> As humorous as winter, and as sudden
> As flaws congealed in the spring of day.
> His temper, therefore, must be well observ'd.
> Chide him for faults, and do it reverently,
> When you perceive his blood inclin'd to mirth;
> But being moody, give him line and scope
> Till that his passions, like a whale on ground,
> Confound themselves with working.   (IV.iv.30-41)

Henry sees that the danger in Hal is not an inclination to sensuality or hot-

16. A. C. Bradley, "The Rejection of Falstaff," in *Oxford Lectures on Poetry* (London: Macmillan, 1963), p. 254. The essay was written in 1902.

blooded passion, but to wintry fury and steely-edged rage. Yet that danger is not much because Hal is capable of far more self-restraint than Henry imagines. When accused and insulted by his father in the deathbed scene, he does not explode in anger as he did in their confrontation scene in *Part I*, and he shows extraordinary self-control when provoked by Williams' insinuations in *Henry V*.[17] In fact, where Richmond is the exemplar of brotherhood and peace at the close of *Richard III*, Harry at the close of *Part II* exemplifies the self-discipline and dedication which England needs after a long period of disorder. Richmond's first official act after gaining the crown is to proclaim a general pardon that welcomes all Englishmen back into the reunited commonweal. Harry's first official act after his coronation is to banish his old companions. He may have a hand open for melting charity, but his conception of charity seems that of the Poor Law and the alms house. When he allows to Falstaff a "competence of life . . .that lack of means enforce you not to evil," he reminds us just a bit of Angelo, who will allow the "fornicatress" Juliet "needful but not lavish means."

Harry's sermon to Falstaff and Shakespeare's treatment of homiletic themes in the *Henry IV* plays cannot be interpreted simply by reference to the Morality tradition. For the moral concerns of *Part II* are less retrospective of earlier plays than prophetic of *Measure for Measure*, and of *King Lear*, in which the homilists are Goneril and Regan, who undertake by proper chastizings to teach their father to recognize his true state. While there is no sympathy for lawlessness in *Part II*, there is a clear-eyed view of the folly of Shallow's judgments, the self-righteousness of the Lord Chief Justice, and the ugliness of the processes of law that demand the services of Fang and Snare. And if an audience sees the world more feelingly in *Part II* than in the earlier History Plays, it may be partly because it glimpses the terror of the law as offenders do, who feel its correction on their backs, and who know the humiliation of the pillory and the pangs of imprisonment.

I am not suggesting that Shakespeare's moral attitudes changed between the writing of the *Henry VI* plays, in which law is the bulwark of the political order, and the writing of *Measure for Measure*, in which the arbitrariness and pitilessness of punitive law are revealed. If we may judge from the courtroom scene of *The Merchant of Venice*, Shakespeare was very early aware of the ironies of judicial principles and processes and conscious that strict measure for measure cannot be the ideal of human relations. It is possible, however, that his

17. Traversi writes very penetratingly about the theme of self-mastery in *Henry V*. See *From Richard II to Henry V*, pp. 168-82.

attitude toward the law as a guarantor of political and moral order evolved in response to the changing circumstances of his society. It is not surprising that he took as his initial subject in the History Plays the violent divisions and contentions of the War of the Roses, because the threat of invasion and the fear of civil war created by the Armada were still vivid memories when Shakespeare began to write the *Henry VI* plays. As the sense of immediate crisis and immediate danger waned, he could see that the fear of Catholic subversion and the harshly repressive measures passed against Catholics in the 1590's posed a greater threat to the unity of England than did the fanaticism of Catholic extremists. He could also see how easily rigor and vindictiveness were officially sanctioned in the name of political security and moral restraint in an age when punishment was savage even for minor offenses. As the sixteenth century drew to its close, the Puritan clamor for reformation in church and state became ever more strident. The most zealous believed that the government had the duty to use its powers to suppress vice and to enforce moral and religious standards; and they were prepared to teach moral lessons with whips or to cast offenders out of the godly state even as the London statutes excluded the profane and idolatrous stage from the precincts of the City.

The Puritan attack on the stage prompted Elizabethan dramatists to savage caricatures of stupid, sanctimonious, and mercenary Precisians. Shakespeare did not join in the counterattack by exposing the hypocrisy of the zealous as did Jonson, Middleton, and Tourneur, among others. Willing to grant the sincerity of motive of those who would raise the level of public morality, he is content to point out in an Angelo the priggery, narrowness, and coldness which disqualify them for the task. Where Jonson imagined himself defending the bastions of civility and art against the onrushing horde of Puritan barbarians, Shakespeare rightly suspected that the enemy is inside our gates and forever among us. For if we did not, like Angelo, think that criminals deserve and need to be punished (as part of their rehabilitation), we could not bear the horror of a system of justice which humiliates and degrades those who are being "reformed" or made "penitent." Although inclined to be self-righteous about Harry's self-righteousness and uncharitable about his uncharity, we have to recognize that his complacent belief that offenders should be punished and "cut off" is the cornerstone of our laws.

Watching Angelo enforce the statutes against fornication, we wonder if any judge or any civil code can deal with the problem of human sexuality without hypocrisy or legalistic evasions. Watching Harry win everlasting glory in France, we understand how decent, honorable men, armed with good consciences and good discipline, have been able for centuries to carry fire and sword into other lands. The next-to-last scene of *Part II* shows the arrest of the Hostess and Doll; the last scene shows the arrest of Falstaff followed immediately by John's prediction of the invasion of France. In the first tetralogy Henry VI's pious meekness was the spiritual antithesis of York's ambition for the throne. In the second tetralogy worldly ambition and devout belief complement each other in the words and acts of the "mirror of all Christian kings." In God's name Harry will go forth to battle, and with earnest humility he will offer up the great victory to God, just as in God's name Elizabethan privateers plundered Spanish shipping and sacked Spanish cities. Until the meek inherit the earth, it will be possessed, I imagine, by men like Harry who think it a sacred duty to expand their power and who believe that the cause of peace depends upon the triumph of their just and hallowed cause.

8. HENRY V

More critics are willing to defend the character of Henry V than to defend the play that bears his name. Those who admire *Henry V* as a rousing patriotic spectacle do not make many claims for it as a work of dramatic art. Those who regard it as a falling off from the History Plays that preceded it declare that it is a complaisant if not shallow play, somewhat simplistic in its subject matter and a bit brassy in its enthusiasms. Some even suggest that Shakespeare was not deeply engaged by or interested in the play, that he probably felt compelled to write it to complete his tetralogy or to satisfy his audience's desire for the heroic story of Agincourt. What evidence is there, however, that *Henry V* was a work of the left hand? Little in it is perfunctory or indifferent; it has none of the muddles and contradictions of *King John*, none of the lapses of inspiration that are obvious in other History Plays. The poetry is always more than adequate to its dramatic purpose; the characterizations are lively and interesting if not fully developed; and the plot is very skillfully contrived and varied in mood and pace. Those who complain that the success of *Henry V* is very limited and conventional underrate Shakespeare's intention as well as his achievement, for the wonder is not that he lowered his artistic sights in *Henry V*, but that it succeeds as well as it does in celebrating English heroism when it makes such damaging admissions about the motives and the methods of the conquerors of France and speaks so candidly of the human cost of their great adventure.

Annoyed that Shakespeare was willing to write a patriotic pageant, readers are not inclined to see what is thoughtful and serious in *Henry V*, and as a result their impressions of it are likely to be shallow and their memories of it

175

mistaken. Those who think of it as a play of physical action, do so not because its scenes are made up of excursions and alarums, but because the Chorus creates such memorable word pictures of epic activity and movement—of the preparations for war, of the gathering and movement of ships and armies, and of the sound and fury of battle. Although the Chorus apologizes several times for the author's feeble attempts to represent the field of Agincourt with "four or five most vile and ragged foils," the apology is as sly as it is gratuitous because Shakespeare makes no attempt in the play to represent an epic confrontation of armies. The war is always offstage, and the one scene of combat at Agincourt that is dramatized is something of a private joke, because it depicts the cowardly Pistol capturing a quaking French soldier. To enjoy the excitement of battle and the clang of sword on armor, we must turn back from *Henry V* to *Henry IV Part I*, where five separate encounters are staged at Shrewsbury. At Agincourt, as at Bosworth, the moral and psychological conflicts that take place on the eve of the battle have more space in the play than the battle itself. The climactic confrontation of *Henry V* finds the King pitted, not against his French enemies, but against English soldiers who debate with him his responsibility for the massacre that threatens on the morrow. Often described in the pages of criticism as a military athlete,[1] Harry not once displays his physical prowess in France. To show him triumphing in chivalric combat at Agincourt, Olivier had to invent a scene for the film of *Henry V* that does not exist in Shakespeare's text.

The abject apology of the Chorus for the failings of the author is just one clue to the artfulness that wears so naive a guise in *Henry V*. Other clues are the ironic juxtapostions which the simple linear plot innocently allows to happen. The Hostess' poignant description of Falstaff's death, for example, is all the more affecting because it follows the cold fury of Henry's diatribe against the traitors at Southampton; in a somewhat similar way, the charming obscenities of Katherine's English lesson provide a comic relief to Harry's threat of rapine and violation at Harfleur. Such ironies do not escape our attention because they are ingeniously hidden in the text but because they are so obvious that one can hardly believe Shakespeare intended them. Scrutinizing his characterization of Harry, critics note the hints of callousness, coldness, self-righteousness, and obtuseness—all the fascinating blemishes which Shake-

1. The most famous critical comment of this kind is Yeats's that "Shakespeare watched Henry V, not indeed as he watched the greater souls in the visionary procession, but cheerfully, as one watches some handsome spirited horse," quoted by Palmer, *Political Characters*, p. 248.

speare added to the Chroniclers' idealized portrait of the hero king. Then they wish that Shakespeare could have seen Harry as perceptively and critically as modern readers do. Or, worse still, they suggest that though Shakespeare did see Harry with all his human imperfections, he idolized him nevertheless. Thus, without any sense of contradiction, E.K. Chambers can speak of Harry on one page as representing for Shakespeare a Hegelian synthesis of all princely virtues, and then a few pages later call him "the prototype of the blatant modern imperialist."[2]

‿Did it never occur to Shakespeare that some would regard his "ideal king" as a blatant imperialist? Or did he, like Machiavelli, regard the empire-builder as the ideal prince? The acclamation of the King in *Henry V* is very explicit and very specific. Echoing the judgment of the Chroniclers, the Chorus declares him a "mirror of all Christian kings," the princes of the Church admire his mastery of divinity and policy, and his captains praise his astuteness as a military commander. Such speeches do not prove, however, that Harry was an ideal ruler—one who brought to his nation the blessings of lasting peace and unity. Although characters speak of Harry's genius at rule, little of that genius is evident when he discusses the French campaign with his councilors, and still less when he leads his army to victory. Our hero is a man on horseback, not a statesman, a military leader who metes out summary judgments, not the bearer of the sacred sword of heaven. The opening Chorus invites us to imagine a "swelling scene" and a Harry as fierce as the Apocalypse, who, letting slip the dogs of war, licenses carnage:

> Then should the warlike Harry, like himself,
> Assume the port of Mars, and at his heels
> (Leash'd in, like hounds) should famine, sword, and fire
> Crouch for employment.   (I.5-8)

The portrait is emblematic, and the emblem is unmistakable—or at least was unmistakable to Shakespeare's audience, for Harry is the very personification of War, a figure described in the Induction to *The Mirror for Magistrates* as standing

>   in glitterying arms yclad,
> With visage grym, sterne lookes, and blackely hewed;
> In his right hand a naked sworde he had,

2. *Shakespeare: A Survey*, pp. 137-38, 143. Like most sensitive critics Chambers is aware of the ways in which Harry's glory is subject in the play to critical scrutiny; nevertheless he suggests that a critical view of conquest is really a modern, not Elizabethan, way of thinking (pp. 142-44).

That to the hiltes was al with blud embrewed:
And in his left, (that kinges and kingdomes rewed)
Famine and fyer he held, and therewythall
He razed townes and threwe downe towers and all.[3]

The Chorus' vision of Harry in the port of Mars could be explained as just a bit of awe-struck rhetoric, except that the apocalyptic image returns again in the scenes where Harry plays the mighty huntsman of war. At Harfleur he describes his troops as "greyhounds in the slips, / Straining upon the start," and urges them to imitate the action of the tiger, even as he was urged by Canterbury to forage like his ancestors in French blood. When imagery of this kind appeared in the battle scenes of *King John*,[4] one could precisely gauge the emotional effect Shakespeare intended because the Bastard was present to anatomize the senseless brutality and waste of life in the war. The Chorus to *Henry V*, who rejoices in Harry's employment of famine, sword, and fire, is a less obvious guide to Shakespeare's attitude. Look as we may beneath the glittering surface of Harry's crusade in France, we cannot find the gross hypocrisy and the blind frenzy for destruction which the Bastard saw in the combatants at Angiers. Only once in France is the King angry, and that is when the French knights slaughter the English camp boys, a cowardly act expressly forbidden by the rules of war. Fluellen, Jamy, and Macmorris have quicker tempers, but they go methodically about the business of war whether the task be to beat the stragglers like dogs into the breach, or, on the King's command, to cut their prisoners' throats. The men who sell their pasture to buy a horse and follow Harry to France are not the "rash, fiery, inconsiderate voluntaries" Chatillon describes in *King John* as having sold their fortunes in England "to make a hazard of new fortunes in France." They are men like Williams and Bates, anxious about their wives and families and their immortal souls, who hope, like Pistol, to profit from the invasion of France; but unlike Pistol, they mean to earn from the wars a respectable living.

The worst that can be said about captains like Fluellen and Gower is that they are pious, conventional, and patriotic. Although they cut throats, they are

3. *Mirror*, pp. 311-12. The Induction, by Thomas Sackville, was added in the 1563 edition of *The Mirror*.
4. Where the Bastard spoke of Death mousing the flesh of men, Exeter speaks of "this hungry war" that "opens his vasty jaws" for poor souls (II.iv.105-6). Where the English Herald at Angiers describes the English army as "a jolly troop of huntsmen come . . . all with purpled hands," the French King speaks of Harry: "The kindred of him hath been flesh'd upon us; / And he is bred out of that bloody strain / That haunted us in our familiar paths" (II.iv.50-52).

not cutthroats, and although they fight in hopes of booty, they are not plunderers. They are professional soldiers, men of good discipline and good cheer, proud of their ancient calling, well versed in its decorums, and scholarly in their knowledge of the campaigns of Caesar and Pompey. They fight honorably as men have fought for centuries, with chaplains by their sides to pray for victory and with regimental flags that will be returned to hallowed places in chapels and cathedrals. They are led by a king of tender conscience who would be convinced before he starts of the rightness of his cause, who calls on Canterbury "justly and religiously" to unfold the truth of his claim to the French crown, and who exhorts him to speak and reason with absolute honesty and candor, with words "wash'd pure" in his conscience. When Canterbury scrupulously unfolds the genealogy of Harry's claim, the King earnestly inquires whether he may "with right and conscience make this claim?" and with equal earnestness Canterbury replies, "The sin upon my head, dread Sovereign."

Knowing that Canterbury, by offering the King a great sum for his French wars, has won his opposition to a bill that would have stripped the Church of the better half of its possessions, a reader may be inclined to mutter about covert extortion and politic bribery. But there is nothing devious in Canterbury's relation with the King and nothing that smacks of hypocrisy in his patriotic fervor. When the King and the Archbishop address one another, they speak from the heart and they play their political hands with scrupulous attention to the rules of the game. Tillyard thinks that Harry allows his councilors to persuade him to the invasion of France: "He hardly interposes [in the debate], much less argues. As a thinker he is quite passive, leaving the business to others."[5] Most readers have the opposite impression: that the King has taken the initiative in pressing his claims in France and is impatient to get his campaign underway. As Dover Wilson puts it, "It is not the Archbishop who sets the King awork, but the King the Archbishop."[6] Neither the puppet of the King nor his manipulator, Canterbury is an astute leader of a church which over the centuries had refined the arts of negotiation, compromise, and accommodation to temporal authorities. Like Ely, he is prudent and discreet, good enough for this world, and as honest with himself as circumstances allow. Both clergymen are ready to render unto Caesar what is Caesar's and to

5. *History Plays,* p. 310.
6. Introduction, *Henry V* (Cambridge: Cambridge Univ. Press, 1955), p. xxi. Wilson labors to convince us that there is "not a hint of a bribe on the Archbishop's part, still less of his provoking the King to war in order to protect Church property!" (pp. xxi-xxii). He succeeds only in turning the play into a Sunday school story.

worship the King this side of idolatry. Knowing that miracles have ceased, they suspect that his miraculous redemption was humanly contrived and admire the way that he "obscur'd his contemplation, / Under the veil of wildness." Tactful men, they will neither impugn the King's motives nor examine too closely their own reasons for supporting his intended campaign. The very thought of preventing the bill of expropriation from becoming law is too grossly politic for their tempers. They must by indirections find directions out; they must begin with the recognition that "the King is full of grace and fair regard," "a true lover of the Holy Church"; then slowly and obliquely they can work their way through praise of Harry toward the "mitigation of this bill." Their taste for dusty quiddities about the Salic law is natural enough, but they are not bloodless pedants. They are patriotic Englishmen, who urge the King to prosecute his hallowed cause with ringing reminders of his ancestors' greatness:

                              Gracious lord,
    Stand for your own, unwind your bloody flag,
    Look back into your mighty ancestors;
    Go, my dread lord, to your great-grandsire's tomb,
    From whom you claim; invoke his warlike spirit,
    And your great-uncle's, Edward the Black Prince,
    Who on the French ground play'd a tragedy,
    Making defeat on the full power of France,
    Whiles his most mighty father on a hill
    Stood smiling to behold his lion's whelp
    Forage in blood of French nobility.   (I.ii.100-10)

A King whose subjects speak in this vein need not busy giddy minds with foreign quarrels or urge his countrymen onward because they are eager "with blood and sword and fire" to win his right. All share the imperial impulse; all are inspired by memories of a glorious past and hopes of crowns and coronets to come; all believe that God and history are on the English side and mean to prove their manhood and improve their condition in France.

    Acts I and II capture the initial swell of excitement and the holiday atmosphere of the first days of a military campaign when the true face of war is hidden behind the waving banners. Confidence in victory is supreme, and the preparations for battle seem a cheerful, productive enterprise, especially to the gentle Archbishop, who gives the most savagely antisocial of human activities the flavor of a church picnic:

    Where some like magistrates correct at home,
    Others like merchants venture trade abroad,
    Others like soldiers armed in their stings,
    Make boot upon the summer's velvet buds,

Which pillage they with merry march bring home
To the tent royal of their emperor.   (I.ii.191-6)

Of a more practical mind, Exeter grapples with the necessities of military
strategy, but he too has the knack of making war seem a rational and natural
activity:

While that the armed hand doth fight abroad,
Th' advised head defends itself at home;
For government, though high, and low, and lower,
Put into parts, doth keep in one consent,
Congreeing in a full and natural close,
Like music.   (I.ii.178-83)

In Exeter's ears the cannon's roar and the groans of dying men sound, not like
the humming of bees, but like the music of the spheres.

Let us say that Harry plays the coy "maid's part" in the council scene. He
raises objections, but allows his followers to push them aside—to seduce or
"incite" him to invade France. If he is too ready, however, to let slip the dogs
of war, Exeter, Westmoreland, Canterbury, and England are straining at the
leash, and if he is not reluctant to be the master of the hunt, he is certainly
more conscionable about it than any of his hounds. Rather than a "pure man
of action, whose thinking is done for him by his counsellors,"[7] Harry stands
out as the most incisive thinker of the play; sober, perhaps even pedestrian in
his thoughtfulness, he is the only one in the council who is able to grasp and be
troubled by the moral issue of the war. He is the only one who can admit that
the "merry march" of conquest is in reality a scene of dreadful carnage.
Canterbury speaks cheerfully of "foraging in French blood," Harry speaks
somberly of the guilt of those "whose wrong gives edge unto the swords / That
make such waste in brief mortality" (I.ii.27-8). His councilors think only of
victory in France; Harry considers the need to defend England against the
ravages of the Scots when his army is embarked, and unlike Westmoreland and
Exeter, who brush aside the danger of the Scots with homely adages of cat and
mice, he can envision the possibility of the Scot marauders "galling the gleaned
land with hot assays." More striking still is his ability to envision the suffering
which his invasion will inflict upon the population of France. When the
Dauphin fatuously insults him with a tun of tennis balls, Harry grimly
prophesies that

                        many a thousand widows
Shall this his mock mock out of their dear husbands,

7. Tillyard, *History Plays*, p. 310.

> Mock mothers from their sons, mock castles down;
> And some are yet ungotten and unborn
> That shall have cause to curse the Dauphin's scorn.   (I.ii.284-88)

"This," Exeter says, "was a merry message."

Innocent in their unexamined enthusiasms, Henry's councilors do not so much evade the moral issue of the war as fail to recognize it. He is a more complex creature, because though he calls solemn attention to the suffering that war inflicts, he allows Canterbury's dusty arguments about the Salic law and Exeter's and Westmoreland's facile optimism to sweep away all compunction. Seeking vindication for a decision one feels he has already made, he finds reasons to do what he intends and scapegoats on which to place the burden of moral responsibility. Whatever else has grown stolid in him, his moral casuistry is as ingenious as ever. In his world-view the problem of ethical choice exists for others, not for him, because his responses are automatic and automatically justified. He begs other men to be merciful, but sees the prosecution of his "just" cause as his only obligation. He never ponders whether his ancient claim to the French throne or the Dauphin's insult really merits the annihilation of cities and peoples. If the Dauphin jeers, then he must properly strike back, even though he knows that thousands of innocent women and children will suffer. If the defense of Harfleur is "guilty," then what is it to him if its citizens are raped and slaughtered by his men? Yet protest as Harry does repeatedly the justness of his cause, he cannot shrug off the problem of guilt quite so casually. When he charges Canterbury to consider the issue of the war with "washed" conscience, he points out that guiltless blood will be shed:

> For never two such kingdoms did contend
> Without much fall of blood, whose guiltless drops
> Are every one a woe, a sore complaint,
> 'Gainst him whose wrongs gave edge unto the swords
> That make such waste in brief mortality.   (I.ii.24-28)

Harry would like to believe that in every war there is a right on one side and a wrong on the other, because he intends to be certain of his "right." Prepared even to deny his responsibility for his soldiers' lives on the eve of Agincourt, he cries out to God against the unfairness of his fate when they refuse to confirm the justness of his cause. Ruthless ambition should be made of stronger stuff!

The consistency of the portrayal of Harry from his first appearance in *Henry IV Part I* to his last words in *Henry V* refutes the accusation that Shakespeare abandoned his conception of Prince Hal when he came to write *Henry V*.[8]

8. Unable to square his conception of Hal as the perfect prince with the portrait of Harry in *Henry V*, Tillyard argues that Shakespeare jettisoned the character of the Prince

Although I spoke earlier of the Aristotelian evolution of Hal's character, I suspect that Shakespeare arrived first at a conception of Harry as the hero of Agincourt and then deduced from it the personality of the Prince who appears in the *Henry IV* plays. He no doubt found suggestions in the Chronicle account of the reign of Henry IV for his portrayal of Hal as a pseudo-libertine; but only in the Chronicle account of the reign of Henry V could he have found clues to his conception of Hal's moral temper. Only in the speeches which Harry made to the traitors at Southampton, to the French at the seige of Rouen, and to his followers on his deathbed, could Shakespeare have seen the need for self-justification which is Hal's distinguishing characteristic from his first appearance in the tavern scenes of *Henry IV Part I.*[9]

The Prince who denied in *Part II* that any strain of pride prompted the taking of his father's crown becomes the King in *Henry V* who seems to consider his claim to the French crown a matter of conscience and "right," but who responds to the Dauphin's insults exactly as he responded to his father's insults in *Henry IV Part I.* The Prince who swore to tear the reckoning of honor out of Hotspur's heart now promises, in a similar crescendo of "I's" to rise in France

> with so full a glory
> That I will dazzle all the eyes of France,
> Yea, strike the Dauphin blind to look on us.   (I.ii.278-80)

Once again Harry promises to imitate the sun in lines aflame with passionate self-assertion, and once again at the height of passion comes the characteristic check—the sudden subduing remembrance: "But this lies all within the will of God."[10] Here as elsewhere Harry's reference to God can be described as an

---

in fashioning his portrait of the all conquering King (*History Plays*, pp. 305-6). This view would be more tenable if we did not see the Prince turning into the King in *Henry IV Part II*, but it is preferable to the notion that Henry V is Shakespeare's ideal, regardless of how he appears to us.

9. See Holinshed, *Chronicles*, III, 70, 102-5, 132-33. Shakespeare found the essence of Harry's personality in his deathbed protestation "that neither the ambitious desire to inlarge his dominions, neither to purchase vaine renowme and worldlie fame, nor anie other consideration had mooved him to take the warres in hand; but onlie that in prosecuting his iust title, he might in the end atteine to a perfect peace, and come to enioie those peeces of his inheritance, which to him of right belonged: and that before the beginning of the same warres, he was fullie persuaded by men both wise and of great holinesse of life, that upon such intent he might and ought both begin the same warres, and follow them, till he had brought them to an end iustlie and rightlie, and that without all danger of Gods displeasure or perill of soule" (pp. 132-33). That Shakespeare had consulted the last pages of Holinshed's commentary on Henry V is evident from his echoing of the phrase "small time," used by Holinshed to describe the glory of Harry, "that in so small time had doone so manie and roiall acts" (pp. 134-5). Cf. Epilogue, line 5.

10. Again and again, Harry first boasts of his intended accomplishment and then recalls God's will. See his pledge to his father in *1Henry IV*, III.ii.149-54, and his boasting speech to the French Herald before Agincourt (IV.iii.115-21).

afterthought, except that the thought of God is again and again the final resting place of his speeches. In the very midst of imperial business he thinks on his end and is harrowed by fear of the final accounting of his responsibility. More extraordinary still, he seeks in victory a personal vindication he no longer needs. All (save the few mercenary traitors) hail his princely genius, and discerning men like Canterbury, Ely, and the Constable of France interpret his past correctly. They know that his profligacy was merely a disguise, a "coat of folly" which covered his youthful discretion. Still Harry is galled by the Dauphin's mocking references to his tavern days, and feels compelled to explain to the French Ambassadors that he gave himself to "barbarous license" because he "never valu'd this poor seat of England." Dismissing all achievement up to the French campaign as plodding "like a man for working days," Harry now looks forward to a holiday in France, where he will play a tennis match that will dazzle the Dauphin and the world. The Prince of *Part I* had predicted correctly enough that his seeming prodigality would provide a foil for his greatness in times to come. Now, however, the legend of his prodigality seems to Harry a blemish that requires radical surgery in France.

Listening to Harry's boastful words to the Ambassadors, one is tempted to speak of a noble mind o'erthrown, of a once acute and critical intelligence grown coarse and infatuated by the vainglorious dream which destroyed Hotspur. Where Hotspur wished to rescue his family honor from shame in future chronicles, Harry declares to his council that

> France being ours, we'll bend it to our awe,
> Or break it all to pieces. Or there we'll sit,
> Ruling large and ample empery
> O'er France and all her (almost) kingly dukedoms,
> Or lay these bones in an unworthy urn,
> Tombless, with no remembrance over them.
> Either our history shall with full mouth
> Speak freely of our acts, or else our grave,
> Like Turkish mute, shall have a tongueless mouth,
> Not worshipp'd with a waxen epitaph.   (I.ii.224-33)

Where Hotspur would be content to wear the crown of honor without corrival, Harry would have all or nothing because without an ample empery his existence is meaningless. This ambition would seem fatuously grandiose did we not suspect that what Harry really wants is something pristine, a baptismal clearness of reputation and place. Regardless of how others view his state, he is conscious of a blot on his heritage, of a stain of blood that only blood can wash away. He is too confident of his own royalty to suffer the insecurity of a

John or a Richard II, but he needs to find in France an ultimate proof of his kingliness: "No king of England, if not king of France."

Could any king be more candid about his motives? Could any king have councilors more frank in their obtuseness? A Falstaff would have had them all at his mercy, but the Chorus whom Shakespeare provides for the scenes of *Henry V* is not one to examine unexamined enthusiasms. Although he stands outside the play, he is too imbued with patriotic pride to criticize the great adventure or recognize its tarnished edges. Just after he exclaims that "honour's thought / Reigns solely in the breast of every man," the disreputable tavern crew walks on stage, full of petty quarrels and greedy purposes. Exeter speaks in the council scene of an English invasion of France as an eagle's flight and compares a Scottish invasion of England to a weasel's sneak attack. Pistol, on the other hand, rallies a band of weasels (or leeches) to the French campaign, "To suck, to suck, the very blood to suck!" It would be wrong, of course, to equate Harry's goals with Pistol's and Bardolph's. They are not the sordid reality that lurks beneath the glittering moral surface of the crusade. They are the basest notes, the parasites swept along on the tide of nobler enthusiasms, and as such perhaps not deserving of the Chorus' attention though they claim a fair portion of the scenes of the play. Far more worthy of the Chorus' scorn is the unholy greed of the English traitors whom Harry exposes at Southampton. Perhaps because the King will anatomize every detail of the traitors' guilt, the Chorus touches only briefly on their vileness and allows himself the liberty to express his outrage in an outrageous pun:

> France hath in [England] found out
> A nest of hollow bosoms, which he fills
> With treacherous crowns; and three corrupted men—
> One, Richard Earl of Cambridge, and the second,
> Henry Lord Scroop of Masham, and the third,
> Sir Thomas Grey, knight, of Northumberland—
> Have for the gilt of France (O guilt, indeed!)
> Confirmed conspiracy with fearful France,
> And by their hands this grace of kings must die,
> If hell and treason hold their promises,
> Ere he take ship for France.   (II.20-30)

Is there not something faintly comic and ironic about this execration of the traitors' greed? While it is monstrous to the Chorus for Englishmen to betray their country for gold, it seems right to him for Englishmen to cut French throats for gold. But then the honorable commerce of war, which holds out the promise of crowns and coronets, cannot make any allowance for the suffering of the enemy. Since war requires substantial investments and entails enormous risks, the Chorus sees nothing wrong with the King's refusal to accept the French King's offer of his daughter and "some petty and unprofitable dukedoms." If the French King is stingy, then French women and children will have to pay for it with their lives.

The Chorus is an interesting figure because in one aspect he is your average patriotic Elizabethan whose eyes moisten at the thought of his nation's triumphs, and in another aspect, he is the author's surrogate, a means by which Shakespeare reflects on his art as well as on England's history. The Chorus plays the latter role in a curious way, because where the Epilogues of Shakespeare's plays are appropriately deferential to his audience, the Chorus to *Henry V* is absolutely obsequious to the "gentles all" whom he addresses and astonishingly apologetic about the limitations of the playwright, the play, and the company. We could imagine an apprentice Shakespeare speaking through a Chorus about his "rough and all-unable pen" as he embarks on the first part of *Henry VI.* We wonder, however, why he doubts his ability to present the glory of Agincourt when he has dazzled his audiences with his depiction of the War of the Roses, and triumphantly staged Bosworth Field, Angiers, and Shrewsbury. Awed by his magnificent subject, he may have been suddenly struck by the inadequacy of his artistic means to present epic action. If so, he soon recovered his confidence, because not many months later he staged the battle of Philippi in *Julius Caesar,* then dared to represent the legendary wars of Troy in *Troilus and Cressida,* and after that he took Rome, Egypt, Asia Minor, and the Mediterranean as his province in *Antony and Cleopatra.*

Shakespeare, I think, never doubted for a moment his ability to deal with epic subjects in drama. What he does "honestly" apologize for through the Chorus is his inability to render on stage the destructiveness of war. Unable to present Harry the huntsman in all his apocalyptic horror—with famine, sword, and fire at his feet—the Chorus asks "pardon, gentles all." Once again before the third act, the Chorus apologizes for the inadequacy of the artistic representation when he asks the audience to imagine the cannon "with fatal mouths gaping" on Harfleur. Since Harry likes not the French offer of terms,

> The nimble gunner
> With linstock now the devilish cannon touches,
> *Alarum, and chambers go off.*
> And down goes all before them. Still be kind,
> And eke out our performance with your mind.   (III.32-5)

If there is a subtle irony in the Chorus' innocent manner, it is directed, not so much against Harry and his men, as against the audience. Assuming that they want a realistic portrayal of patriotic gore, that they would like to hear the cannon's roar, to see the walls crumbling, the houses burning, the swords whistling through the air, the Chorus asks the "gentle" spectators nevertheless to "still be kind." He even promises to digest the "abuse of distance" so that the gentles present will have a gentle pass to France, because "we'll not offend one stomach with our play."

The immediate justaposition of the plea for kindness and the cannon's roar and the recurrent appeals to the gentleness of the audience remind us that from the beginning of civilization war has been an aristocratic enterprise as well as an exalted literary theme. For centuries the hunt of battle has left an "unnatural" trail of devastation through the world, and for centuries the impulse to the hunt has been native to man—bred in his blood, enshrined in his history, and celebrated in his art. Before Agincourt, Canterbury recalls, there was Cressy; before Cressy there was the Norman Conquest, to which the French nobility refer; and long before the Norman Conquest were the "pristine wars of the Romans," the campaigns of Caesar and Pompey, and the famous victories of Alexander the Great, which Fluellen learnedly cites. Since time immemorial the battlefield has provided the supreme test of nobility. Just as Harry proved his princeliness at Shrewsbury, he will prove at Agincourt his right to an imperial title, and those who shed their blood with him, he promises, will also gentle their condition, be they "ne'er so vile."

The Chorus bids us "gently to hear, kindly to judge the play." If we have any doubt what kindliness of judgment is we can take our cue from the King, who stands in judgment over the traitors at Southampton and over the citizens of Harfleur, who confirms the sentencing of Bardolph and pardons Williams. Unless we see that kindness is a theme in *Henry V,* we will wonder why Shakespeare allows so much space to the scene at Southampton and why he amplifies the Chronicle account of this episode by inventing the cat-and-mouse game which Harry plays with the traitors before he condemns them. Once again, as in the rejection of Falstaff, Harry's behavior is unimpeachably correct; the earls confess their shameful guilt, and their punishment exactly fits their crime. Once again, however, Harry's manner is somewhat priggish if not heartless. He entraps the traitors in their hypocrisy in very much the way that the Duke, at the end of *Measure for Measure,* entraps Angelo; but, unlike the Duke, Harry makes no attempt to reform the traitors, who, like Angelo, are stunned into confession and repentance. Where the Duke's game of cat and mouse has its moral and psychological purposes, Harry's game simply allows him to enjoy his mastery of those who would have betrayed him. Their crime he regards as a breach of personal faith, but his rage he considers wholly impersonal. It is the law, he explains (as Angelo does to Isabella) that condemns wrongdoers, not he; and he sees himself as the helpless instrument of the law, though just before he showed that he has the godlike office of charity. But even as he protests that he seeks no revenge "touching our person," he turns on the traitors with a fury that is barely contained by the conventionalities of his pulpit rhetoric. Sixty-five lines are scarcely enough to express his outrage at their offence, which seems to him so hellish, so damned, so fiendish and unnatural that it can only be compared to the original disobedience in the Garden. Three times the mirror of all Christian kings calls on God to have mercy on the traitors because, though he promises that he will weep for them, he offers no mercy himself. Or, rather, he explains that he was filled with mercy for the drunken soldier who merely railed against his person, a mercy that was "suppress'd and kill'd" by the traitors' own counsel. Just as he despised Poins's vulgar judgment yet made it his reason for not weeping for his father, so now he rejects the traitors' hypocritical counsel of severity and then uses it as the justification for executing them.

Immediately before and after this scene, the tavern crew gathers on stage to speak of the dying Falstaff, whose heart the King broke. Unless God is merciful, the traitors, Harry thinks, will end in hell. Where Falstaff will ultimately rest is a more dubious matter, but the Hostess, who sends him to his last reward, is sure that it will not be in hell. Like Harry, she also was betrayed; she was fobbed off, cheated, and mocked by the Falstaff whose last hours she tenderly comforted. Where Harry could enumerate every detail of the traitors' guilt, the foolish, forgetful Hostess cannot remember even the crimes Falstaff committed against her own person, though she reluctantly admits that Sir John "did in some sort, indeed, handle women." Where Harry invokes God's name repeatedly, the Hostess describes how she bid Falstaff not trouble himself before times with the thought of God:

So a' cried out, "God, God, God!" three or four times. Now I, to comfort him, bid him a' should not think of God; I hop'd there was no need to trouble himself with such thoughts yet.   (II.iii.21-3)

Are we to assume that the Hostess' muddle-headed sentiments are a foil to Harry's deeply religious and clear-sighted judgment? Or are we to wonder if there is not more tenderness of heart and Christian charity in this gross vessel than in the mirror for all Christian kings?

At his most self-righteous with the traitors, Harry is not quite John of Lancaster, who sneered at the rebels' pose of piety and then betrayed them with pious protestations and finely spun casuistry. Where John could not see that good faith was at issue in his dealings at Gaultree Forest, Harry is well aware that mercy is the rarer action, but his moral awareness is of the mind, not of the heart. He knows intellectually the obligations he does not feel. Thus when he exhorts the citizens of Harfleur to surrender, he can describe the horror that threatens them with extraordinary detachment:

> If I begin the batt'ry once again,
> I will not leave the half-achieved Harfleur
> Till in her ashes she lie buried.
> The gates of mercy shall be all shut up,
> And the flesh'd soldier, rough and hard of heart,
> In liberty of bloody hand shall range
> With conscience wide as hell, mowing like grass
> Your fresh-fair virgins and your flow'ring infants.
> What is it then to me if impious war,
> Array'd in flames like to the prince of fiends,
> Do with his smirch'd complexion, all fell feats
> Enlink'd to waste and desolation?
> What is't to me, when you yourselves are cause,
> If your pure maidens fall into the hand
> Of hot and forcing violation?   (III.iii.7-21)

Just before, Harry had urged his men to imitate the action of the tiger; now he asks what it is to him if they act like raging beasts. He can promise Harfleur grace if he gets what he demands—and gets it immediately. Otherwise, he will turn his soldiers loose like dogs on a quarry and, once they taste blood, he will not be able to control them or be responsible for their savagery. Just as Harry could dissociate himself from the sentencing of the traitors, so too he can dissociate himself from the horror he threatens at Harfleur by abstracting the violence of war so that it seems to have a life and agency beyond his control. The raging beast will not be his army but "impious war." The women will be ravaged, not by his soldiers, but by "the hand of hot and forcing violation." And what rein, he asks, "can hold licentious wickedness / When down the hill he holds his fierce career"? (III.iii.21-3). Here as always Harry sees the moral issue as a problem in casuistry. If he can find himself not guilty, he thinks his course justified, however many will suffer because of it. Some critics are confident that he would not have carried out his threat, and he does prove merciful to the citizens of the surrendered city. But the fact remains that Harry was capable of making the terrible threat—and in good conscience—because he does not see the horror of war feelingly.

Promising mercy and threatening destruction at Harfleur, Harry reminds modern readers (as he no doubt reminded Shakespeare) of Marlowe's Tamburlaine,[11] who offered the citizens of Damascus the same choices. But where Tamburlaine has the simplistic morality of a mythological titan—his will is a universal law—Harry is all too human in his moral equivocations. Although he refers again and again during the play to his just and hallowed cause, and dedicates his victory to God, he speaks with conviction at Harfleur of the unholy desolation, and the hellish lusts and "liberties" of war. He describes the "filthy and contagious clouds / Of heady murther, spoil, and villany" that o'er hang Harfleur and compares the impending slaughter of women and children to Herod's murder of the innocents. Yet even as the "base contagious clouds" of his tavern cronies helped to create Harry's radiant future, so too the filthy and contagious clouds of murder, rapine, and villainy at Harfleur will bring him closer to a dazzling greatness. And whatever happens, the burden of guilt for the slaughter of innocents will be on the heads of the leaders of Harfleur if they persist in their "guilty defence."

Harry's ability to turn his consciousness of the horror of war into a weapon of coercion is fascinating. His men are not more tenderhearted, just less sensitive. Fluellen and the others beat their men into the breach, summarily condemn Bardolf to death for stealing, and adore their gallant king when he worthily commands them to cut their prisoners' throats. Even as the gentle Canterbury can in his mind's eye picture war as a May game, Harry's followers, honest Christian men all, can give themselves to the bestiality of war in good conscience and go about the business of slaughtering their enemies, as Macmorris can at Harfleur, with the name of Christ on their lips:

The town is beseech'd, and the trumpet calls us to the breach, and we talk, and be Crish, do nothing. 'Tis shame for us all. So God sa' me, 'tis shame to stand still, it is shame, by my hand! and there is throats to be cut, and works to be done, and there ish nothing done, so Crish sa' me, la!   (III.ii.115-21)

Such men do not disobey the Christian ethic; they are, like Harry, Christians as well as soldiers who, going about their good works on the field of battle, prove there is no activity so savage that men cannot reduce to sober order and to humane rules and disciplines. The discrimination of just and unjust wars was

11. Dover Wilson speaks of Harry as "a kind of English Tamburlaine" (*Henry V*, p. xxvi); Ribner calls Harry "Shakespeare's Christian Tamburlaine, noteworthy for his mercy rather than his cruelty" (*English History Play*, p. 185).

centuries old by Shakespeare's time. The rules of battle, which allowed captured populations to be expelled from cities and territories, to be sold into slavery or slaughtered, were carefully prescribed and scrupulously obeyed by honorable and courteous combatants. According to these rules, Harry's position at Harfleur was impeccable: a hopeless resistance to a seige was "guilty" because it needlessly cost the attackers' blood; and it thus gave the captors the right to slaughter or sell into captivity those who did not surrender. But, while the slaughter of babes at Harfleur would have been "right," the killing of the English camp boys was, as Fluellen remarked, "expressly against the law of arms," and angers the King.[12]

Shall our guide to *Henry V* be medieval and Renaissance treatises on the proprieties of war? Or shall we see war feelingly through Shakespeare's eyes and recognize that, despite the appeals in *Henry V* to God and Christ, despite the references to justice and mercy and the talk of ancient disciplines and rules, war is an assault on the foundations of civilization. It is a breach in the structure of moral restraints, a hunt in which the pack as well as the quarry are dehumanized, and the most primitive bloodlusts and sexual appetites are unleashed. Armies have their camp followers; conquerors take their choice of women, and maidenheads become as cheap as stinking mackerel, because women, caught up in the sexual excitements of war, are ready to offer their bodies even to the enemy soldiers. When what is animal in man is deliberately summoned forth and praised, other values, including that of mercy, are necessarily debased. Grace is equated, as in Harry's speeches to the French Ambassadors, not with angelic love but with a checked fury or a fettered passion.[13] The King who mercifully spares the inhabitants of Harfleur shows equal "grace" at Agincourt when he allows the French to sort out their dead.

In his oration at Southampton, Harry equated treason with hell. In his oration at Harfleur he equates war with hell. Yet the slaughter of women and children at Harfleur, like the slaughter of the outnumbered English envisioned

---

12. I thought of Fluellen's speeches when I read Barbara Tuchman's account of the rage of German officers at the civilian resistance in Belgium in World War I, which they countered with wholesale executions and burnings of occupied cities (*The Guns of August* [New York: Dell, 1963], pp. 350ff.). Mrs. Tuchman writes: "The Germans were obsessively concerned about violations of international law. They succeeded in overlooking the violation created by their presence in Belgium in favor of the violation committed, as they saw it, by Belgians resisting their presence" (p. 354). Where Harry speaks of "guilty resistance," the Germans spoke of "perfidious street fighting contrary to international law" (p. 353).

13. "We are no tyrant, but a Christian king," says Harry to the Ambassadors in the council scene, "Unto whose grace our passion is as subject / As are our wretches fett'red in our prisons" (I.ii.241-43).

around the campfire on the eve of Agincourt, is a dread possibility that never materializes. By keeping the battle offstage, Shakespeare spares us the horror of war. Instead of hearing the moans of the dying, we listen to the good-natured wrangling of Fluellen, Gower, Macmorris, and Jamy. We are told that the French dead cover the field after Agincourt but we do not see them. They are part of the body count, of the statistics which testify to English courage and divine providence. Taking his cue directly from Holinshed, the author of *The Famous Victories* depicts ordinary French soldiers dicing for and gloating over the prisoners and booty they expect to win at Agincourt. Shakespeare, however, never allows his audience to see the French equivalents of Williams and Bates. Juxtaposing the wretchedness of simple English soldiers against the foppish overconfidence of French generals who wager on the number they will kill, he never shows the answering fires of the French camp where other men like Williams and Bates await the morrow. If an audience is to rejoice in the victory, it cannot feel too much for those who will litter the field. All that it can know is the hubris, folly, and effeteness of the French leaders, who, in the judgment of some historians, were nearly as incompetent as Shakespeare describes.

I do not mean that as we read *Henry V* we expect to see a French campfire scene on the eve of Agincourt and are conscious of its omission. Since our view of the English army has included from the beginning such volunteers as Bardolph and Pistol, it seems natural enough that we eavesdrop on Williams and Bates at Agincourt. We do not expect to see ordinary French men at arms because our view of the French is confined from the beginning to noblemen and princes. It is artistically appropriate, moreover, that the moral issue at Agincourt be debated among Englishmen and be focused on the fate of the English soldiers, because here as elsewhere in the History Plays the crucial question is the King's responsibility for the well-being of his subjects. Accused of malfeasance by Gaunt and York, Richard II literally stood trial before his peers at his deposition. In like manner Hal was accused of irresponsibility and disloyalty by his father in both *Henry IV* plays. Once again on trial in *Henry V*, he is indicted first by the French Herald, who accuses him of misleading and betraying his ragged army. Sharper still are the accusations of falsehood made by Williams and Bates, who doubt the King's statement that he refuses ransom. Now that the glittering chivalric adventure threatens to become a shambles there is cause for recriminations. The tables have turned; the hunters of crowns and coronets have become the prey. The once eager greyhounds who strained at the leash are lank-cheeked, hungry, sick; their coats are shabby and worn. As the Chorus describes them waiting like cattle to be slaughtered, we remember the wretched company Falstaff led to Shrewsbury and wonder at the irony of fate that finds the cautious, calculating Harry in the shoes of the reckless Hotspur. Like the harebrained Percy, Harry seems to rejoice at Agincourt in the odds that lend a greater luster to the enterprise, and he announces to his men that he covets the honor that will be won at such a risk.

In war as in peace the end crowns all: the reckless winner is balladed for his daring; the reckless loser is scorned for his folly. It would have been amazing, however, if Hotspur had won at Shrewsbury, because his cause was shabby, his allies unfaithful, his council of war divided, and his leadership faulty. Conversely, Harry's triumph at Agincourt is not a piece of incredible luck. His leadership is inspiring and his men are splendid soldiers, brave and faithful to one another unto the last. Although hungry and sick in body, the English army does not droop from the infection of spirit that sapped the rebel cause at Shrewsbury. The wrangling around the campfire expresses the anxieties of men who are determined to fight the next day as bravely as they can for themselves and their king. Furthermore, though Harry says that he welcomes the great odds, because the fewer the men the greater the share of honor, he does not, like Hotspur, call recklessness security or refuse to calculate the risk. Not one to court danger for its own sake, he tells the French Herald that he would rather not fight at Agincourt, even as he confesses to his men that they are like shipwrecked men who can expect to be washed away by the tide. Wanting no reluctant men by his side, he invites those who have "no stomach to this fight" to depart with passport and crowns for convoy in their purse. If there is an analogue to Hotspur at Agincourt is is not Harry; it is the Dauphin, who echoes Hotspur's contempt for Hal and who wagers with his barons for men's lives. Or rather, the Dauphin is a counterfeit Hotspur who chatters about his horse and armor and courtly mistresses but whose only gest is the slaughter of the English camp boys.

Shrewsbury was a personal victory for Hal, who, dressed in glittering armor and plumed like an estridge, slew Hotspur in single combat. Agincourt is a victory in which all England shares, a victory won by men who received from their leader on the dark night before the battle "a largesse universal" like the sun. Although he has his doubts about the morrow, Harry does not parade them, and though he feels the weight of responsibility for the fates of the men under him, he does not shrink from their presence. Not the greatest of military strategists, he can inspire those who follow him—plain, outspoken warriors for the working day. He has the very accent of their manly pride, their gruff good humor, and their understated courage. He knows how they observe their feast days, the words and ceremonies with which they commemorate their times of fellowship and victory. At Shrewsbury the King's body became again a mystical host because devoted men marched in Henry's suits and died for his sake. At Agincourt the bond between the King and his men is of a humbler sort; it is symbolized by the cloak which disguises Harry's royalty from Williams and Bates and which allows them to speak as equals and share for a while their common fears and hopes.

One would like to say that at the moment of supreme crisis Harry discovers his humanity or grows companionable again. But though he can disguise his majesty with a cloak, he cannot shrug off the consciousness of his majesty and of his soldiers' commonness. Even when he speaks to Bates of the King, with "his ceremonies laid by, in his nakedness" appearing "but a man," he cannot see himself as but a man. On the morrow he will proclaim to the army that those who shed their blood with him will be his brothers; on the eve of the battle he expresses in soliloquy a very different point of view: a contempt and disgust for ordinary men which recalls his treatment of Francis, Poins, and Falstaff in the *Henry IV* plays. He bemoans the hard condition of greatness, "subject to the breath / Of every fool." He compares the uneasy sleep of kings with the sound sleep of "the wretched slave," "Who with a body fill'd, and vacant mind, / Gets him to rest, cramm'd with distressful bread" (IV.i.286-7). He meditates on the life of the "lackey," the "slave," the "gross brain," who does not know "What watch the king keeps to maintain the peace."

Although he has learned the language of common men in the tavern, Harry cannot sympathize with the lowly born. He is not really moved by the prospect of his soldiers' fates, nor does he grieve for the lonely impoverished widows and orphaned children they will leave behind. What agonizes him is the thought that he will be accountable for all this suffering. He joins the men about the campfire partly to confess the anxieties he dare not reveal as King and partly to be absolved by them of guilt for the impending disaster. Much more honest about his situation than Hotspur, Harry nevertheless seeks out the soul of goodness in things evil and discovers the moral uses of adversity. Forgetting that his army has invaded France, he speaks to his commanders of the French as bad neighbors who make the peaceful English early risers. And he plays the King's counsel at the campfire as deftly as he played the prosecutor of the traitors at Southampton. Like a clever advocate, he can argue both sides of the same question. At Harfleur he spoke of impious war that carries its foul contagion of murder and rapine. At the campfire he describes war as God's beadle who takes vengeance upon the sinners killed in battle. On the morrow he will embrace his men as brothers, but now he meditates on their likely crimes of murder, seduction, riot, and robbery. Unable to accept his responsibility for having led them to the brink of disaster, he would like to attribute their fates to the fortunes of war, or, rather, to the risks of life, because he would compare their plight to that of men who miscarry at sea or are assailed by robbers.

To judge Harry fairly we must recognize that he did not have to debate this issue with his men, nor did he have to tolerate their insinuations about his honesty. Where a hypocrite would have had his revenge on Williams and walked away more convinced than ever of his righteousness, Harry is stricken by his soldiers' refusal to absolve him. At Southampton he had relished the role of the betrayed king—a role which Henry VI, Richard II, and Henry IV had played before him in the History Plays. But he cannot bear to be cast in the role of Judas by his own men when he was prepared to play Pilate and wash their blood from his hands. When they reject his facile arguments, he complains, as so often before, that he is misunderstood. Perhaps he is right, because his soldiers are at least as obtuse as he is. Just as he would shrug off responsibility for their deaths, they would place the burden of their immortal souls on him. He would forget that he led them to the edge of a catastrophe; they would forget their eagerness to be led. Unlike the wretches Falstaff commanded, they were not impressed; they were volunteers eager to seek their fortunes in France. Yet when Harry insists upon the righteousness of the King's cause—"his cause being just and his quarrel good"—they insist on their ignorance of such matters: "That's more than we know." They cannot be duped by his talk of fathers and sons because they do not want a royal father or brother; they want a royal scapegoat. And though (like Henry IV and Falstaff before them) they accuse Harry of untruth, they would not think of disobeying him, because obedience is their moral absolution: "we know enough if we know we are the King's subjects. If his cause be wrong, our obedience to the King wipes the crime of it out of us" (IV.i.137-9).

For Williams and Bates ignorance of the King's cause is bliss. For Harry there is no comparable escape. Without a single confidant, he can only ruminate on the unfairness of life which makes the royal destiny so much harder than that of common men:

> And what have kings that privates have not too,
> Save ceremony, save general ceremony?
> And what art thou, thou idol Ceremony?

What kind of god art thou, that suffer'st more
Of mortal griefs than do thy worshippers?
What are thy rents? what are thy comings-in?
O Ceremony, show me but thy worth!
What is thy soul of adoration?
Art thou aught else but place, degree, and form,
Creating awe and fear in other men?
Wherein thou art less happy being fear'd,
Than they in fearing.
What drink'st thou oft, instead of homage sweet,
But poison'd flattery? O! be sick, great greatness,
And bid thy ceremony give thee cure!   (IV.i.255-69)

  Shall we say that under great duress Harry, like his father, and like Richard
II and Henry VI, discovers the disillusioning vanity of the royal office? Or shall
we say that the prince who complained that he had been misinterpreted by
Poins, by his father, and by his brothers now complains that he is maligned by
the gross vacant minds of his brothers in arms? In *Henry IV Part II* Harry spoke
of the crown as a golden scalding care and protested his uneasiness in the
gorgeous garments of majesty. Now when he expounds the mockery of the Idol
Ceremony, we are once more unconvinced because again and again he returns
to the thought of those who stoop before him: he speaks of "homage sweet,"
of "flexure and low-bending," of commanding "the beggar's knee." Even as he
denies the satisfactions of power and the pleasure of rule, his rhetoric swells to
a crescendo that proclaims the oceanic splendor of majesty:

'Tis not the balm, the sceptre, and the ball,
The sword, the mace, the crown imperial,
The intertissued robe of gold and pearl,
The farced title running fore the king,
The throne he sits on, nor the tide of pomp
That beats upon the high shore of this world—   (IV.i.277-82)

It is all vanity, every last drop of it, but Harry never thinks of renouncing it.
Having led his army to the pit in search of empire and everlasting fame, he
speaks with heavy heart at Agincourt of the thankless burden of keeping the
peace.[14]

  While his father lived Harry avoided his presence. When his father lamented
the way he met the crown, Harry seemed not to understand. On the eve of

  14. See Palmer's discussion of the humanity of Shakespeare's portrayal of Harry at
Agincourt (*Political Characters,* pp. 241-44).

Agincourt, however, he begs God not to think "upon the fault / My father made in compassing the crown!" (IV.i.310-11). Characteristically, it does not occur to him that Agincourt may be a fitting retribution for his own vainglory. Insisting on his blamelessness, he can only attribute the impending catastrophe to the sins of his father. Hearing him speak of his father's guilt, one understands the rage with which he had turned upon his would-be assassins at Southampton; their plot to assassinate him would strike him as a primal and original sin, because just such a crime has "left a kind of blot" on his own title, which had been gained by treason and murder. Accustomed to measuring out his moral obligations, Harry would strike a bargain with God, [15] but he is not so crass as to think that he can buy absolution. Even as he enumerates his acts of contrition and the prayers he has commissioned "to pardon blood," he knows that these ceremonies are "nothing worth." All is finally in God's hand and God's will; only from God can come the absolution of a miraculous victory.

The attempted communion about the campfire ends in bitterness. The next morning, however, Harry and his men stand together against the enemy, and though their fellowship cannot last, for the brief time of the battle they are the few, the happy few, the band of brothers. Finding his redemption in the great triumph, Harry is, as after Shrewsbury, at peace with himself and able to relax and joke with his men. He allows Fluellen and Williams to appeal one another and to hurl gauntlets of defiance and accusations of treason at one another, as Mowbray and Bolingbroke did in the opening scene of *Richard II;* but he makes certain that no blood is spilled in this last of his practical jokes. Fearing no treason from his subjects, and desiring no revenge on the loyal men who insulted his majesty, he fills Williams' glove with crowns and thus plays one last time the king of courtesy and good fellows. Never again will the past return to haunt him: Falstaff is dead; Nym, Bardolph, and the Page die in France; and the Hostess, we soon hear, "is dead i' the spital / Of the malady of France." The only survivor of the Boar's Head is Pistol, who is beaten for his cowardice and destined for a beggarly end. The true heroes of Agincourt will, on Crispin's day, show their wounds to family and friends; the cowardly Pistol, who came to France the very blood to suck, will exhibit his patches for alms. Like the

15. Una Ellis-Fermor somewhat unfairly describes Harry's prayer as an attempt to "bargain with his God like a pedlar" in "Shakespeare's Political Plays," *The Frontiers of Drama* (London: Methuen, 1948), p. 47. But it is true that Harry enumerates every jot of the penance he has paid, and Miss Ellis-Fermor's essay is a splendid piece of criticism.

crippled survivors of Falstaff's company at Shrewsbury, all he will have for his pains is a license to beg, and what he did not learn of charity at Harfleur he will learn from the London citizenry at the town's end.

A journey's end for Harry and his men, the victory of Agincourt would have been a logical place for Shakespeare to end the plot of *Henry V*. What better ending for the play could he have wanted than the scene of comradeship which concludes Act IV? And what better epilogue could he have fashioned for the play (and the tetralogy) than the Chorus to Act V, which, describing Harry's triumphal return to London, shows England once again strong and united? As soon as the last act begins, the glow of Agincourt begins to fade, for the cudgeling of Pistol ends the brief time of fellowship, and the negotiations for the peace treaty reveal that Harry is less attractive as a lover than as a soldier. Perhaps Shakespeare missed his mark in the brief last act; perhaps he set out to humanize and domesticate his mighty hunter of battles and succeeded only in making Harry too hearty and downright a wooer. More likely, however, he knew precisely what artistic effect he aimed at. If Harry's wooing lacks the tender humor and intimacy of Hotspur's moments with Kate, it is because the conqueror of Agincourt cannot, even in his "passion," forget his royal self; and he will not allow the others to forget that Kate is one of the prizes of war, his "capital demand." We prefer the captain with his men to the rough-and-ready wooer because the former is more natural than the latter. When he pleads his love Harry is not unbuttoned and unselfconscious, the "naked" man with his ceremonies laid by. He is the victor consciously savoring the pleasures of his victory, certain that whatever approach he takes this French princess will be his. Having proved his greatness beyond all doubt, he deliberately underplays his royalty and takes a kingly pleasure in seeming the rough-edged boor, the country squire who sold his farm to buy a crown. Certain now that all men acknowledge his royalty, he can joke about the original sin of his father's ambition, which before he spoke of only to God:

Now beshrew my father's ambition! he was thinking of civil wars when he got me; therefore was I created with a stubborn outside, with an aspect of iron, that, when I come to woo ladies, I fright them.   (V.ii.241-5)

Though a fine mimic of common men, Harry has too much taste for privilege ever to be a king of good fellows. For all his rough-and-ready manner, he insists that Ceremony bow before his greatness; he will have from Kate the kiss which custom forbids, because, as he puts it, "nice customs curtsy to great kings." And though he plays the plain fellow to Kate, he is, like his father, adamant about receiving the full measure of his royal title. Just as Bolingbroke asked York to look on him as a father and forced Richard to adopt him as his heir, so Hal, who took the Lord Chief Justice as his foster father, insists that the King of France adopt him and name him his "tres cher fils Henry roi d'Angleterre, heritier de France."

In the first act of *Henry V* Harry speaks eloquently of the suffering that war will exact. In the last act Burgundy describes the devastation of France, whose land and people have been reduced to a state of near savagery. Harry, it would seem, is unmoved by Burgundy's appeal. Insisting that the business of war is business, he reminds the French that peace is a commodity to be bargained for, not a blessing to be bestowed:

> You must buy that peace
> With full accord to all our just demands;
> Whose tenures and particular effects
> You have, enschedul'd briefly, in your hands.   (V.ii.70-3)

What is it to the victor if the French people are brutalized? As Pistol sucks blood, he will show mercy. As Harry gets what he demands, he will prove "charitable." To be sure, he seems no less humane than the other princes who meet to determine the articles of peace. Like Harry in the first act, Burgundy raises the moral issue of war and peace but does not really press it; and he and Harry obviously understand one another perfectly. Men of the world, they are accustomed to the realities of power and sophisticated in their view of politics and women, subjects they handle with equal ease. Undaunted by his brush with catastrophe at Agincourt, Harry still dreams of martial glory and of founding a dynasty of warriors. Since he has won Kate with "scambling," he is confident that she "must therefore needs prove a good soldier-breeder" and with him "compound a boy, half French, half English, that shall go to Constantinople and take the Turk by the beard" (V.ii.221-3). But though Harry can bequeath his piety to his son, he cannot hand down his imperial abilities. He proves in France that he has all the qualities of a thoroughbred save one: he cannot breed true. The descendant of warrior-kings, he will father an heir more fit for a monastery than a throne room.

Harry has won a place for himself in Chronicles in time to come. He has not, however, called back yesterday; he has not recreated the stable political order which fell with Richard II. Where Richard's authority rested on the great pyramid of feudal privileges, Harry stands alone in the play as sovereign of England; more like a Tudor than a Plantagenet monarch, he is adored by his followers as Elizabeth was adored, as a person not as a god. Fluellen tells the

King that he need not be ashamed of him "so long as your majesty is an honest man," and whatever private thoughts Harry may have about his imperial greatness, he must publicly admit that with his ceremonies laid by, he is merely human. Defending himself against the charge of lese majesty, Williams claims that he did not insult the King on the eve of Agincourt, because Harry came to the campfire as a man, not as a king. In accepting this excuse, Harry implicitly admits that majesty is a garment worn, not (as Richard II imagined) an inherited mystery that exalts one man above other mortals. The royal office is anointed, not the man who fills it.

Like *Richard III*, *Henry V* concludes with a prayer that a royal marriage will make friends of foes and secure the blessings of peace for future generations, but it is hard to believe that Harry's marriage to Katherine was made in heaven when she is so obviously a political pawn. Although the hand of hot and forcing violation will never threaten her as it does the women of Harfleur, she will endure handling because she is a trophy of the hunt, a maiden princess identified with cities "girdled with maiden walls that war hath never ent'red." In possessing her, Harry possesses France; in compounding with her a boy, he improves his own breeding. Urged by Canterbury to look back to his mighty ancestors, Harry exhorts his men at Harfleur to remember their "fathers of war-proof," to dishonor not their mothers, and to prove that they were worth the breeding. And breeding is important to those who imitate the action of the tiger because it distinguishes friends from foes, Englishmen from Frenchmen. Why should the English, Bardolph asks, keep knives to cut each other's throat, when together they can cut the enemy's throats in France. Clipping English crowns is a capital offense, but, as Harry declares, it is "no English treason to cut French crowns, and tomorrow the King himself will be a clipper" (IV.i.245-6). Nevertheless, the differences in breeding between Englishmen and Frenchmen will not bear too close a scrutiny. For if Harry looks back to his distant ancestors, he may remember that he is a descendant of a Norman conqueror of England. As the Duke of Bourbon contemptuously puts it, what are the English but "Normans, bastard Normans"; similarly, the Dauphin describes them as "a few sprays of us, / The emptying of our fathers' luxury," some rude graftings from the best garden of the world. There are other mixed breeds among the fierce mastiffs and bulldogs in Harry's ranks—Welsh, Scots, and Irish, each proud of their blood and ancestry and sensitive to insults. Fluellen's mention of Macmorris' "nation" touches a nerve so raw that bloodshed threatens:

Of my nation? What ish my nation? Ish a villain, and a basterd, and a knave, and a rascal. What ish my nation? Who talks of my nation? . . . I do not know you so good a man as myself. So Chrish save me, I will cut off your head.

(III.ii.132-34, 144-45)

Can Englishmen and Frenchmen, ancient enemies, learn to be brothers when English, Welsh, Scot, and Irish squabble in Harry's army, and when private quarrels break out among Harry's men as soon as the victory is won? Even the brotherhood of the fallen does not long endure, because the French Herald begs permission to sort out the bodies of nobles and commoners so that princes will not "lie drown'd and soak'd in mercenary blood" and the "vulgar drench their peasant limbs / In blood of princes." Harry, of course, stands above petty national prejudices and antagonisms. He speaks as easily of brotherhood to his French enemies in the last scene as he does to his English soldiers before the battle. He is no closer, however, to his brothers Bedford and Gloucester in *Henry V* than he was in *Henry IV Part II*, where he met them like strangers after his father's death and had to reassure them that a Harry succeeds a Harry, not an Amurath an Amurath.

No sooner does Harry win his empire than the Chorus enters to speak in the Epilogue of the "small time" of his greatness. Nevertheless, as Harry prophesied it would, the memory of Agincourt will endure as a precious reminder of the courage and determination that can sustain a people in the face of terrible adversity. "Old men forget," says Harry to his troops at Agincourt, "yet all shall be forgot," but the memory of Agincourt will live. Its story

shall the good man teach his son;
And Crispin Crispian shall ne'er go by,
From this day to the ending of the world,
But we in it shall be remembered.   (IV.iii.56-9)

To the ending of the world is a long time, however, for feast-days to be observed, and no man can be absolutely certain how his fame will be bruited in future times. Just as Alexander is remembered in *Henry V* as the man who conquered the world and in a drunken rage killed his friend, Harry is remembered by Shakespeare and his readers as the hero king who triumphed at Agincourt and turned away the fat old knight. Although we are advised by critics not to linger over the rejection of Falstaff, Shakespeare refers to it a half dozen times or more in *Henry V*, and though we are warned not to sentimentalize Falstaff's fate, Shakespeare makes the Hostess' description of Falstaff's death the only moment in the play that touches the heart.[16]

Where the last lines of *Richard III* look ahead to an Elizabethan present, the

16. Most would agree with Chambers that her description is the only thing in *Henry V* that is intimate and "touches the depths" (*Shakespeare: A Survey,* p. 145).

last lines of *Henry V* look back on a legendary past which the playwright's art has for a time restored to present memory. In a retrospective if not valedictory mood in his Epilogue, Shakespeare meditates not only on Harry's epic achievement but also on his own epic achievement in the History Plays. Recalling to his audience's minds the plays of the first tetralogy, "which oft our stage has shown," he whimsically begs his listeners to look kindly on *Henry V* for their sake. Apologize though he may for his "rough and all-unable pen," he must have known that his art would last longer than the small time of Harry's empire. He must also have suspected that if the memory of Agincourt were to last unto the ending doom, it would be because his powerful rhyme would outlive the gilded monuments to Harry's victories. As he came to the ending of *Henry V*, Shakespeare's thoughts returned to the sonnets in which he had posed the tender living memory of art against the speechless ironies of statues overturned. Appropriately enough, his last words about the king who wielded Fortune's sword are an Epilogue composed in sonnet form.

9. HENRY VIII

Until the nineteenth century Shakespeare's authorship of *Henry VIII* was unquestioned. But ever since James Spedding argued, in 1850, that there are two different poetic voices and dramatic styles in the play, one Shakespeare's, the other apparently Fletcher's, critics have debated what is Shakespearean or un-Shakespearean in *Henry VIII* and have argued over stylistic, linguistic, and metrical evidence supporting the thesis of collaboration.[1] Because this evidence is wholly internal, and Shakespeare's colleagues included *Henry VIII* in the First Folio, I could put aside the authorship controversy and discuss the play "as if it were Shakespeare's," except that, like many other scholars, I am convinced that Fletcher collaborated with Shakespeare in *Henry VIII* and that Fletcher's role in the collaboration was by far the preeminent one. Spedding's division of the play, which has been confirmed by investigators using more

---

1. Spedding's article "Who Wrote Shakespeare's *Henry VIII*?" appeared in *Gentleman's Magazine* (August 1850). The same year Samuel Hickson came independently to the conclusion that *Henry VIII* was a collaboration by Shakespeare and Fletcher (*Notes and Queries*, II [24 August 1850]). In a recent book, Paul Bertram has argued that the controversy over the authorship of *Henry VIII* is really a dead issue which retains some semblance of life only because scholars are still burdened by "the worn-out assumptions of the past" (*Shakespeare and the Two Noble Kinsmen* [New Brunswick, N.J.: Rutgers Univ. Press, 1965], pp. 124-79). To read the introductions to the new Arden and new Cambridge editions of *Henry VIII* is to realize, however, that the authorship controversy is not a last flickering of the discredited disintegrative scholarship of the Victorian period. Many expert and objective textual scholars have studied the question in recent years and come to contrary conclusions about the authorship of *Henry VIII*. In the new Arden edition (London: Methuen, 1957), R. A. Foakes presents the evidence and arguments supporting Shakespeare's sole authorship of the play. In the new Cambridge edition (Cambridge: Cambridge Univ. Press, 1962), J. C. Maxwell persuasively marshalls the case for the thesis of collaboration.

refined and reliable methods of textual analysis, attributes about three-fourths of the text to Fletcher and gives only one and a half scenes of the last three acts to Shakespeare.[2] Even in the first two acts, Shakespeare's contribution, I think, is limited to the working out of a conception which is in every essential respect Fletcherian.

Retired from the stage and willing to collaborate with Fletcher in *The Two Noble Kinsmen* and the lost *Cardenio*, Shakespeare would not have been reluctant to lend his pen and, more important, his great name to one last History Play commissioned by the King's Men.[3] No doubt it was easier for him to adapt to Fletcher's courtly manner than for Fletcher to imitate his way with history, though Fletcher tried in a superficial way to do so and pieced together his conception of *Henry VIII* from Shakespeare's History Plays. He found the inspiration for Cranmer's vision in the prayer by Richmond that concludes *Richard III*; and he makes a show of dealing in *Henry VIII* with the themes of treason, justice, and royal favoritism, that were of paramount importance in the tetralogies. Even with these Shakespearean flourishes, *Henry VIII* is so lacking in essential substance that critics wonder what it is about.[4] A tour de force, it pretends to seriousness only in the way that a trompe l'oeil painting pretends to depth, and its representation of political issues is so vague that it leaves Wolsey's role in English history very much in doubt. We cannot tell whether he was a force for good or evil because the evidence within the play is quite contradictory, and his personality as well as his deeds are ambiguous. In a like way, the nature and political significance of Buckingham's treason remain elusive, and the very question of his guilt is unresolved. One could forgive Fletcher for blurring or evading the political issues of Henry's reign if he

2. Shakespeare is credited with writing I.iⅈ II.iii&iv; III.ii.1-203; and V.i. All other scenes, the Prologue, and Epilogue are attributed to Fletcher.

3. When one considers the greatness of Shakespeare's reputation as a writer of History Plays, it is perhaps not surprising that his colleagues in the Kings Men would advertise *Henry VIII* as by his authorship and that they would think of the play as "his" despite Fletcher's very large share in its authorship. As a writer of romance, Fletcher's reputation was as great as, if not greater than, Shakespeare's, but he had no reputation as a writer of History Plays, whereas Shakespeare was the supreme master of the genre.

4. In an article entitled "What is Shakespeare's *Henry VIII* About?" Frank Kermode argues that the play is a latter-day version of *The Mirror for Magistrates*—that is, a collection of tragic falls. Kermode's article appeared in the *Durham University Journal,* IX (1948), 48-55, and was reprinted in *Shakespeare: The Histories,* ed. E. M. Waith (Englewood Cliffs, N.J.: Prentice Hall, 1965), pp. 168-79, from which my citations are taken. In his article Kermode, who thinks *Henry VIII* wholly Shakespearean, does not explain why Shakespeare regresses in it to a more primitive dramatic form than that used in *Henry VI Part I.* Nor does he consider whether there is any other play by Shakespeare so loosely constructed and so amorphous in substance that a critic must speculate as to what it is about.

greatly realized the historical figures who appear in his scenes. But, except for Katherine (and she only in the early Shakespearean scenes), the characterizations are either shallow or opaque. More often than not, scenes are fashioned as successions of emotional closeups: one watches the menace of a frown, the welling of a tear, the curling of a lip, or the breathing of a passion. The dramatic portraiture is so conventionalized, however, that it is hard to distinguish Buckingham's noble posture of resignation from that which Katherine and Wolsey finally assume. Instead of character in action, Fletcher provides an artfully choreographed ballet of emotional gestures.

The concern with elegantly contrived surfaces in *Henry VIII* is most apparent in the extraordinarily elaborate stage directions and descriptions of courtly spectacle. This lovingly detailed attention to pageantry and ceremony has no parallel in the earlier History Plays or in the late romances. Although banners, fanfares, processions, and rituals of various kinds play an important part in the staging of the History Plays, and though masques and shows have an integral part in the moral and dramatic actions of *The Winter's Tale* and *The Tempest*, only in *Henry VIII* is the glitter of pageantry its own excuse for being. No strain of discord or act of rage is allowed to mar the graceful forms of ritual at Henry's court; no irony shadows the brilliant displays of pomp or interferes with the audience's pleasure in gorgeous costumery and heraldry. Where the ritual moments of the *Henry VI* plays, of *Richard III* and *Richard II,* engage the minds and emotions of the audience, the spectacles of *Henry VIII* merely feast the eye. The emphasis is not, as in the earlier History Plays, on the decorums symbolized by ritual, but on the niceties which only a connoisseur of courtly spectacle would appreciate: who stands next to the King, who by his right side, who by his left; who enters first in a procession, who last; who wears a golden coronal and who plain circlets of gold. Such authenticity of detail is superfluous to the representation of politics and history; it exists to give an audience or a reader the thrill of a vicarious closeness to luxury and power—to bring them within the charmed circle of the Court, which is in *Henry VIII* a very heaven.[5]

Although many of the scenes of the earlier History Plays take place in throne rooms and halls of state, their actions move out of the Court into the streets and taverns of London, to other shires, cities, and villages of the realm. There

5. The only other Shakespearean play in which there is something like this detail of stage directions is *The Two Noble Kinsmen,* entered in the Stationers' Register and printed in 1634 as a play by John Fletcher and William Shakespeare. An elaborateness of stage directions is no more characteristic, however, of the plays of Fletcher than of Shakespeare.

are scenes of Gloucestershire, Kent, and Northumberland, and characters who speak with the accents of Wales, Scotland, and Ireland and who create an imaginative sense of the different regions and peoples of Britain. Only in *Henry VIII* is the *mise en scène* confined to the precincts of the Court, and only in *Henry VIII* does the backstairs politics of the Court—the plotting against adversaries and maneuvering for royal favor—become the actual focus of plot. Where the drama of courtly faction and favoritism in the tetralogies encompasses large political and moral issues, the drama of courtly intrigue in *Henry VIII* remains on the level of personal animosities. We watch the courtly pack close in on Wolsey when he has been brought to bay by the King's displeasure, and we listen in the dialogue to a gazette of courtly gossip about who's in, who's out, whom the King frowned on or leaned on, whom he met or danced with. This is the reporting of an insider, one who knows the kind of jokes courtiers tell about the King's "conscience," and who is so sophisticated in his own values and attitudes as to be incapable of criticizing the malice and vanity of courtiers. There is not the slightest suggestion in *Henry VIII* that the greedy scrambling for the King's favor may damage the body politic; and though every ordinary person in the play is grossly caricatured, not one satiric glance is directed at courtly snobbery or affectation.[6] We look in vain for an Iden or a Fluellen or even a Feeble—for any of the common men who have their full share of decency, shrewdness, good humor, and humanity in the other History Plays. The several commoners who do appear in *Henry VIII* are unpardonably common in their behavior. The lascivious chatter and greediness of the Old Lady contrasts sharply with Anne's gentility, even as the Judas-like "treachery" of the Surveyor heightens sympathy for Buckingham, who accepts his martyrdom with touching grace. Lest there be any doubt about the vulgarity of the crowd, the Porter and his man, coarse clowns in themselves, walk out to lampoon the mob at the christening of Elizabeth as a fry of fornication, a herd of rutting animals whose heads and buttocks were created to be knocked with staves.

Although Shakespeare's view of men was hardly egalitarian, his ideal of nobility was untainted by the courtly snobbery that is a characteristic of *Henry VIII* and of Fletcher's drama. Identifying nobility with courtliness and caste, Fletcher makes refinement appear a cardinal virtue and boorishness a deadly

6. By contrast, Shakespeare's late romances make telling satiric comments on courtly vanities and affectations. One thinks especially of the characterizations of Antonio and Sebastian in *The Tempest*, of Iachimo in *Cymbeline*, and of Autolycus' incomparable parodying of courtly "airs" in IV.iv of *The Winter's Tale*. In a larger sense, *The Winter's Tale* is a profound comment on the oversophisticated sensibility of the Court.

sin. Thus, the treason attributed to Buckingham in *Henry VIII* seems less dreadful than the *arriviste* greed and insolence of Wolsey, a butcher's cur who has risen above his place and betters. Whatever crime the well-bred Buckingham may have committed, he seems a nobler figure than Wolsey because he has a finer spirit, or at least a finer manner. Even those who learn the vanity of great titles in *Henry VIII* never lose their concern with manner and manners. The dejected Katherine can forgive and cherish the husband who unjustly divorced her, but she turns with rage on a Messenger who fails to kneel when he approaches her. Similarly, Henry will allow Cranmer's enemies to invent spurious charges against him, but he stops the judicial proceeding when he discovers that the councilors treat Cranmer as if he were a "lousy footboy."

Where Shakespeare values the nobility of mind that is expressed in steadfast loyalties and courageous acts, Fletcher finds the quintessence of nobility in exquisite gestures of submission. Thus, while the courtiers of *Henry VIII* strike postures of manly defiance now and then, the highest form of nobility in the play is expressed by "feminine" acquiescences. Where Shakespeare and other Jacobean tragedians celebrate a stoic acceptance and readiness to endure, Fletcher, in *Henry VIII* and other plays, is uniquely the laureate of emotional surrender. He alone enshrines his characters' failures of will and makes the instinct to self-abasement in an Aspatia in *The Maid's Tragedy* or a Katherine in *Henry VIII* seem sublime. In those scenes of Acts I and II which can confidently be attributed to Shakespeare, Katherine has the courage of her convictions. Devoted to the principles of justice and concerned with the welfare of her people, she is a noble queen as well as a loyal wife. Like Hermione in *The Winter's Tale,* she knows her royal worth, and outraged, as Hermione is, by her husband's desire to cast her off, she also refuses to admit the legality of her trial. The lyric pathos of the song which opens Act III, however, announces Fletcher's attenuation of Katherine's nobility. Once again she turns on Wolsey as she did at the arraignment, but her indignation burns low and she lacks the will to defend her place and her dignity. Before the scene ends, she turns from Hermione into patient Griseld, from a dramatic personality into a sentimental stereotype of feminine helplessness. Even as she again declares her constancy and her royalty, she admits that she is "a woman friendless, hopeless":

What will become of me now, wretched lady?
I am the most unhappy woman living.
[*To her Women*] Alas, poor wenches, where are now your fortunes?
Shipwrack'd upon a kingdom where no pity,

No friends, no hope, no kindred weep for me,
Almost no grave allow'd me! Like the lily
That once was mistress of the field and flourish'd,
I'll hang my head and perish.   (III.i.146-53)

This poetic accent is unmistakable: it is the sadness of Ophelia and Desdemona
remembered and transmuted in the characterization of the forlorn Aspatia.
"When I am dead, good wench," the dying Katherine says,

Let me be us'd with honour. Strew me over
With maiden flowers, that all the world may know
I was a chaste wife to my grave.   (IV.ii.167-70)

The same lyric poignancy invests Aspatia's dirge in *The Maid's Tragedy*:

Lay a garland on my hearse
    Of the dismal yew.
Maidens, willow branches bear;
    Say I died true.[7]

We cannot object that this Katherine, who is abjectly grateful for any scrap
of comfort sent by Henry, is not the Katherine who the Chronicles said
"stood stiffelie in hir first opinion, that she was his true and lawfull wife, and
from the same would not by anie meanes be remooved."[8] For Fletcher, like
Shakespeare, must be granted an artistic freedom with history and a right to
conceive of Katherine as an Aspatia rather than a Hermione—or perhaps as a
Hermione whose resoluteness is sapped by loneliness and misery. But we must
object when Fletcher on the one hand exploits the pathos of Katherine's
"wrong," and on the other hand obfuscates Henry's role in the divorce.
Even in the trial scene (which Shakespeare wrote), Katherine is a Hermione
without a Leontes, or rather she is a Hermione who blames her wrong on
Wolsey (a somewhat degraded Camillo), although in fact her oppressor is
Henry, who instigates the divorce proceeding and chafes at its slowness. With
remarkable legerdemain, Fletcher first makes Wolsey seem the villainous
engineer of the divorce; then he makes him appear disloyal to the King because
he opposes the divorce. He makes an audience sigh over the wrong that is being
done to Katherine, and not much later he allows it to to think Cranmer a

7. Like Katherine in *Henry VIII*, Aspatia has been cast aside by her lover, who marries
another woman; and like Katherine, she remains absolutely devoted to the man who has
betrayed her. See my discussion of *The Maid's Tragedy* in *Moral Vision of Jacobean
Tragedy*, pp. 173-79.
8. Holinshed, III, 774.

"worthy fellow" because he obtains the divorce which Henry desires. The "ambiguity" of Wolsey's role in the divorce proceeding is in a sense permitted by the Chronicles, which report that rumors of his machinations were current at the time of the divorce, and that Katherine accused him of instigating it.[9] Where Holinshead leaves little doubt that Wolsey acted as Henry's agent in the divorce, Fletcher deliberately enhances the ambiguity of his role. Even though Wolsey protests his innocence at the trial and is vindicated by the King, he appears nevertheless to be Katherine's enemy. Three times he is accused by Katherine of wronging her, and these accusations are seconded by Henry's courtiers. Even more damning is the scene (invented by Fletcher) in which Henry meets Anne at Wolsey's palace, for it creates the impression that Henry's infatuation with Anne is in part one of Wolsey's contrivances. In other words, Fletcher does not simply dramatize the historical "fact" that Wolsey was thought by many to have instigated the divorce proceeding; he contrives the scenes of *Henry VIII* so that the audience shares the mistaken impression that Wolsey, not the King, is Katherine's persecutor. As Paul Bertram observes, "Through a remarkable piece of Shakespearean sleight-of-hand, never in the play are we made aware of Henry rejecting Katherine; indeed, he usually speaks as her advocate."[10] The sleight-of-hand is remarkable; that it is Shakespearean is extremely doubtful because such manipulation of appearances is the very hallmark of Fletcher's dramaturgy.

Because Shakespeare's political and psychological insights were profounder than those of the Chroniclers, he may invite us to look beneath the surface of the Chronicle account, as he does when he depicts the banishing of Suffolk in *Henry VI Part II*. But if he makes this episode more ambiguous than it seems in Hall, he precisely defines the characters of the Nevils, Suffolk's accusers, and he brings into focus the struggle for power that culminated in Suffolk's banishment. In like manner, he makes the character of Bolingbroke far more distinct in *Richard II* than it is in Holinshed, even though he deepens the ambiguity of Bolingbroke's motive for returning from exile. Fletcher, in contrast, again and again makes the historical personalities in *Henry VIII* more opaque and ambiguous than they appear in the Chronicles. Where Shakespeare seeks to fathom the contradictions of a Richard II, Fletcher deliberately creates contradictory impressions of Buckingham, Wolsey, and Henry, because his goal is to intrigue and tantalize his audience, not to explore the mysteries and paradoxes of human personality. In suggesting, for example, that

9. See Holinshed, III, 736-40.
10. *Shakespeare and The Two Noble Kinsmen,* p. 168.

Buckingham is ensnared by Wolsey's machinations, Fletcher seems merely to follow Holinshed, who reports that "the cardinall boiling in hatred against the duke of Buckingham, and thirsting for his bloud," devised his destruction, and entrapped him by suborning his surveyor. According to Holinshed, Buckingham denied ever being a traitor at his arraignment, but at his execution "he said he had offended the kings grace through negligence and lacke of grace, and desired all noble men to beware by him, and all men to pray for him, and that he trusted to die the kings true man." The pity Holinshed feels for Buckingham does not prevent him from condemning the Duke's disloyalty:

Alas that ever the grace of truth was withdrawne from so noble a man, that he was not to his king in allegiance as he ought to have beene! Such is the end of ambition, the end of false prophesies, the end of evil life, and evill counsell; but speciallie the end of malice, which grew to so huge and monstruous a fire in the hautie hart of the proud cardinall, that nothing could asswage it, but the bloud of this noble duke, against whome he had procured this processe in iudgement ended with the execution of death . . . .

In Holinshed's view, Buckingham's "offense was traitorous and therefore deserved as law had provided."[11]

More "neutral" than Holinshed, Fletcher makes his portrait of Buckingham a masterpiece of artistic equivocation. On the one hand there seems to be uncontrovertible proof of Buckingham's treason: a Gentleman who was present at the trial reports that there were evidence, proofs, and "confessions of divers witnesses," which Buckingham could not fling from him. On the other hand the charges seem to be trumped up by Wolsey, and when Buckingham appears on his way to execution he earnestly protests his innocence and devotion to the King. What shall we say of Buckingham: that he is a wronged innocent? a cunning dissimulator? a dreamer who has convinced himself of the fantasy of his innocence? These questions would be germane if the characterization were by Shakespeare, Chapman, Jonson, Webster, or any dramatist concerned with psychological and moral truths.[12] They are irrelevant to Fletcher's portrait of Buckingham, which is all facade—a study in noble anger and saintlike resignation. Holinshed draws a fairly conventional de casibus moral about

11. *Chronicles,* III, 657, 662-63.
12. Compare, for example, the opaqueness of the treatment of Buckingham with the clarity of the treatment of the traitorous Duke Byron by Chapman in *Byron's Tragedy.* Like Buckingham, Byron protests his innocence, but he is clearly guilty; and though Byron is entrapped by his enemies, his insistence upon his innocence is a fascinating portrayal of megalomania. By contrast, there is no artistic "reason" for the ambiguity of Fletcher's portrait of Buckingham except to allow the noble attitudinizing with which Buckingham greets his fate.

Buckingham's ambition and evil life. Fletcher, however, takes the occasion of Buckingham's fall to comment on the slipperiness of baseborn men. On his way to the scaffold Buckingham warns others, not against the vanity of ambition, but against the folly of placing one's trust in vulgar men. He laments that his father and he

> Fell by our servants, by those men we lov'd most—
> A most unnatural and faithless service!
> Heaven has an end in all. Yet, you that hear me,
> This from a dying man receive as certain:
> Where you are liberal of your loves and counsels,
> Be sure you be not loose; for those you make friends
> And give your hearts to, when they once perceive
> The least rub in your fortunes, fall away
> Like water from ye, never found again
> But where they mean to sink ye.   (II.i.122-31)

Are we to think that the servant who turns state's evidence is more treacherous than the peer who plots against the king? Or are we simply to commiserate with Buckingham, whose family has had such bad luck with their retainers?

The ambiguity of the portrayal of Buckingham teases an audience only for a handful of scenes. The vagueness of the portrayal of the King is more irritating because it spans the entire length of the plot, and it is more disastrous because Henry's role as monarch and judge is the only connecting link between the first scenes and the last, between Buckingham's fate and Cranmer's. The problem is not just that Henry is a contradictory figure, here seemingly earnest, there seemingly hypocritical, but that the contradictions are all that we know of his nature. Apart from them and from some superficial mannerisms of speech, he does not exist as a man, as do the monarchs of the other History Plays. Critics cannot debate, therefore, whether Henry is compassionate or callous, noble or contemptible; they can only debate whether the amorphousness and ambiguity of his characterization are artistically defensible and appropriate. Although some would have us believe that a certain vagueness of characterization enhances Henry's symbolic role as an earthly providence in the play, attempts to treat him as a Prospero of the History Plays fail,[13] because there is no comparable moral ambiguity in Prospero's nature. Prospero can be peremptory at times with Ariel and harsh with the unregenerate Caliban, but his severity with Ferdinand is obviously pretended, and the first scene in which he appears

13. "Like Prospero," R. A. Foakes remarks, "[Henry] has a kind of vagueness, not a lack of solidity, but a lack of definition, as a representative of benevolent power acting upon others" (Introduction, *Henry VIII*, p. lxi).

with Miranda establishes the fundamental tenderness of his feelings. Although he plots "revenge," he is careful that no harm comes to those whom his tempest washes ashore, and though his words sometimes threaten, his deeds are always gentle. In contrast, Henry's words are kind but his deeds harsh. Even Frank Kermode, who would have us look on Henry as an exemplar of the divine, must admit that there is an undeniable element of hypocrisy in the King's character in the first half of the play; among other flaws to be found in this Godlike figure, Kermode lists susceptibility "to flattery, to adulterous passions," choler and extravagance.[14] As we would expect, Holinshed did not dare to suggest that Elizabeth's father was guilty both of hypocrisy and adulterous lust. It is Fletcher who simultaneously elevates and degrades Henry's character by suggesting here that his acts are divinely graced and there that his behavior is contemptible.

While protesting his desire that the divorce proceeding be just, the King fumes at Cardinal Campeius, who will not try the cause in Katherine's absence. He publicly declares his love for Katherine and his admiration for her wifely virtues; he even praises her as a bedfellow and insists that he divorces her out of a scruple of conscience regarding their marriage. Yet even as the King declares his pious motive, his courtiers insinuate that his conscience lies in his codpiece. One gentleman remarks that the King's conscience "has crept too near another lady"; another gentleman, admiring Anne's beauty, comments that he cannot blame the King's conscience. The purity of Henry's scruple about his marriage is unsullied in Holinshed, who places the divorce proceedings before Henry's acquaintance with Anne. It is Fletcher who creates the innuendoes about Henry's motives by reversing this chronology and by depicting a Henry hotly affected of Anne at their first meeting.

When Shakespeare portrays Henry V, who seems both ruthless in ambition and tender in conscience, he illuminates a particular kind of moral sensibility. When Fletcher deliberately blurs the character of Henry, whom Van Doren calls a "dummy king,"[15] he sacrifices moral insight and psychological verisimilitude to sophisticated wit. Artfully playing with royalist attitudes in *Henry VIII* as in *The Maid's Tragedy,* he makes an object of veneration of a king whose scruples are questionable and whose "conscience" is a source of amusement to his courtiers. Of course, Fletcher is too politic a playwright to

14. "What is Shakespeare's *Henry VIII* About?" *Shakespeare: The Histories,* pp. 173, 178, 179.

15. Mark Van Doren, *Shakespeare* (New York: Henry Holt, 1939), p. 332. His discussion of the emptiness of theme and characterization in *Henry VIII* is illuminating.

sneer at Tudor monarchs. He does not suggest that the jokes about Henry's lust point to the true motive that lies beneath the King's gestures of piety and scruple. On the contrary, he seems to insist, despite the courtiers' innuendoes, that we take Henry's noble protestations at face value, because his mercy and goodness are attested to by those who have the least reason to venerate him: Buckingham, Katherine, and Wolsey. Yawning over his task in *King John,* Shakespeare is quite capable of pushing aside the question of the King's responsibility for Arthur's fate, but he never seeks to amuse his audience as Fletcher does with equivocal characterizations—with heroes like Philaster and Henry VIII who are both ridiculous and sublime.

To enjoy *Henry VIII* as it was meant to be enjoyed, we first must recognize that it is an extended *double-entendre.* The spiritually inclined will find in it an abundance of conventional piety—of spiritual striving and turning away from the tinsel pleasures of the world. The worldly sophisticate will find in it an intense preoccupation with the magnificence of courtly life. While Wolsey's valedictory speeches strike the proper note of resignation and world-weariness, his beatitudes have, on close examination, a curiously worldly taint. Stripped of wealth, position, and power, he advises his follower Cromwell to

> fling away ambition!
> By that sin fell the angels. How can man then
> (The image of his Maker) hope to win by it?
> Love thyself last. Cherish those hearts that hate thee;
> Corruption wins not more than honesty.   (III.ii.412)

Just twenty-five lines earlier, however, he had advised Cromwell in a contrary vein:

> Go get thee from me, Cromwell!
> I am a poor fall'n man, unworthy now
> To be thy lord and master. Seek the King.
> That sun, I pray, may never set! I have told him
> What and how true thou art. He will advance thee.
>   . . . . Good Cromwell,
> Neglect him not; make use now, and provide
> For thine own future safety.   (III.ii.412-21)

Exactly what spiritual lesson Wolsey preaches is difficult to say. He does not urge Cromwell to find some humble place away from the corrupting vanity of the Court; instead he would be remembered by Cromwell as the master who "Found thee a way (out of his wrack) to rise in— / A sure and safe one, though thy master miss'd it" (III.ii.437-8). Like Buckingham, who preaches security not loyalty, Wolsey preaches security not humility. Given the choice of contemning worldly pomp or of securing his courtly future, Cromwell, with Wolsey's blessings, takes the latter path and next appears as a member of the council that tries Cranmer.

Deliberately ambiguous, *Henry VIII* can seem different things to different viewers.[16] The sober bourgeois no doubt enjoyed the play because he could gawk at the glitter of the Court (knowing that it is slightly tarnished) and savor the pleasure of pitying great noblemen. He could also rejoice in the apparent glorification of his own moral sentiments and shed a tear at the redemption of even the most hardened of sinners. The more sophisticated viewer could admire the authentic representation of courtly elegance and intrigue and relish the witty innuendoes about the royal conscience. To satisfy both sentimentalist and cynic Fletcher willingly sacrifices the integrity of his characters and of his plot. Without warning the audience of the miracle to come, he transforms Wolsey from a grasping overreacher into a contrite moralist whose sweetness of temper and acceptance of adversity passeth understanding. Having seen earlier in the play how nobly Buckingham and Katherine respond to calamity, we may be ready to grant that being hurled down in Henry's court brings extraordinary spiritual benefits. We may be equally ready to grant that someone as thoroughly despicable as Wolsey seems to be may be instantaneously redeemed, though nothing in his character hints of the possibility of such a sea-change. But we must balk at Fletcher's attempt to alter at the end of Act III our very memory of Wolsey's personality. Before this point in the play, scene after scene testifies to Wolsey's ruthlessness, pride, malice, and cynicism. Suddenly, however, another Wolsey appears, who is earnest, tenderhearted, devoted, and careful of his immortal soul. We no sooner enjoy the emotional satisfaction of witnessing Wolsey's exposure and richly deserved downfall than we are allowed the contrary satisfaction of discovering his saintliness. Where the modern sentimentalist invents a trollop with a heart of gold, Fletcher imagines a Machiavel who lived by the Sermon on the Mount. But having seen not one fleeting sign of Wolsey's devotion to Henry, we can scarcely believe his lament:

> Had I but serv'd my God with half the zeal
> I serv'd my king, he would not in mine age
> Have left me naked to mine enemies.   (III.ii.455-57)

The new Wolsey is no more convincing as a human being than the old one;

16. I have noted the way in which Beaumont and Fletcher's *Philaster* and *The Maid's Tragedy* are constructed in the manner of optical illusions in *Moral Vision*, pp. 178-79.

once a cliché of malevolent policy, Wolsey becomes next a cliché of Christian piety, and it is precisely because he has no character at all in a Shakespearean sense but merely a set of rhetorical postures that the impression of his character can be so easily altered.[17]

Unless we are willing to debase the coinage of Shakespeare's art, we cannot place the stamp of Shakespeare characterization on figures like Wolsey, Buckingham, and Henry. Nor can we allow the loosely connected episodes of *Henry VIII* to pass current as Shakespearean dramatic form. It is significant that one apologist for *Henry VIII* sees in it a regression to the naive tragic themes and artistic form of *The Mirror for Magistrates*,[18] while another sees in it a ritual drama of penance and reconciliation comparable to that found in the late romances.[19] The latter view would be acceptable if one saw in Henry any of Leontes' painfully won self-recognition, or if Henry showed the slightest remorse at the misery he inflicts on those he casts off, or if he acknowledged in some slight way Wolsey's years of service. But where Henry's victims are so reconciled to their bitter fates that they bless the hand that strikes them down, Henry is capable of only the meagerest gestures of charity: he sends comfort to the dying Katherine by an emissary, a kindness which, Katherine remarks, comes like pardon after execution. Some would see in the plot of *Henry VIII* the spiritual growth and education of a King who becomes maturely responsible as he shrugs off his reliance on Wolsey. I fail to recognize the difference between the King who fumes at Campeius and frowns on Wolsey and the King who rages at Cranmer's accusers. Whatever Henry learns during the course of the play, he does not, like Cymbeline, Leontes, and Prospero, learn the vanity of power or the preciousness of mercy. Supposedly an exemplar of mercy, he is as scornful, petty, threatening, and quick to anger at the end of the play as at the beginning.

While Shakespeare could imagine willful and peremptory characters, he could not, I think, imagine characters like Buckingham, Katherine, and Wolsey, who find that being wronged is a spiritual blessing. Some of his noblest characters—Cordelia, Desdemona, Kent, and Hermione—continue to love those who wrong them, but they do not thank their oppressors for wronging them. The innocent and generous Desdemona may be unable to admit to herself how brutally she is being mistreated by Othello, but she knows that she does not

17. E. M. Waith comments incisively on the substitution of rhetorical effect for psychological truth in the portraits of Wolsey and Buckingham, which he attributes to Fletcher in *The Pattern of Tragicomedy in Beaumont and Fletcher* (New Haven: Yale Univ. Press, 1952), pp. 119-24.
18. Kermode, in *Shakespeare: The Histories*, pp. 173-76.
19. Foakes, *Henry VIII*, pp. xxxvii-xlv.

deserve brutality, and she does not willingly submit to it. To find analogues to Buckingham, Wolsey, and Katherine we must turn to Fletcher's drama, to characters like Arethusa and Bellario, who continue to worship Philaster after he falsely accuses them and wounds them both in attempts to kill them. Just as Wolsey thanks the King for "curing" him of vanity, Bellario, when stabbed by Philaster, exclaims, "Blessed be that hand! / It meant me well."[20] Such ludicrous hyperboles of devotion have nothing to do with the reality of moral experience; they are romantic fantasies acted out by story-book characters.[21]

It is precisely because Shakespeare places a supreme value on the fidelity that is tested by time and circumstance that he will not sentimentalize or caricature it in this fashion or equate it, as Fletcher does, with emotional surrender. Loyal beyond measure and even beyond reason to the Lear who wrongs them, Cordelia and Kent insist nevertheless on their truth and will no more abase themselves before Lear's peremptory will than Hermione will feed on any crumb of regard offered by the husband who defames and rejects her. If we can imagine Shakespeare treating Hamlet's abuse of Ophelia as a beneficent act because it indirectly helps bring about the downfall of Claudius, then we can imagine him suggesting in *Henry VIII* that Henry's mistreatment of Katherine is divinely inspired to bring about England's good. Because Fletcher has no consistent moral viewpoint or serious moral purpose in his art, he can allow us to rejoice in Katherine's loyalty to Henry at the same time that we rejoice that Henry's callousness to her insures England's future greatness.

In Shakespeare's late romances nothing is forgotten of pain, suffering, and guilt in the final scenes of reconciliation. If there is a second chance for Leontes, it is earned by the death of his son, the loss of his wife and daughter, and by the years of loneliness, misery, and sorrowing penance which prepare him spiritually for the moment of forgiveness and rediscovery. We believe in the possibility of spiritual change because we see it occur; we watch the young, willful, arrogant king change into the humble, aging, careworn monarch whose only thought is of the blessed wife he wronged and the son whom he destroyed. Spiritual change comes more easily in *Henry VIII*, where sudden miraculous conversions occur even though there is no corresponding change in the spiritual climate of Henry's court, no abatement of pettiness, envy, and malice as the plot draws toward its close. In the very midst of world vanity,

20. *Philaster*, IV.iv.26-7. The heroines of Beaumont and Fletcher's plays have a nice taste for masochistic satisfactions. They enjoy being wounded by their lovers' sword, on which Aspatia finds her quietus in *The Maid's Tragedy*. This kind of perverse eroticism is kept out of *Henry VIII*.

21. Una Ellis-Fermor writes superbly of the fairy-tale quality of Fletcherian romance in *The Jacobean Drama* (London: Methuen, 1947), pp. 206-21.

however, visionary experiences take place. Even before Cranmer looks through the veils of time, the art of the stage is enlisted in the service of supernal mysteries. When Katherine dies, the hidden music sounds, the hidden chorus sings, and the crown of heaven descends on a golden cord from a machine. Where Horatio can only hope that flights of angels will sing Hamlet to his rest, the dying Katherine is granted a "Vision" of "personages, clad in white robes," with "golden vizards on their faces," who make "reverend curtsies," and present her with the garland of heaven, at which "(as it were by inspiration) she makes (in her sleep) signs of rejoicing, and holdeth up her hands to heaven" (IV.ii. 82 s.d.). Can there be any doubt that Katherine's fall is fortunate when this scene indicates that she will be more elevated in heaven than she was dejected on earth, and when she is promised courtly masques and homages forever more?

For a play which ventures so confidently into the realm of the supernal and the visionary, *Henry VIII* is astonishingly shallow in its religious concerns. So cursory and superficial is its treatment of the religious issues of the Henrician reformation that Pandulph's debate with John at Angiers seems by contrast a profound consideration of the question of papal hegemony. All that we know of Wolsey's attachment to the Old Faith is his remark that Anne is "a spleeny Lutheran, and not wholesome to / Our cause," and all that we know of the attack on Wolsey's Catholicism is Surrey's scurrilous threat to startle him

> Worse than the sacring bell, when the brown wench
> Lay kissing in your arms, Lord Cardinal.   (III.ii.295-6)

Some dozen lines at Cranmer's arraignment make vague references to heresies and new opinions, but one cannot distinguish the Protestant stance from the Catholic, because Gardiner's assault on Cranmer duplicates Surrey's attack on Wolsey. When Surrey presses the attack on Wolsey, the Chamberlain warns, "Press not a falling man too far!" When Gardiner waxes vehement against Cranmer, Cromwell protests that he is too sharp: " 'Tis a cruelty / To load a falling man." In both instances breeding, not theology, is the real issue. Just as Wolsey contemns Anne's lowliness of birth more than her Protestant faith, he is hated more for his vulgar opportunism than for his religious convictions. It is not surprising, therefore, that Henry's anger is directed not at the Catholicism of Cranmer's enemies but at the lack of manners they show in making "This honest man, wait like a lousy footboy / At chamber-door" (V.iii.139-40).[22] Unwilling to tolerate such boorishness, Henry charges the malicious Gardiner,

22. Of course, the incident is so described in the historical source from which it was taken, John Foxe's *Acts and Monuments* (see the new Arden *Henry VIII*, pp. 214-15). But

who thirsts for Cranmer's destruction, to "embrace and love" Cranmer, and
Gardiner does so "with a true heart / And brother's love." Unlike Prospero,
who cannot educate Caliban or redeem Sebastian and Antonio, Henry has
limitless powers of spiritual persuasion. When he frowns, a man's entire
character is transformed. If there is a Shakespearean analogue to this moment
of "reconciliation" in *Henry VIII* it is to be found, not in the last plays, but in
Richard III, where at Edward's command, Buckingham and Hastings pledge
their undying love to the Queen's relatives.

The way that Henry rescues Cranmer from his persecutors leaves no doubt
that the unforgivable sin in *Henry VIII* is bad form, not bad theology. Or,
perhaps, in *Henry VIII* bad form demands bad theology, because, having failed
to create a unified and coherent plot, Fletcher must pretend in the last scene
that his play discovers the providential design of English history and thereby
justifies the ways of God (and kings) to men. The tragic falls in *Henry VIII*, we
are to think, are fortunate not only because they produce remarkable spiritual
benefits, but also because they make possible the blessing of future generations. Who can fail to see that partial evil is general good when it is
obvious that Henry's lust shall provide England's salvation? Even before
Cranmer's prophecy, there are minor Annunciations of the blessedness to come
by men who see the soul of goodness in Anne's beauty. Suffolk remarks that
she is

> a gallant creature, and complete
> In mind and feature. I persuade me, from her
> Will fall some blessing to this land, which shall
> In it be memoriz'd.   (III.iii.49-52)

Equally prophetic is the Chamberlain, who remarks of Anne just after the
divorce proceeding:

> Beauty and honour in her are so mingled
> That they have caught the King; and who knows yet
> But from this lady may proceed a gem
> To lighten all this isle?   (II.ii.76-9)

At Anne's coronation a Gentleman protests, as he has a soul, that she

> is an angel!
> Our king has all the Indies in his arms,
> And more, and richer, when he strains that lady.   (IV.i.44-6)

---

it is Fletcher who chose to make this episode of central importance in his plot, even as he
changed Foxe's report that Henry accused the councilors of making Cranmer "waite at the
counsaile chamber doore amongst serving men" to "wait like a lousy footboy." The
sneering view of serving boys is Fletcher's, not King Henry's as Foxe recorded it.

Who then can blame the King's "conscience?"

To hope that Providence may bring good out of evil is not to confuse evil and good, or to praise the unconscionable motive that somehow issues in a prosperous result. Kermode argues that the fact that Elizabeth "could not have existed but for the tragedy of a good woman must not be allowed to detract from the pleasure the auditors are expected to feel at the end of the play, which is of course related to the happy dynastic progress of English history since that birth, a progress which might have been very different if Henry had not put away Katherine."[23] By the same token, the happy dynastic progress of English history under the Tudors would have been different if Richard III had not "put away" the innocent sons of Edward IV. At best "all's well that ends well" is a specious theology because if Providence can manifest itself in Henry's "conscience," it can manifest itself equally well in the "impartiality" of a Pilate, who by washing his hands of Christ's blood made possible the Sacrifice. The belief that all in history—the suffering, the brutality, and the injustice—is for the best is a sentimentality alien to Shakespeare's temper. He does not attempt to justify the pattern of the past or of the present. He does not try to explain away the pain and the misery of men's lives, nor would he argue the necessity and utility of callousness or cruelty. Aware that men appeal to the heavens to vindicate their acts and desires, he shows us a Margaret who thanks God for Richard's villainies, a York who sees God's will in Richard II's public degradation, and a Prince John who attributes the "victory" at Gaultree Forest to God. He never intimates, however, that the divine plan is furthered by atrocity and deceit, nor does he ask us to believe that God rewards Henry V for his princely virtue by helping him to despoil the world's best garden.

There is good reason to think that Fletcher derived the inspiration for Cranmer's vision from Richmond's prayer, which similarly links the historical past in *Richard III* with the Elizabethan present. Where Richmond prays that a new era of peace and reconciliation will come to a reunited England, Cranmer envisions an England secure, triumphant, and prosperous under Elizabeth and James. Richmond prays that his heirs may "enrich the time to come with smooth-fac'd peace, / With smiling plenty, and fair prosperous days." Cranmer predicts that good will grow with Elizabeth:

> In her days every man shall eat in safety
> Under his own vine what he plants, and sing
> The merry songs of peace to all his neighbors.   (V.v.34-6)

But where the "pastoralism" of Richmond's speeches is a fitting consummation

23. Kermode, in *Shakespeare: The Histories,* p. 178.

to the agrarian motif that echoes through the poetry of *Henry VI Part III* and *Richard III,* Cranmer's scene of rustic bliss is a sentimental cliché conjured into incongruous being amid the artificiality of the Court. Despite its pious rhetoric, Cranmer's speech lacks the moral substance of Richmond's prayer, which somberly recalls the dreadful anarchy of civil war. Its only purpose is to exploit the nostalgic memories of Fletcher's audience so as to provide the sense of an ending and of mighty consonances which the plot of *Henry VIII* fails to provide. Where Richmond's prayer is but one element in the great design of *Richard III,* Cranmer's prophecy is the only thing that saves *Henry VIII* from trailing off into insignificance. Take that single speech out of the text, and the failure of coherence and meaning in Fletcher's plotting is nakedly exposed.

If we assume that Cranmer's vision is Shakespeare's last comment on English history, we may also assume that in 1613 he decided that the millennium had arrived under the wisest fool in Christendom, whose incompetence to deal with political and religious problems was every year becoming more obvious. If we wisely doubt that Shakespeare wrote Cranmer's speech—if we doubt, in fact, that he was capable of its fulsome flattery of James and of its facile optimism—then we can speak with less certainty of his conclusions about England's destiny. Of one thing I am certain: having made the conscience of the king a central moral concern from *Henry VI Part I* to *Henry V,* Shakespeare would not have made it the subject of titillating jests in *Henry VIII.* The similarities in the portraits of Henry V and Henry VIII, both of whom can be described as royal paragons whose pious motives are sometimes suspect, are only superficial. Critics have not argued vehemently about the characterization of Henry VIII, because he strikes modern readers as a Jacobean waxwork figure, one that no longer seems lifelike but that can possibly be explained by reference to outworn royalist ideas. But critics continue to argue bitterly about the character of Henry V, because he seems all too contemporary and familiar. Those who see through Henry V's easy talk of brotherhood are eager to point out that the mirror of all Christian kings was not his brother's keeper. They are less eager to admit that Harry is our brother, though evidence of our kinship with him is written in the self-righteous political rhetoric and the bloodstained history of our days.

10. CONCLUSION

Because the tetralogies, so far as is known, were never performed as such on the Elizabethan stage, Shakespeare had no practical artistic reason or professional obligation to concern himself with their unities. Few members of his audiences would have recognized and objected to inconsistencies of characterization from play to play, just as few would have been able to appreciate the continuities, parallelisms, and symmetries which a critic can discern. Nevertheless, there are in the tetralogies, as in almost every Shakespearean play, reaches of art that lie beyond the grasp of most theatergoers: for example, the echoes of *Richard II* in *Henry IV Part II* and *Henry V* that contribute to the unity of the second tetralogy. I stress the artistic coherences of the second tetralogy because critics suggest that Shakespeare completed it mainly to satisfy his audiences' tastes and expectations. They also suggest that having reached an artistic impasse in *Henry V*, he found a new direction in *Julius Caesar* and the great tragedies that followed.[1] If it is useful to divide Shakespeare's career into its different stages, then one may say that the line between the "early" Shakespeare and the "mature" Shakespeare falls somewhere between *Henry V* and *Julius Caesar*. Yet there is as immediate a link between the concerns of the History Plays and those of *Julius Caesar* as there is between *Julius Caesar* and *Hamlet*. Even as the characterization of Brutus points directly toward the profounder study of idealism in Hamlet, so also the studies of political motive and conscience in the History Plays prepare the way for the psychological and moral delineation of Brutus.

1. Granville-Barker suggests that *Henry V*, "like many successes . . . brought its writer to a 'dead end,'" "From *Henry V* to *Hamlet*," p. 73.

221

Since Elizabethan poets and dramatists found much of their tragical matter in the Chronicle accounts of the falls of princes, it is often difficult to say whether an Elizabethan play is a historical tragedy or a tragical history; and the very effort to make this distinction may seem downright Polonian. So inextricable was the link between history and tragedy in Elizabethan dramatic theory and practice[2] that few Chronicle plays lack a tragic theme; and so necessary was tragic theme to the plotting of Chronicle plays that Shakespeare alone was able to create a satisfactory aesthetic form for historical drama that does not depend upon a tragic denouement. Forgetting that history and tragedy commingle in the Roman plays as well as in the plays of the tetralogies, critics sometimes argue that the "public" orientation of the History Plays is incompatible with the tragic vision of Shakespeare's maturest art. Where the tragedies testify to the supreme importance of personal values and relationships, the History Plays supposedly define the impersonal necessities of political order; where the tragedies question the very foundations of belief, the History Plays, it is said, bear witness to the Providential design of English history.

It should be possible to acknowledge the different emphases of the History Plays and the tragedies without sacrificing the integrity and wholeness of Shakespeare's perception of experience. From the beginning his artistic thought is all of a piece, and from the beginning his interest in human behavior and in political and moral issues cuts across the boundaries of dramatic genre.[3] He places as great a value on the sanctity of personal relations in the History Plays as in the tragedies, because he intuits that order depends, not on concepts of hierarchy and degree, but on the fabric of personal and social relationships which is woven by ties of marriage, kinship, and friendship, by communal interests, and ideals of loyalty and trust. Accordingly, he sees the archenemies of political order, not as subversive ideologists, but as individualists who cast off all bonds of blood or affection—who hunger for power because they cannot love. Chaos comes in the History Plays as in the tragedies, not when doctrines of obedience are questioned, but when the most intimate human ties disintegrate: when brother turns on brother, when a son becomes his father's

2. See the illuminating discussion of the relation between history and tragedy in Elizabethan drama and critical theory in chapter 6 of Madeleine Doran's *Endeavors of Art: A study of form in Elizabethan drama* (Madison: Univ. Wisconsin Press, 1954).

3. One cannot trace Shakespeare's treatment of honor or law, for example, without stepping again and again across the boundaries of dramatic genre. The way to the heath scenes in *King Lear,* in which justice itself is accused, begins in *Henry VI Part II* and continues in *The Merchant of Venice, Henry IV Part II,* and *Measure for Measure.* To find Shakespeare's last words about justice and mercy, moreover, one must look beyond *King Lear* to *The Winter's Tale* and *The Tempest* if not to *Henry VIII.*

enemy. The political conflicts which Samuel Daniel treats as impersonal struggles for power, Shakespeare portrays as personal and familial antagonisms which pit cousin against cousin, uncle against nephew, and father against son. The breach between Henry and his heir is a central theme of the *Henry IV* plays; more radical still is the dissolution of familial bonds in the Percies, who are untrue to those closest to them in blood. So much meaning is attached to personal truth and obligation in the second tetralogy that the height of treachery in *Henry IV Part I* is not Worcester's conspiracy against the King but his betrayal of his nephew Hotspur at Shrewsbury; and the ugliest moment of *Henry IV Part II* is John's Worcester-like equivocation to the rebels at Gaultree Forest.

If we think that Shakespeare looked beyond the "official" values of the History Plays in the tragedies that followed, then we may say that, where *Henry V* celebrates the victory of the English Caesar, *Antony and Cleopatra* suggests that 'tis paltry to be Caesar. But we do not thrill in *Henry V* to the fulfillment of Harry's ambition to be sole sir of England and France. What we rejoice in is the small time of brotherhood which Harry and his soldiers share at Agincourt; and what redeems the warlike Harry are precisely those human needs which we cannot imagine in the coldblooded Octavius: the anguish of conscience and the loneliness that prompts him to confess his fears and to seek the companionship of his men around the campfire. Thus, in its own way *Henry V* celebrates the same human bond that *Julius Caesar* and *Antony and Cleopatra* celebrate: the devotion that wins the happy few (Harry and his men; Brutus and his loyal followers; Antony, Cleopatra, and their faithful retainers) "a place i' the story." Although the tragedies speak far more eloquently than the History Plays of the irony of imperial ambition, we cannot imagine that Shakespeare turned away from his study of English history contemptuous of "men of action," when the great soldier *is* the tragic hero in *Othello, Macbeth, Antony and Cleopatra*, and *Coriolanus*—when it is force of arms that redeems Edgar's lost humanity in *King Lear*, and when Hamlet, who sees through the absurdity of martial conquests,

> Imperious Caesar, dead and turn'd to clay,
> Might stop a hole to keep the wind away,

receives the tribute of the soldiers' music and the rites of war.

To believe that Shakespeare turned away from the History Plays disillusioned with political ideals or political heroes,[4] we must also believe that, despite his

---

4. In her penetrating essay, "Shakespeare's Political Plays," Una Ellis-Fermor suggests that the chilling impersonality of Henry V expresses Shakespeare's recognition that the

apparent shortcomings, Henry V was Shakespeare's ideal of royalty. Shakespeare, I think, had too strong an instinct for the truth of experience to fashion models of virtue, and he had too much artistry to make his "perfect prince" repellent to sensitive readers. Disappointed with utopian hopes, modern ideologues may proclaim that political ambition uniquely corrupts and dehumanizes. Shakespeare's insight into human nature is deeper: he knows that the will to power, which can manifest itself in any human relationship or activity, is not a peculiarly political vice. He has, moreover, too clear a sense of the force of personality in politics to imagine that events are shaped by mechanistic necessities to which men must bow.[5] Fluellen, Williams, and Bates are for him, not the insignificant cogs of Harry's juggernaut, but the men whose patriotic and soldierly pride and whose appetite for booty and adventure make possible the conquest of France. Other Elizabethans understood the role of Commodity and of ruthless calculation in politics, but none saw as well as Shakespeare that political calculations are only as logical as human vanity, arrogance, fear, and ambition will allow them to be.

It is perhaps easier now to appreciate the personalism of the History Plays than it was some decades ago, when political scientists spoke of ideological movements and economic determinants and described totalitarian regimes as monolithic states. Then literary prophets could imagine a future in which whole populations would be so regimented and dehumanized that individuality would disappear and personal life become vestigial. Now another utopian millennium seems more probable—one in which millions will enjoy the nearly absolute freedom that anomie grants. As traditional codes of behavior lose their authority in modern society, the pressures for conformity lessen. As our sense of community erodes, a tolerance based on indifference to the lives of others licenses almost every idiosyncrasy of speech or dress or life style. Haunted by the increasing loneliness of contemporary life, we glimpse the possibility that the outward forms of political order will outlast the personal, familial, and communal relationships which create our social lives. Ripping apart the very fabric of civilized order, modern war has forced millions out

---

demands of political success are opposed to the essential qualities of the individual human spirit (pp. 43-54). Granville-Barker also sees in the portrayal of Henry V signs of Shakespeare's disillusion with the "perfect man of action," "From *Henry V* to *Hamlet*," pp. 79-81.

5. The most extraordinary misconception of the History Plays that has recently appeared is Jan Kott's view that Richard III is a victim of the "Grand Mechanism" of history. See *Shakespeare Our Contemporary*, trans. B. Taborski (New York: Doubleday, 1964), pp. 31-33.

onto the heath. Millions of others have found no place in the civilized order except the urban heath where man's life is cheap as beast's.

To suggest that the failure of relationships—the loneliness and isolation—pictured in *Henry IV Part II* has its modern counterpart is not to say that the vision of the History Plays grows increasingly bleak. On the contrary, there is more sweetness and light in the second tetralogy than in the first, where savagery becomes a norm. But there is also a recognition in the second tetralogy that political choices are rarely as simple and clear-cut as that between Richard III and Henry Richmond; more often than not men must choose between Richard II and Henry Bolingbroke—or an Archbishop of York and an Earl of Westmoreland. Melodramatic villains like Richard III are scapegoat figures who permit us to believe that unscrupulous ambition is a human aberration. The more realistic and subtly shaded characterizations of the second tetralogy suggest how intrinsic to our humanity are the problems of relationship and order, how easily suspicion, antagonism, duplicity, and greed warp the most intimate ties. Whatever ideal of nature man may conceive, the bloodstained pages of his history indicate that restlessness, selfishness, and aggressiveness may be as natural in him as the cooperative impulses on which a peaceful and humane order depends.

It is ironic that *Henry V* should be condemned for its jingoism when it is the only History Play to intimate that the patriotism of a Faulconbridge may not be enough, because it blinds men to their kinship with those whose throats they cut. It is ironic too that the insularity of viewpoint in *Henry V* should be decried when its perspective is large enough to suggest a connection between Agincourt, Cressy, the Norman conquest of England, the campaigns of Caesar and Pompey, and the famous victories of Alexander. These reminders of ancient conflicts allow no easy confidence about the future, for they predict that as long as honor and patriotism can summon decent men to support all-hallowed causes, so long will the chase of battle continue; and so long will the sacrifice of lives on the battlefield provide a more compelling motive for political action than the Sacrifice itself. Although war conducted by the most Christian rules mocks the Christian ideal of brotherhood, it creates, Shakespeare realizes, the primal tribal bond of kinship in those who shed their blood together and who have a common memory of heroism and victory.

One may wish that Shakespeare had taken a more explicit and absolute stand in the History Plays against the horror of war, but he speaks as eloquently as any of his contemporaries of the need for peace. He cannot be condemned for loving his threatened country or for believing that courage and fidelity deserve celebration in a Williams and a Fluellen as well as in a Kent and a Cordelia. Perhaps by the time he wrote *Henry V* he had given up the hope of reconciliation and brotherhood which Henry Richmond embodies, but he knew that princely greatness demands more than victories gained by fire, sword, and famine. Those who argue that Shakespeare could not imagine or believe in a royalty more perfect than that of the warlike Harry forget that he lived under Elizabeth, a vain, politic, devious, occasionally ruthless queen who won the praise of her wisest subjects because for nearly half a century she kept her beloved England at peace.

INDEX

INDEX